W9-BFN-655

Parallel Programming

Parallel Programming

An Introduction

Thomas Bräunl

Prentice Hall
New York London Toronto Sydney Tokyo Singapore

First published 1993 by
Prentice Hall International (UK) Limited
Campus 400, Maylands Avenue
Hemel Hempstead
Hertfordshire, HP2 7EZ
A division of
Simon & Schuster International Group

© Thomas Bräunl 1993

All rights reserved. No part of this publication may be reproduced, stored in a retrieval system, or transmitted, in any form, or by any means, electronic, mechanical, photocopying, recording or otherwise, without prior permission, in writing, from the publisher.
For permission within the United States of America contact Prentice Hall Inc., Englewood Cliffs, NJ 07632

Printed and bound in Great Britain at the
University Press, Cambridge

Library of Congress Cataloging-in-Publication Data

Bräunl, Thomas.
Parallel programming: an introduction/Thomas Bräunl.
p. cm.
Includes bibliographical references (p.) and index.
ISBN 0-13-336827-0
1. Parallel programming (Computer science) I. Title.
QA76.642.B75 1993 93-2097
005.2—dc20 CIP

British Library Cataloguing in Publication Data

A catalogue record for this book is available from
the British Library

ISBN 0-13-336827-0 (pbk)

---

2 3 4 5 97 96 95 94

Contents

Preface

This book provides an introduction to the subject of parallel programming and is directed at 3rd or 4th year computer science students. The topics are divided into four major parts. After part I on fundamentals follow parts II and III on 'conventional' asynchronous parallel programming and synchronous 'massively parallel' or data-parallel programming with thousands of processors. Part IV contains other parallel models which cannot be placed into one of the previous parts, as well as automatic parallelization/vectorization and performance analysis.

The book originated from the class notes of a course, given by the author for the first time in the fall semester of 1990 at the University of Stuttgart. Accompanying labs and seminars have supplemented the material; exercises at the end of each part are oriented towards these. This textbook was translated from the original German manuscript by Brian Blevins and the author.

My special thanks go to Prof. Dr. Andreas Reuter for his support and inspiration for this book project, Astrid Beck, Brian Blevins, Stefan Engelhardt and most importantly Claus Brenner for proof-reading the manuscript and numerous suggestions for improvements, as well as Christine Drabek and Hartmut Keller for word-processing the first version. I would also like to thank Prof. Dr. Jürgen Nehmer, Prof. Dr. Ewald von Puttkamer and Prof. Dr. Kai Hwang, whose lectures gave me a series of inspirations for this book.

Many thanks go to the assistants and students, who with much enthusiasm and enormous amounts of work translated the programming language concepts for Modula-P and Parallaxis used in this book into programming environments, which have been put to use world-wide as public domain software. Ingo Barth, Frank Sembach and Stefan Engelhardt developed an extensive programming environment with a compiler, simulator and debugger for Parallaxis, while Roland Norz developed a compiler for Modula-P. Michael Ancutici designed a Petri net simulation tool, which is very helpful in testing large networks or complex synchronization protocols.

All those wishing to try out the parallel algorithms shown in this book can obtain a free copy of the compilers and simulation systems for the parallel languages Modula-P and Parallaxis, as well as the Petri net simulation system via 'anonymous ftp'.

The Internet address is:

`ftp.informatik.uni-stuttgart.de` (currently: 129.69.211.2)

The directories are:

`pub/modula-p`	Modula-P compiler and sample programs
`pub/parallaxis`	Parallaxis compiler, debugger, and sample programs
`pub/petri-nets`	Petri net simulation system

A supplementary booklet with solutions to the exercises in this textbook is available from the publisher to faculty members using this book in lectures.

Stuttgart
August 1993

Thomas Bräunl

PART I

Fundamentals

Parallelism may be considered from several points of view. Parallel computer systems can be classified according to their machine structure, while parallel operations may be grouped by their level of abstraction or by the types of argument they accept. These provide fundamentally different views of parallelism. From this basis, sequential programming appears to be just a special case of parallel programming. Petri nets are a useful tool for the definition of asynchronously parallel tasks. They help to discover dependences and solve problems, before the design of a parallel systems is transferred into a parallel program. The most common language concepts for handling parallelism in programming languages, together with the most important connection structures used in parallel computer systems, are the fundamentals for understanding parallel computation.

CHAPTER 1

Introduction

The world is parallel! This principle is illustrated in the following examples. Natural systems, complex technical processes, and even societal changes are all highly parallel processes. The growth of a plant is simultaneously influenced by a large number of factors. The starting of a motor requires the coordination of many components. On the stock market, share prices depend on the positions of thousands of purchasers and sellers. Interestingly, parallelism shows up not only in the concrete physical world but in abstract processes as well.

Parallel supercomputers belong to the latest developments of computer science. However, one should not overlook that even in simple personal computers many operations are carried out in parallel: among these are input/output channels, direct memory access (DMA), and the parallel control of functional elements of the central processing unit (CPU) in microcode. Even a normal 16 bit arithmetic unit works in parallel when one considers each bit as a separate element.

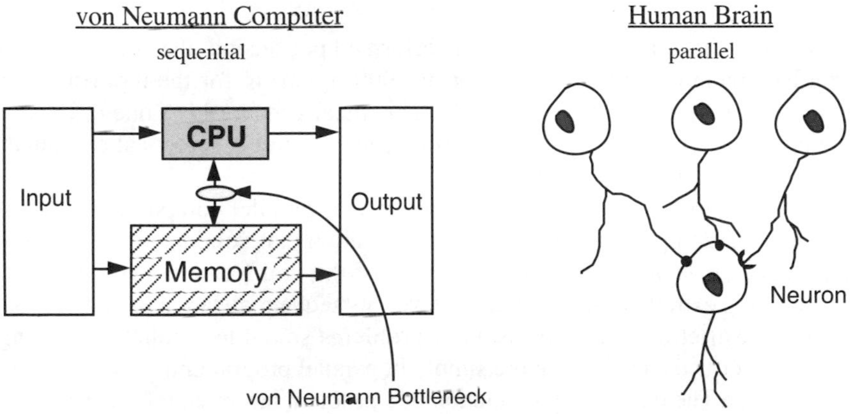

Figure 1.1 Von Neumann computer versus brain (neurons)

The human brain works in parallel as well. The illustration in Figure 1.1 shows a comparison between a sequential von Neumann computer and a brain which consists of a (natural) parallel neural network:

The table in Figure 1.2 illustrates the incongruity of a von Neumann computer between a single active CPU and a large number of passive memory cells. This contrasts with the homogeneous brain structure where all of the components are constantly active.

von Neumann Computer	Human Brain
Number of elements: $\approx 10^9$ transistors for: 1 CPU (10^6 trans.), always active 10^9 memory cells, mostly inactive	$\approx 10^{10}$ neurons ('CPU + memory') constantly active
Switching time: 10^{-9} s = 1ns	10^{-3} s = 1ms
Total switching operations per second: [10^{18} / s *(theoretical value, if all transistors were simultaneously active)*] 10^{10} / s (practical value, due to inactive memory cells)	10^{13} / s

Figure 1.2 Performance comparison

In terms of the number of operations performed per second, the brain is superior to the von Neumann computer by a factor of 1000, ignoring for the moment the more complex switching functions of a neuron. This means that at least one of the reasons for the higher performance of the brain (in terms of purely theoretical computational power) lies in parallel processing.

From these observations evolves the thesis that parallel computing is the natural form of information processing. The sequentialization that dominates today's programming practices is simply a historical outcome of the von Neumann computer model. This model was extremely successful; however, its sequentialization of all processing is an artificial restriction. The expression of problems suited to parallel processing can usually be described and solved more simply in parallel programming languages than in sequential ones. The parallel representation of a problem has more information from the problem itself in comparison with the easily constructed sequential variation. The goal is therefore to code parallel problems in a parallel programming language, in order to achieve more understandable programs on the one hand, and a considerably faster execution of these programs on parallel computer systems on the other hand.

CHAPTER 2

Classifications

In this chapter, three different classification systems will be introduced. First, parallel computers will be classified according to their processing structure. Then a classification of concurrent actions according to their level of abstraction is shown. Finally, parallel operations are classified by their argument types.

2.1 Computer System Classification

Flynn's classification system [Flynn 66] divides the entire computer world into four groups: SISD, SIMD, MISD, and MIMD (see Figure 2.1). In our context the two most interesting classes are SIMD (synchronous parallelism) and MIMD (asynchronous parallelism). The SISD class are von Neumann computers with just a single processor, while applying a quite free interpretation makes the MISD class cover pipeline computer systems.

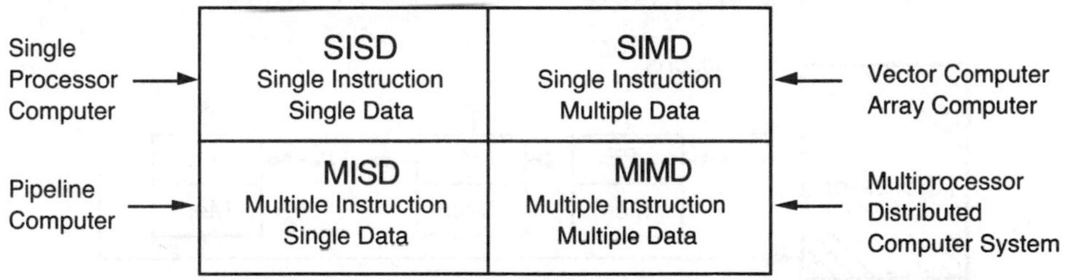

Figure 2.1 Computer system classification according to Flynn

Synchronous parallelism means that there is only a single thread of control. So a special processor executes the program, while all other processors with a simpler structure execute the 'master processor's' commands in lock step (synchronously). Asynchronous parallelism, in contrast, indicates that there are multiple threads of control. In this way, each processor executes an individual program. For a data exchange between two asynchronously working processors, some kind of synchronization operation must be performed. In this classification scheme, it is also useful to divide both of the classes, MIMD and SIMD, into two subclasses according to the interconnections between their processors.

MIMD

- Coupling via shared memory
  (tight coupling)
  → Multi Processor System
- Coupling via an interconnecting network with message exchange
  (loose coupling, distributed memory)
  → Distributed Computer System

SIMD

- No coupling or only a chain between processor elements (PEs)
  → Vector Computer
- Coupling via an interconnecting network
  → Array Computer

Pipeline systems, as well as MIMD and SIMD systems, will be considered more closely in the following sections.

Figure 2.2 shows the structure of a simple pipeline computer. The sketch in Figure 2.3 (adapted from [Perrot 87]) illustrates the step-wise processing of commands in a pipeline computer with a single pipeline.

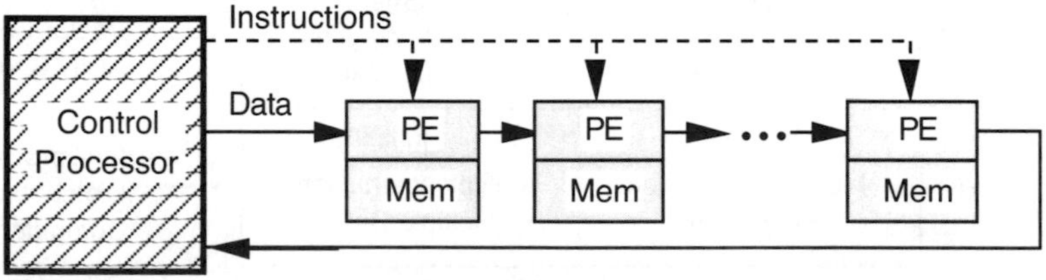

Figure 2.2 Pipelined computer system

Sequential and parallel execution are contrasted with one another in Figure 2.3 . The pipeline has three stages A, B, and C corresponding to different parts of one task. These might correspond for example to 'load values x and y', 'multiply x by y', and 'add the product to s'. If this set of instructions is carried out many times, the total computation time for *sequential execution* sums each loop through this set of instructions. Using pipelined parallel execution one set of instructions will be finished with each cycle, after an initialization phase (loading the pipeline).

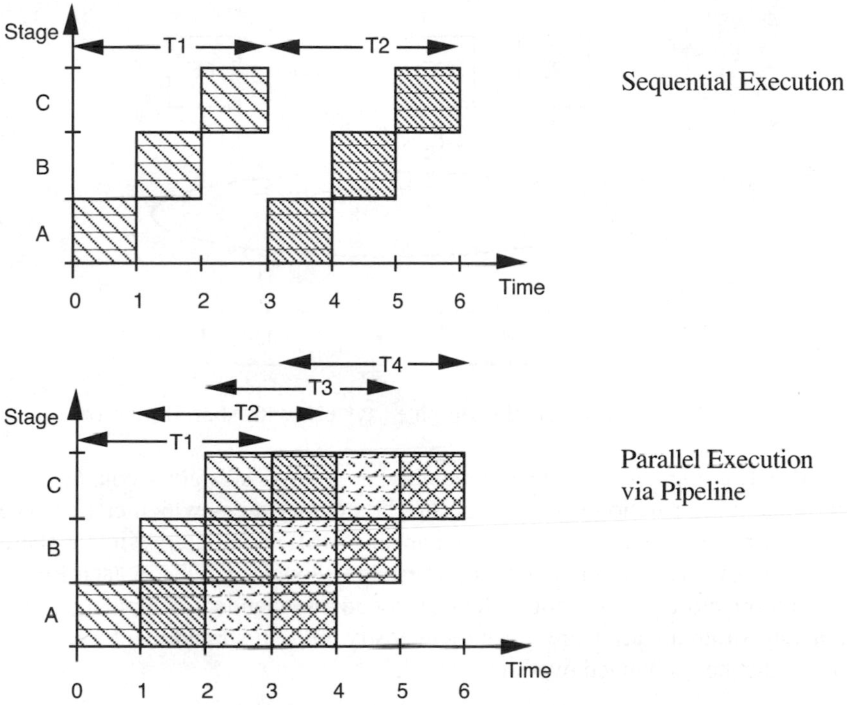

Figure 2.3 Program execution in a pipelined computer system

An *n*-stage pipeline accomplishes, after the load phase of $(n-1)$ cycles, one result in each cycle. This amounts to a parallel speedup by a factor n. Pipelines are specific machine structures that are only applicable to specific tasks. These tasks always involve recurring sets of instructions that show up for example in program loops. Due to phased execution, instruction interdependence is not allowed here. Furthermore, the list of instructions must be coordinated with the size of the pipeline. Detailed information on the structure of pipeline computer systems can be found in [Hockney, Jesshope 88].

A simple pipeline computer with just one pipeline has just one control flow. It is just a single-processor system with an attached arithmetic/logic vector pipeline unit (see Figure 2.2). If two or more independent pipelines are present, then the computer is an MIMD system with pipelines (multiple-pipeline system).

MIMD (multiple instruction, multiple data)

Computers in this class have in comparison to SIMD computers a more general structure and always work asynchronously. Each processor executes its own program with an individual control flow, so multiple control threads are executed simultaneously. One differentiates between MIMD computers with shared memory (see Figure 2.4) and MIMD computers without shared memory (distributed memory, see Figure 2.5).

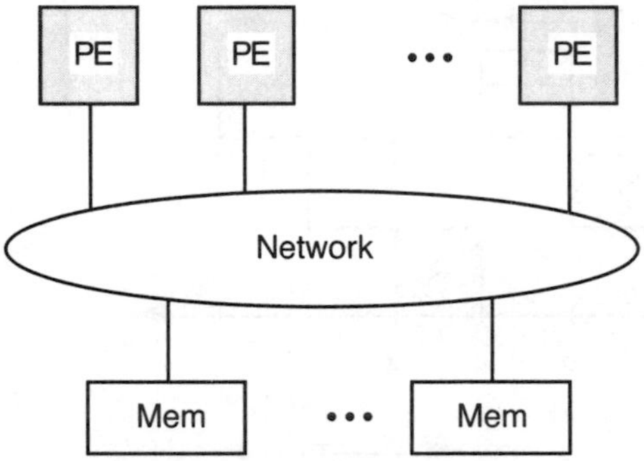

Figure 2.4 MIMD computer system with shared memory

MIMD computers with shared memory are known as 'tightly coupled'. Synchronization and information exchange occur via memory areas which can be accessed by different processors in a coordinated manner. MIMD computers without shared memory are known as 'loosely coupled'. These have local memory in each PE and correspond more closely to a group of loosely bound, independent computers. Synchronization and communication are much more costly without shared memory, because messages must be exchanged over the network.

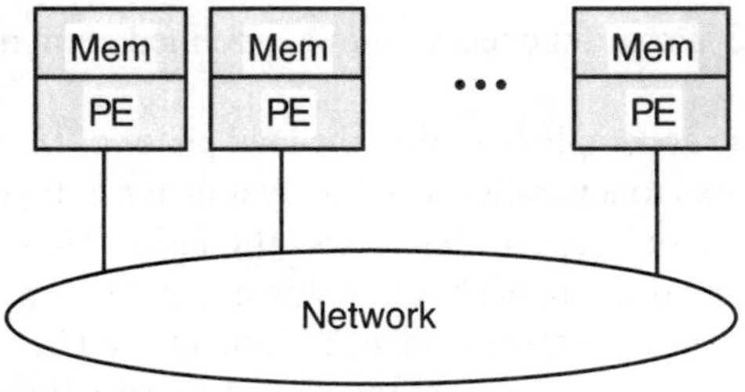

Figure 2.5 MIMD computer system without shared memory

SIMD (single instruction, multiple data)

Array computers, for which the term SIMD computer is often used as a synonym, are constructed more simply than MIMD computers. The hardware for the command cycle (instruction fetch, decode, program counter control) is only required *once* in the central control processor (also known as the 'array control unit', ACU, or 'sequencer'). In this case the PEs are made up of just an arithmetic/logic unit (ALU), local memory and a communication unit attached to the interconnection network. Since only one instruction decoder is present, the execution of a SIMD program is always synchronous. That is, there can exist only one control flow for the whole parallel program (in contrast to MIMD). Each PE either executes the *same instruction* as the other PEs on its local memory or it is inactive.

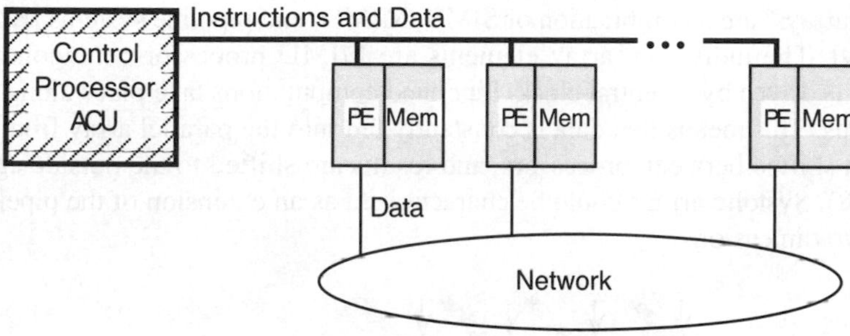

Figure 2.6 Array computer system

A vector computer (see Figure 2.7) is constructed more simply than the array computer described above (see Figure 2.6), because the global interconnection network between the PEs is not present. The 'local data' is implemented as vector registers, where operations are executed component-wise. Simple data exchange operations, like shifts and rotations, are executed via special data links between the PEs.

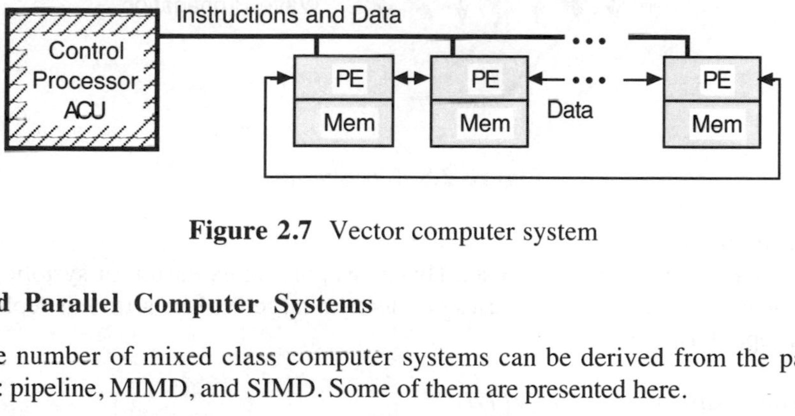

Figure 2.7 Vector computer system

Hybrid Parallel Computer Systems

A large number of mixed class computer systems can be derived from the parallel classes: pipeline, MIMD, and SIMD. Some of them are presented here.

Multiple-Pipeline
As has been mentioned before, a pipeline computer can have two or more independent pipelines and use them in parallel. This makes it a combination of pipeline and MIMD computers.

Multiple-SIMD
In a multiple-SIMD system (MSIMD), there are several control units (ACUs) present, each being responsible for a subset of the PEs. This is equivalent to a (MIMD-like) connection of several independent SIMD computers.

Systolic Arrays
'Systolic arrays' are a combination of SIMD, MIMD, and pipeline systems [Kung, Leiserson 79]. The individual array elements are MIMD processors; the computation, however, is driven by a central clock. Pipelined computations take place along all array dimensions. This means that data is constantly fed into the parallel array from the outside, then shifted between processors, and results are shifted to the outside again (see Figure 2.8). Systolic arrays could be characterized as an extension of the pipeline concept to two dimensions.

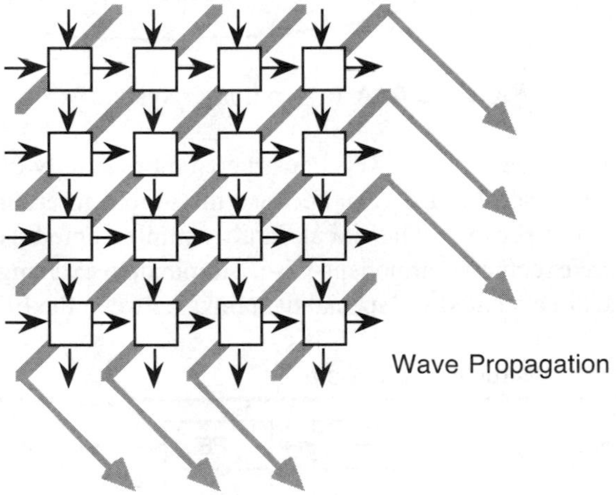

Figure 2.8 Systolic array

Wavefront Arrays
'Wavefront arrays' [Kung, Lo, Jean, Hwang 87] are an extension of systolic arrays. Here, the central clock, which causes problems in large systolic arrays, is replaced by the concept of data flow.

Very Long Instruction Word (VLIW)
Another hybrid form consisting of MIMD and pipeline computers is the 'very long instruction word' or VLIW computer, such as the Multiflow Trace Parallel Computer (see [Fisher 84] and [Hwang, DeGroot 89]). In this computer system, parallelism is achieved with a unusually long instruction format in analogy to horizontal microcode. Several arithmetic/logic operations, contained in one instruction word, are carried out simultaneously and independently of one another. In this way, several scalar operations are executed at the same time without vectorization. A number of problems crop up

with this form of processing, among them the filling of the wide instruction words and the pre-fetch of instructions before (!) a conditional branch. The packing of the individual operations into one VLIW determines the usage level and therefore the level of parallelism and efficiency of this type of parallel computer. The conversion of sequential instructions into a VLIW can only be performed by an 'intelligent' compiler, and since the optimal packing cannot be determined at compile time, heuristics must be applied. Multiflow Trace was not a commercial success and is no longer on the market. The system probably failed in its pretension of having an efficient parallelization of sequential programs, which is a task that might not be possible in this form.

Same Program Multiple Data (SPMD)
A very promising mix of SIMD and MIMD is the SPMD model ('same program multiple data', see [Lewis 91]). As the name suggests, the parallel computer system is controlled by a *single* program (or more exactly by a *single* logical flow of control). This should combine the ease of SIMD programming with MIMD flexibility. While the SIMD model is sufficient, despite its restrictions, for a broad range of applications, it is very inefficient for a simple, parallel `IF–THEN–ELSE` selection. On a SIMD computer system, the two branches of a selection with local condition have to be executed *one after the other* for the '`THEN` group' and the '`ELSE` group' of PEs. This would not happen when executing the same program on a SPMD computer system. The different branches of a selection can be executed *at the same time*, since only one or the other case applies for each individual processor. The same argument holds for different numbers of loop executions between PEs. Each processor of the SPMD system executes the same SIMD program on its local data and with an individual flow of control. While doing this, the computation may be switched between SIMD lock step and asynchronous MIMD operation, according to the structure of the SPMD system. Unlike SIMD lock step with its single thread of control, each of the processors of a SPMD computer system has to synchronize with other processors only whenever a data exchange operation is encountered in the program. The Connection Machine CM-5 can be regarded as a SPMD system, although quite often SPMD is considered to be only a MIMD programming style rather than a classification for parallel computer systems.

2.2 Levels of Parallelism

In a number of publications, for example [Kober 88], a classification of parallelism at different levels is presented (see Figure 2.9). In this scheme, the parallelism present is differentiated by the level of abstraction. At lower levels, the parallelism is more fine-grained, while it is more coarse-grained at higher levels.

Each level deals with a totally different aspect of parallel processing. Methods and constructs of one level are limited to application at that level and in general cannot be applied to other levels. The individual levels are briefly introduced below. Of particular interest are the procedure level (coarse, asynchronous parallelism) and the expression level (fine or massive, synchronous parallelism).

coarse-grained ↕ fine-grained

Level	Executed Object	Example System
Program Level	Job, Task	Multitasking Operating System (e.g. time sharing)
Procedure Level	Process	MIMD System
Expression Level	Instruction	SIMD System
Bit Level	within Instruction	von Neumann Computer (e.g. 16 Bit ALU)

Figure 2.9 Levels of parallelism

Program Level

At this level, complete programs execute simultaneously (or are at least time-sliced) (see Figure 2.10). The host computer is not restricted to a parallel system, but at least a multitasking operating system is required (e.g. implemented via *time sharing*). In this system each user process obtains a time-slice from the operating system (scheduler) according to its priority. Each process gets to use the CPU for a short time, after which it must wait again in the process queue. If – as usual – not enough processors are available for all user processes, parallel processing is simulated through 'quasi parallel' operations.

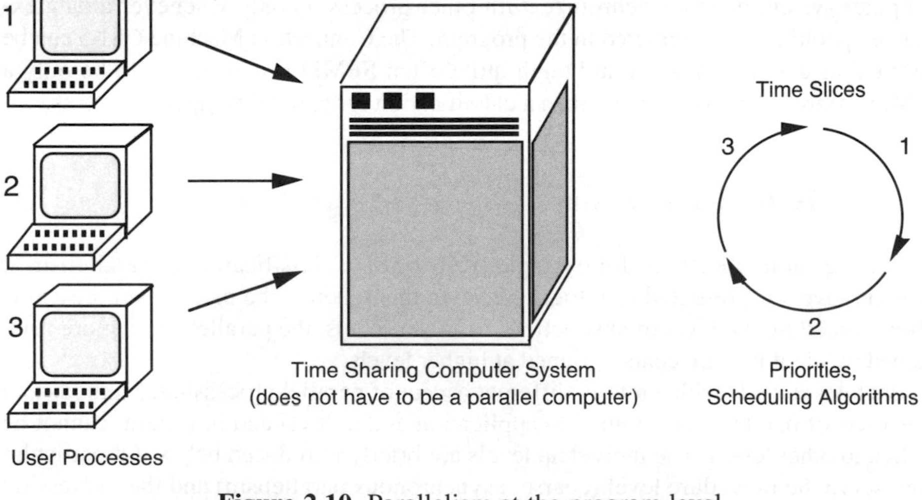

Figure 2.10 Parallelism at the program level

Procedure Level

At this level, several sections of the same program execute in parallel. These program sections are known as 'processes' and correspond approximately to sequential procedures. Problems are divided into largely independent subproblems, so that the relatively expensive exchange of data between processes is minimized. From the fields of application below, it is obvious that this level of parallelism is in no way restricted to the parallelization of sequential programs. A much larger set of applications exists that requires this type of parallel structure, even when only one processor is physically available (similar to the problem at program level).

Fields of Application:

- Real Time Programming
  Control of time-critical technical processes
  e.g. power plants

- Process Control System
  Simultaneous control of multiple physical components
  e.g. robot control

- General Purpose Parallel Processing
  Breaking down a problem into sub-tasks, which are distributed onto several processors for performance enhancement
  (see example in Figure 2.11)

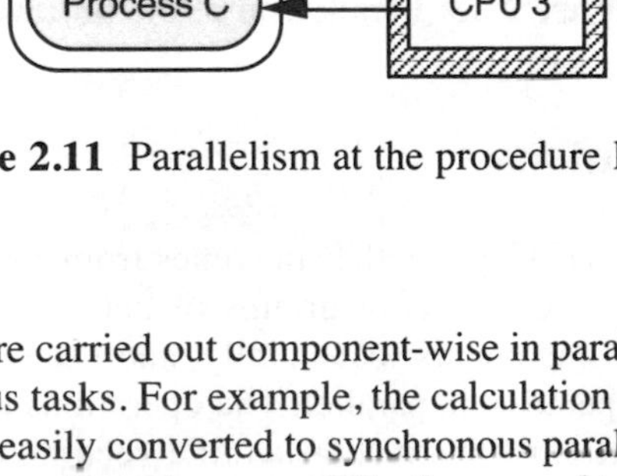

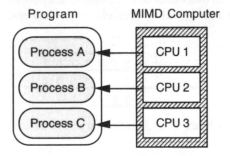

Figure 2.11 Parallelism at the procedure level

Expression Level

Arithmetic expressions are carried out component-wise in parallel. These can be executed in simple synchronous tasks. For example, the calculation of a matrix addition (see Figure 2.12) can be very easily converted to synchronous parallelism by assigning each processor a matrix element. By using $n \times n$ PEs, the sum of two $n \times n$ matrices can be calculated in the time required for a single addition (without considering the time required to load and store the data). The concepts used at this level are vectorization and so-called 'data parallelism'. The expression *data parallelism* has been coined to reflect the fine-grained parallelism at this level. Almost every data element can be assigned a processor of its own, so the 'passive data' elements of a von Neumann computer become 'active processing elements'. This will be dealt with in greater depth in later chapters.

$$\begin{pmatrix} 1 & 2 \\ 3 & 4 \end{pmatrix} + \begin{pmatrix} 1 & 1 \\ 2 & 0 \end{pmatrix} = \begin{pmatrix} 2 & 3 \\ 5 & 4 \end{pmatrix}$$

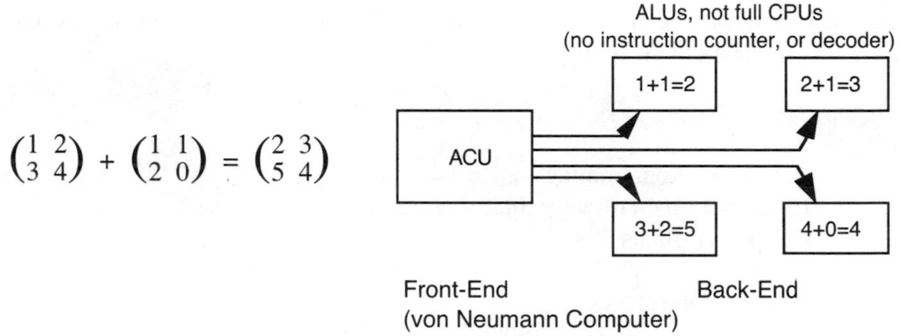

Figure 2.12 Parallelism at the expression level

Bit Level

The parallel execution of bit operations on one word occurs at the bit level (see Figure 2.13). Bit level parallelism can be found in every ordinary microprocessor; for example, in an 8 bit ALU the individual bits are operated upon simultaneously by parallel hardware. Parallelism at this level is relatively easy to understand and will not be considered further.

	0	1	0	1	1	1	0	1
AND	1	1	0	1	1	0	0	0
	0	1	0	1	1	0	0	0

Figure 2.13 Parallelism at the bit level

2.3 Parallel Operations

A totally different way of viewing parallelism comes from analyzing mathematical operations on individual data elements or groups of data. One distinguishes between scalar data, whose processing occurs sequentially, and vector data, which can be processed by the specified operation in parallel. The operations listed below are the basic functions that may be part of the instruction set of a vector computer or an array computer.

Simple operations on vectors, for example the addition of two vectors, can occur directly via synchronous parallelism. In this case a processor could be applied for each vector component. With complex operations, like the construction of all partial sums, the mapping of processors to vector elements for an efficient parallel algorithm is not directly obvious. In the following overview monadic operations are distinguished from dyadic operations. A typical example is given for each type of operation.

Monadic Operations

a: Scalar → Scalar — Sequential processing
Example: 9 ↦ 3 — 'square root'

b: Scalar → Vector — Replication of a data value
Example: 9 ↦ (9,9,9,9) — 'broadcast'

c: Vector → Scalar — Reduction of a vector to a scalar
Example: (1,2,3,4) ↦ 10 — 'summation'

d: Vector → Vector *(with simplifying assumption: vector length remains constant)*

i. Local Vector Operation — Component-wise monadic operation
Example: (1,4,9,16) ↦ (1,2,3,4) — 'vector square root'

ii. Global Vector Operation by Permutation
Example: (1,2,3,4) ↦ (2,4,3,1) — 'exchanging vector components'

iii. Global Vector Operation (General) — (often constructed from simple operations)
Example: (1,2,3,4) ↦ (1,3,6,10) — 'partial sums'

Dyadic Operations

e: (Scalar, Scalar) → Scalar — Sequential processing
Example: (1,2) ↦ 3 — 'scalar addition'

f: (Scalar, Vector) → Vector — Component-wise application of operation on a scalar and a vector
Example: (3, (1,2,3,4)) ↦ (4,5,6,7) — 'addition of a scalar'

Identical to :	3 ↦	(3,3,3,3)	replication	*b)*
		+ (1,2,3,4)	vector addition	*g)*
		(4,5,6,7)		

g: (Vector, Vector) $\rightarrow$ Vector — Component-wise application of operation on two vectors

Example: ((1,2,3,4), (0,1,3,2)) $\mapsto$ (1,3,6,6) — 'vector addition'

The application of these operations will be illustrated through a simple example, the calculation of the dot product of two vectors. This can be achieved though the execution of an operation of type *g* (component-wise application of an operation on two vectors, multiplication in this case) and an operation of type *c* (reduction of a vector to a scalar, using addition in this case) in sequence.

Example: Dot product

$$((1,2,3),\ (4,2,1)) \overset{g}{\mapsto} (4,4,3) \overset{c}{\mapsto} 11$$

$\uparrow$ component-wise multiplication (g) — $\uparrow$ vector reduction through addition (c)

CHAPTER 3

Petri Nets

Petri nets were developed by C. A. Petri in 1962 to define the coordination of asynchronous events (see [Petri 62], [Peterson J. 81] and [Baumgarten 90]). Petri nets are often used for describing interdependence between and synchronization of parallel processes.

Definition

A Petri net is a *directed*, *bipartite graph* with *tokens* (markings).

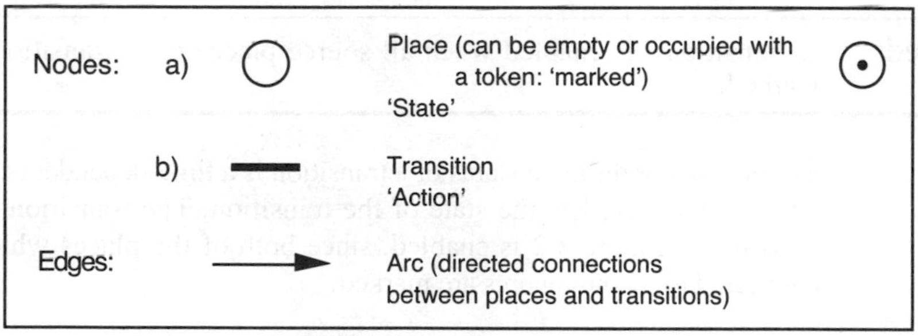

Figure 3.1 Elements of a Petri net

This definition can be understood in the following way (see Figure 3.1): Every Petri net is a graph that consists of two separate types (bipartite) of nodes (places and transitions). Between places and transitions run directed arcs; however, arcs are not allowed to connect two places or two transitions. For each place-transition pair, there may be at most one arc from the place to the transition (*incoming arc*) and at most one arc from the transition to the place (*outgoing arc*). The places can be either free or *marked* (containing tokens); the transition nodes, however, cannot be marked. The places with outgoing arcs to a transition t will be known hereafter as *source places of transition t*. The places with incoming arcs from a transition t will be known hereafter as *drain places of transition t*.

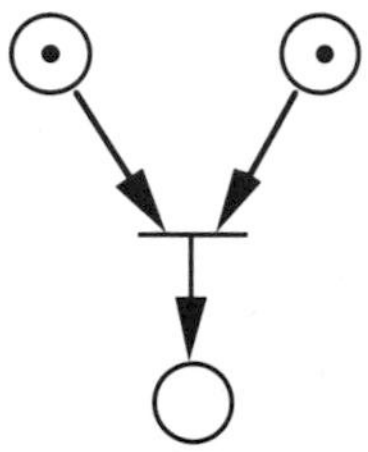

Figure 3.2 Petri net

Figure 3.2 shows a simple Petri net, consisting of a transition node and three places, of which two are marked and one is unmarked. Each place is connected to the transition with an arc. The operation of a Petri net will be explained through the definitions in the next section.

3.1 Simple Petri Nets

Definitions

Enabled: *(State)*	A transition t is enabled when all source places p_i of transition t are marked.

The enabled or disabled status of a transition is a time-dependent characteristic and describes the state of the transition. The transition of the Petri net in Figure 3.2 is enabled, since both of the places which are connected to incoming arcs are marked.

Firing: *(Action)*	An activated transition t may fire. Then all of the source places p_i of t will lose their token (become unmarked), and all of the drain places p_j of t receive a token (become marked).

The process of firing requires that the transition be in the enabled state. Through this process the tokens in the places of a Petri net are altered. Figure 3.3 shows an example of this process: the transition is enabled, since the two places being connected to incoming arcs are marked. After the transition fires, the tokens in the places at the top of the Figure (sources) have disappeared, while a new token has been generated for the place at the bottom (drain).

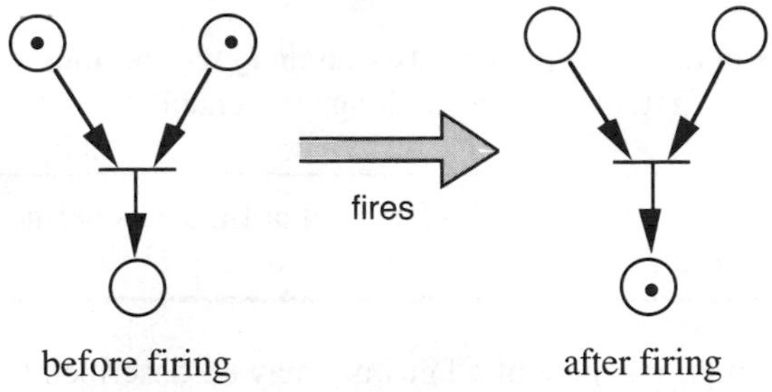

Figure 3.3 Firing of a transition

The total number of tokens in a Petri net does not remain constant. If a drain place already has a token, it will be overwritten, which means it has a token just as it did before the transition fired.

Nondeterminism:	If multiple transitions are simultaneously enabled, then it is not specified (*not determined*) which of them will fire first.

The definitions above do not state in which order multiple, simultaneously enabled transitions will fire. The **concurrent firing** of several transitions is **not** possible! This is illustrated in Figure 3.4, where two different outcomes are possible. Which of these actually occurs is not defined by this Petri net formalism. Since the firing of one or the other transition may not be forced by outside parameters, this Petri net contains a nondeterminism.

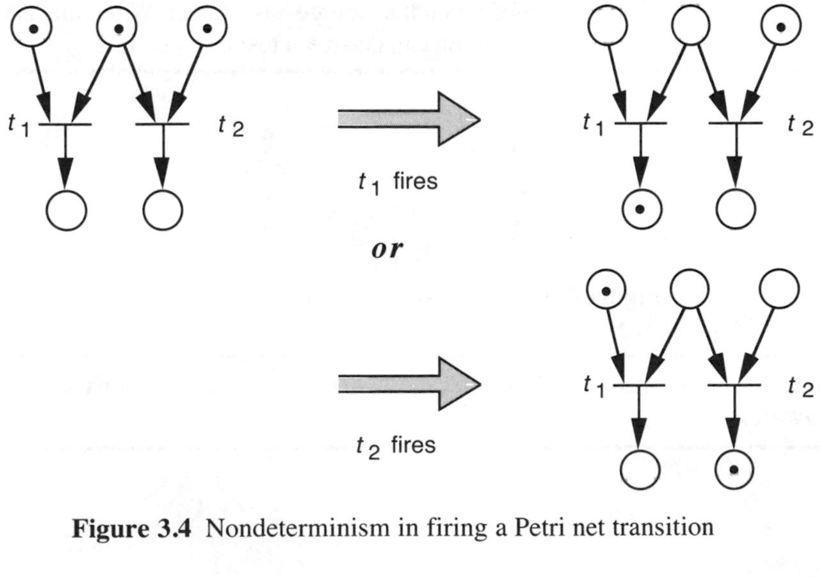

Figure 3.4 Nondeterminism in firing a Petri net transition

If t_1 in this example fires first, then t_2 will no longer be enabled; and if t_2 fires first, then t_1 will no longer be enabled.

State: The (marking) state of a Petri net at time T is defined as the entirety of all markings of each singe place in the net.

The marking state of a Petri net may be described by a sequence of binary digits (a bit string) for simple Petri nets. The firing of a transition is then expressed by a successor state. If there are multiple enabled transitions, as in Figure 3.4, then there exist multiple successor states.

$$ (111\ 00) \overset{(001\ 10)}{\underset{(100\ 01)}{\diagdown}} $$

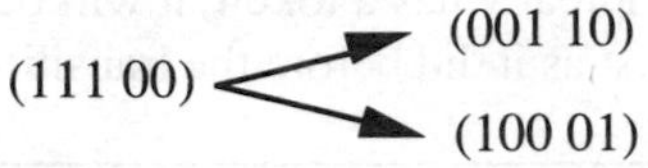

Describing each possible firing of all transitions by such a rule, all successor states from a given start state may be 'computed'. If blockings occur (see below), they can be detected automatically.

Token generation: A transition that has no sources (no incoming arcs) is always enabled and can always generate new tokens for its drains (places to which it has outgoing arcs).

Token destruction: A transition that has no drains and only one source is always enabled when that source has a token. When this is the case, the transition can destroy a token at any time.

Figure 3.5 Generation and destruction of tokens

Dead: A Petri net is dead (blocked) when none of its transitions are enabled.
(Blocking)

A dead Petri net is static in that there can be no new following states. For example, both of the Petri nets on the right-hand side of Figure 3.4 are dead.

Live:	A Petri net is live (unblocked at all times) when at least one of its transitions is enabled and this is true for all possible following states.

It should be noted here that being 'live' is not the opposite of being 'dead'. A live Petri net is not blocked and will never become blocked in successive states, however a non-blocked Petri net is not necessarily live. It could become blocked after several firings. Figure 3.6 shows two examples.

The Petri net on the left-hand side of Figure 3.6 is live; its token moves from place to place, but is never lost. Therefore a transition will always be enabled. In the Petri net on the right-hand side, this is not the case. Either transition *u* can fire (in which case the net is immediately dead) or transition *s* can fire. After *s*, transitions *t* and *u* can fire, but then the net is dead as well.

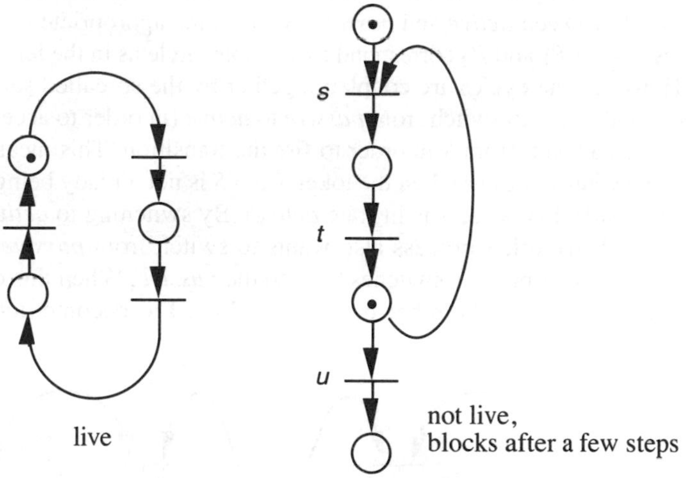

Figure 3.6 Live and blocking Petri nets

As has been mentioned before, Petri nets may be used to describe the synchronization of asynchronously parallel processes. This may be necessary to avoid deadlocks or inconsistent data in cases where two processes need to access shared memory (see Figure 3.7).

Process P_1 (*producer*) in the Figure generates data independent of process P_2, writes it into the buffer area, and would like to continue further processing without having to wait. Process P_2 (*consumer*) reads the data from the buffer area and processes it in parallel to process P_1. In order to avoid inconsistent data, the following restriction must be maintained:

Through the synchronization required to achieve this, one of the processes might eventually be forced to wait for a short period of time.

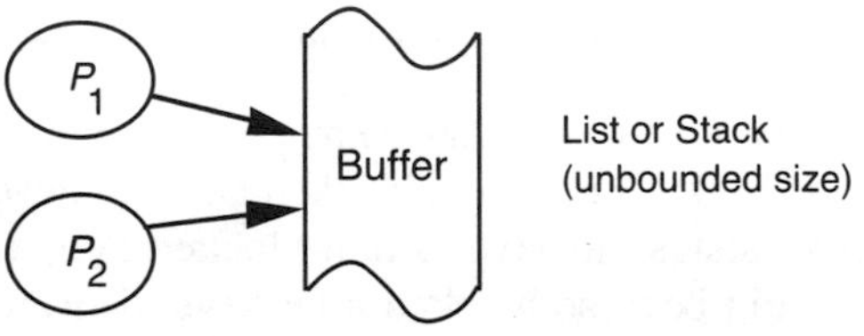

Figure 3.7 Two processes accessing shared memory

The processes must not be allowed to access the buffer area simultaneously.

Figure 3.8 shows a simple example of this situation where two processes P_1 and P_2 are synchronized in order to allow access to shared memory. Each process has two states, *active* and *passive*, symbolized by two places. A process always is in the state that is indicated by its token (in Figure 3.8 both processes are passive). Both processes can switch between *active* and *passive* by firing the appropriate transition. Both of the state cycles for P_1 and P_2 correspond to a simple circle as in the left-hand side of Figure 3.6. However, the cycles are coupled together by the so-called semaphore place S. A process that wants to switch from *passive* to *active* (in order to access the shared memory), needs a token from S in order to fire the transition. This means that it is only allowed to switch to *active* when the token from S is not already being taken by the other process (while this process is in state *active*). By switching to *active*, the token in S is destroyed. If the other process also wants to switch from *passive* to *active*, it has to wait until the first process switches back to the *passive*. When this occurs, the token in S is regenerated, and the other process is allowed to become *active* and access the shared memory.

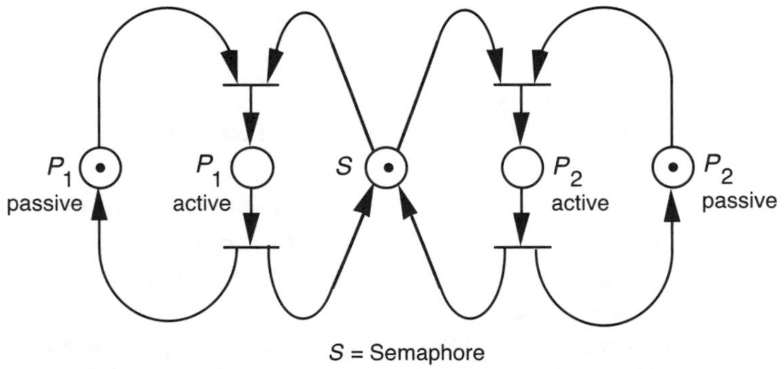

Figure 3.8 Petri net for the synchronization of processes

The synchronization provided by this Petri net reliably excludes more than one of the processes from being in state *active* at any time. If the processes request to enter state *active* simultaneously, their accesses will be sequentialized. Under no condition can a deadlock occur.

3.2 Extended Petri Nets

The simple Petri nets that have been introduced up to this point are fully sufficient for the description of a large set of applications. However, with three simple extensions, these nets can be made considerably more powerful. Hopcroft and Ullman showed that (even without the arc weights, introduced below) extended Petri nets are as powerful as the Turing machine [Hopcroft, Ullman 69], which means that they can be used as a general model of computability.

Extensions:

i) Multiple Tokens

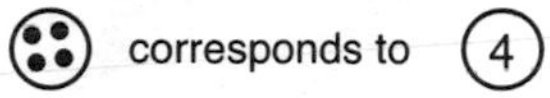

Each place can contain an arbitrary number of tokens (a number greater than or equal to zero). When drawing a Petri net, the tokens can be abbreviated by a number. The rules for firing and enabled transitions are correspondingly adapted:

- A transition is enabled if and only if the number of tokens in each of its sources is greater than or equal to one.
- When a transition fires, the number of tokens in each of its sources is decremented by one and the number tokens in each of its drains is incremented by one.

In this way, the number of tokens in a place can always increase; however, it can never be less than zero.

ii) Inhibitory Arcs
An inhibitory arc is a special kind of incoming arc and is represented by a dot at the transition end of the arc (see Figure 3.9); the earlier defined regular arcs will be called positive arcs. Inhibitory arcs run from a place to a transition, but never in the other direction. The introduction of inhibitory arcs requires a new adaptation of the rules for firing and enabled transitions:

- A transition is enabled if and only if the number of tokens in each of its sources connected by a positive arc is greater than or equal to one and the number of tokens in each of its sources connected by an inhibitory arc is equal to zero. (In Figure 3.9, transition *t* is enabled, since P_1 is marked and P_2 is unmarked.)

- When an activated transition fires, the number of tokens in each of its sources connected by a positive arc is decremented by one while the number of tokens in each of its sources connected by an inhibitory arc remains unchanged during this step. As defined earlier the number tokens in each of its drains will be incremented by one during the second step.

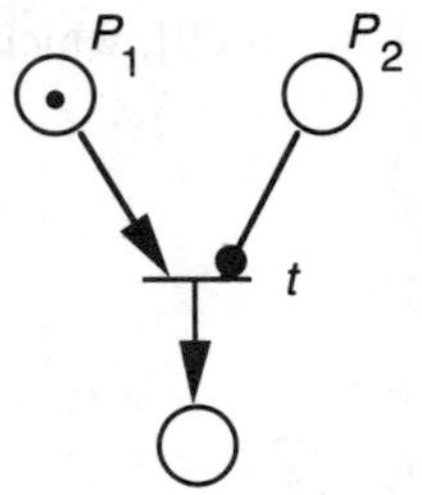

Figure 3.9 Inhibitory arc

iii) Arc Weights

Each arc that is *not* an inhibitory arc may have a constant integer weight greater than or equal to one (default value). The following now holds for enabling and firing of a transition:

- A transition is enabled if and only if the number of tokens in each of its sources is greater than or equal to the corresponding arc's weight or it is equal to zero in case of an inhibitory node.

- When a transition fires, the number of tokens in each of its sources is decremented by the corresponding incoming arc's weight (or remains unchanged for inhibitory arcs) and the number of tokens in each of its drains is incremented by the corresponding outgoing arc's weight.

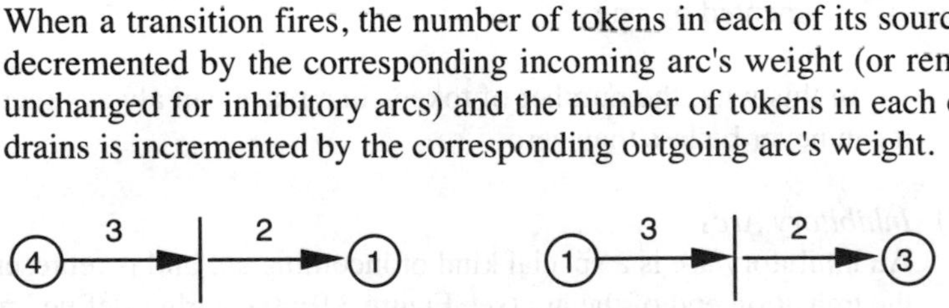

Figure 3.10 Arc weights

Extended Petri Net Summary

p denotes the number of tokens in place P.

***t* is enabled**	:⇔	for all regular sources P of t:	$p \geq$ arc_weight(P,t)
		for all inhibitory sources P of t:	$p = 0$

***t* fires** ⇒	1. step:	for all regular sources P of t:	$p := p -$ arc_weight(P,t)
		for all inhibitory sources P of t:	(* do nothing *)
	2. step:	for all drains P of t:	$p := p +$ arc_weight(P,t)

Note that a place P can be an inhibitory source and also a drain for transition t. This makes two steps necessary in executing a firing.

The following series of examples of extended Petri nets are partially based on [Krishnamurthy 89]. Theoretically any program written in any programming language can be converted into an extended Petri net. It must be noted, however, that the 'token memory' of a place can only contain a positive number or zero. Negative numbers could be represented, for example, by using a separate place to indicate the sign of the value. Each of these examples has a separate, marked place *start* with which the calculation is started and a place *finish*, which indicates that the result has been produced and the calculation is donc. Separate *start* and *finish* places are particularly important when a complex Petri net is to be built from existing components.

Petri Net Adder

The first Petri net in Figure 3.11 adds the tokens in place Y to the tokens in place Z, that is, it calculates the sum $Z + Y$. The distinguished start place will be preset with a value of '1'. After the firing of transition s, this token disappears, and a token appears in place *finish* only after the procedure is completed and place Z contains the sum.

After the start transition s fires, the middle place in the Petri net is marked. With each firing of transition t, the number of tokens in place Y is decremented (source) and the number of tokens in place Z is simultaneously incremented (drain). The middle place remains marked because it has an outgoing and an incoming arc from transition t $(1 - 1 + 1 = 1)$. Nevertheless this place is not superfluous because it ensures that the addition will take place in an orderly fashion after the function is started via the insertion of a token into place *start*. When $Y = 0$ at the end, Z contains the sum of Z and Y, and transition t is no longer enabled. Instead, transition u is now enabled. When u fires, the token in the middle place is removed and a token is generated in place *finish*. This indicates that the calculation has been completed.

It should be noted in this example and in the following one as well that the starting value of Y is deleted (in this case it becomes zero) and is not available for further calculations. If a value is needed later during a calculation, the Petri net must be designed so that the original value is kept.

Adder

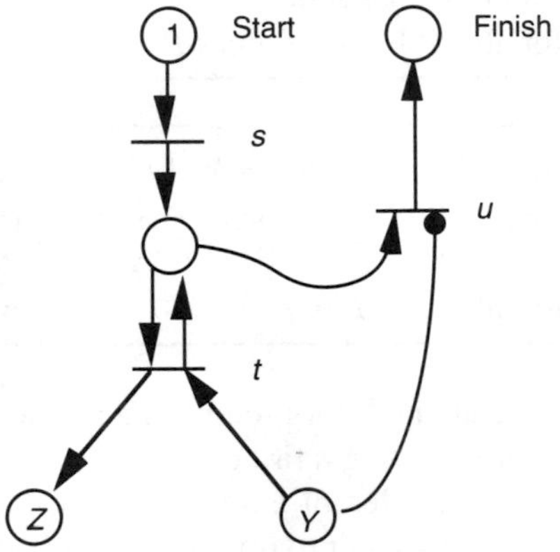

$$Z := Z + Y$$

Figure 3.11 Petri net adder

Subtracter

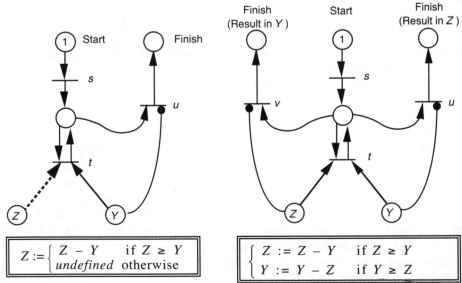

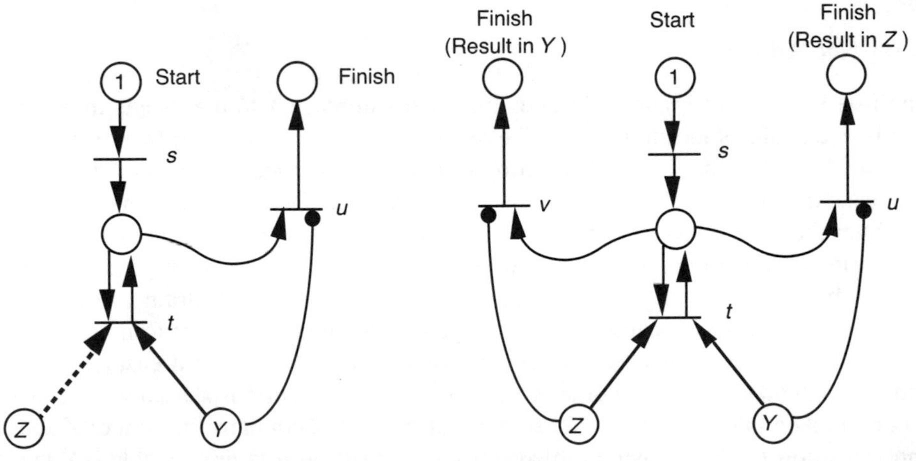

$$Z := \begin{cases} Z - Y & \text{if } Z \geq Y \\ \textit{undefined} & \text{otherwise} \end{cases}$$

$$\begin{cases} Z := Z - Y & \text{if } Z \geq Y \\ Y := Y - Z & \text{if } Y \geq Z \end{cases}$$

Figure 3.12 Two Petri net subtractors

Petri Net Subtractor

A simple subtractor (Figure 3.12, left) can be derived from the adder (Figure 3.11) by simply reversing the arrow to Z (shown as a broken arrow). With this change a token will be removed from Z in each step instead of being added to it. However, this solution only works correctly if $Z \geq Y$. Otherwise the processing stops without putting an end token in place *finish*! Naturally this does not make much sense; therefore the subtractor was extended in Figure 3.12 (right), to calculate a symmetric difference.

Under the symmetric subtraction, the difference $Z - Y$ is generated in Z if $Z \geq Y$ and the difference $Y - Z$ is generated in Y if $Y \geq Z$. The Petri net was correspondingly symmetrically completed by the addition of transition v.

Petri Net Multiplier

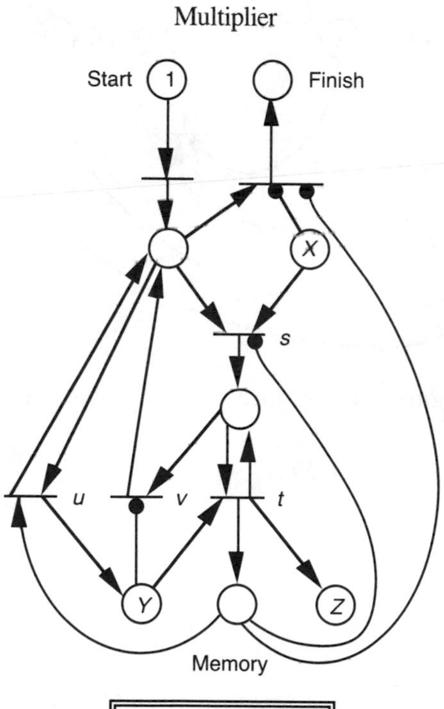

Figure 3.13 Petri net multiplier

The multiplier (Figure 3.13) proves to be somewhat complex. However, one can see the frame of the adder in transitions s, t, and v. This betrays the operation of the multiplier: With each pass, X is decremented by one and Y is added to Z. The original value of *Y* is copied into the 'memory' place during each addition and then transferred back to *Y* via transition *u* in preparation for the next addition. When the 'memory' place becomes equal to zero, the next pass starts, since transition *s* is enabled via the inhibitory arc from the 'memory' place. The passes are carried out until *X* equals zero; therefore the value $X * Y$ is added to *Z*.

Replication

Multiple operations can easily be executed by connecting them with an activation chain. This can be accomplished by connecting their *start* and *finish* places in the desired sequence or in parallel. With multiple read accesses to the same memory cell, the processing must occur sequentially and each operation must replace the original value of the cell. This condition was required only by the multiplier example for variable *Y*. Figure 3.14 shows a general method of replicating the value of a variable.

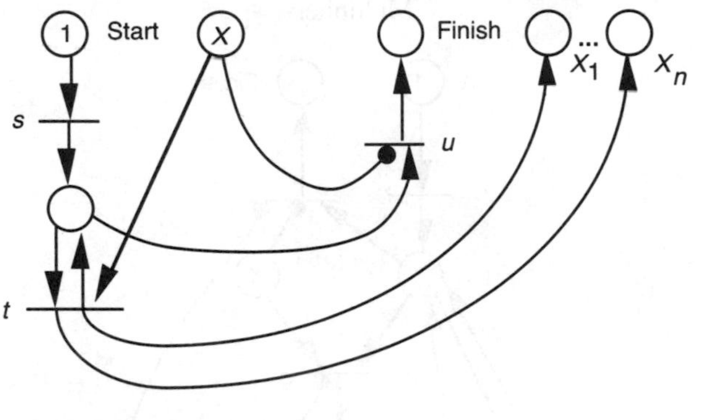

Figure 3.14 Replication of variable values

Sequential and Parallel Petri Nets

i) Sequential Processing

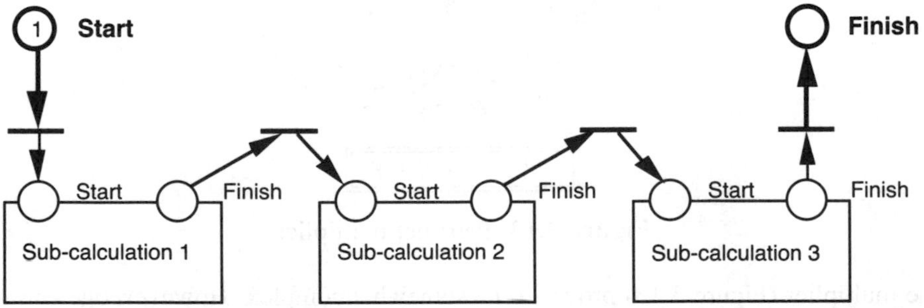

Figure 3.15 Sequentially composed Petri net

Figures 3.15 and 3.16 show examples of complex Petri nets, which are constructed from simpler modules that are treated like *black boxes*.

ii) Parallel Processing

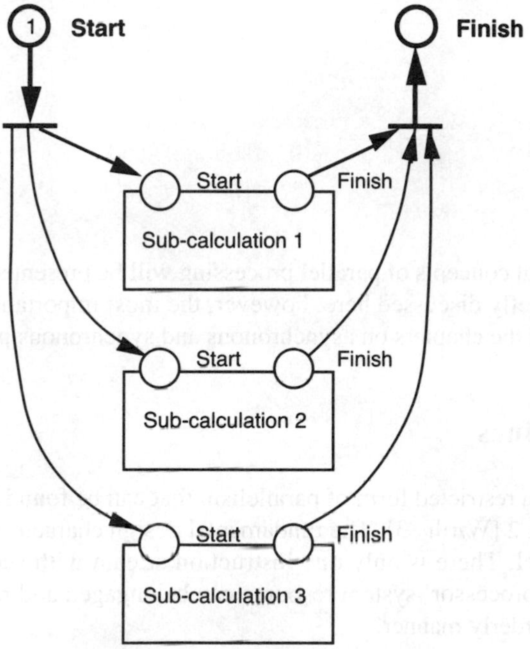

Figure 3.16 Parallel composed Petri net

CHAPTER 4

Parallel Processing Concepts

The fundamental concepts of parallel processing will be presented in this chapter. They will only be briefly discussed here; however, the most important concepts will be further explored in the chapters on asynchronous and synchronous parallelism.

4.1 Coroutines

Coroutines are a restricted form of parallelism that can be found among other places in Wirth's Modula-2 [Wirth 83]. The fundamental design characteristic here is the single-processor model. There is only one instruction stream with sequential flow control. However, the 'processor' system resource can be engaged and released by a set of coroutines in an orderly manner.

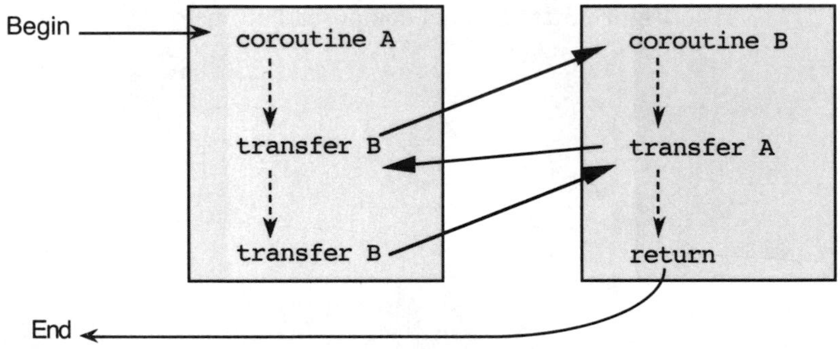

Figure 4.1 Coroutines

A 'quasi-parallel' execution takes place between two or more coroutines. They can be seen as a kind of procedure, whose local data is kept between calls. Execution starts with the call of *one particular* coroutine. Each coroutine may contain any number of `transfer` statements that switch the flow of control to a different coroutine. This is *not* a procedure call, that is the coroutine called does not have to return control to the calling coroutine, but may switch to another coroutine. If a previously active coroutine regains control, execution is resumed at the statement following the `transfer` statement. In case an active coroutine terminates, the execution of all coroutines is terminated. The transfer of control has to be explicitly specified by the application programmer. Therefore, he also has to take care that each coroutine will be reached and that the flow of control is transferred at the correct points.

Since this concept is based on one processor (and cannot be extended to multiple processors), it avoids the overhead of multitasking. The branching of the control flow must be explicitly defined by the application programmer. However, true parallel processing does not occur!

The procedure `transfer` is provided in order to switch control flow between coroutines in Modula-2:

```
PROCEDURE TRANSFER (VAR Source, Destination: ADDRESS);
```

For each flow control switch, the current and next coroutine's name must be explicitly specified.

4.2 Fork and Join

The `fork` and `join` constructs (which are known in the Unix operating system as `fork` and `wait`) were introduced by Conway and Van Horn. They are among the earliest parallel language constructs ever used (see [Conway 63] and [Dennis, Van Horn 66]).

It is possible to start parallel processes in the Unix operating system [Kernighan, Pike 84] with the `fork` operation and to wait for the end of them with the `wait` operation. In contrast to coroutines, this is an example of true parallel processing. However, execution may also be performed through time-sliced multitasking on one processor, if multiple processors are not available.

In this type of parallel programming, two fundamentally different concepts are mixed: first, the declaration of parallel processes; and second, the synchronization of processes. Since this deals with totally different conceptual problems, it would be better according to the fundamentals of software engineering clearly to separate these concepts in a programming language with distinct language structures.

Actually the functionality of the `fork` operation in Unix is not as general as shown in Figure 4.2. Instead, an identical copy of the calling process is generated, which then executes in parallel to the original. The values of all variables and that of the program counter in the new process are identical to those of the original process. The only possibility for a process to determine its identity (either parent or child process) is to read the process identification number being returned by the `fork` operation. For the child process this number will be zero; whereas for the parent process this value will be the same as the Unix process number, which can never be zero. This method cannot be said to constitute clear and safe programming.

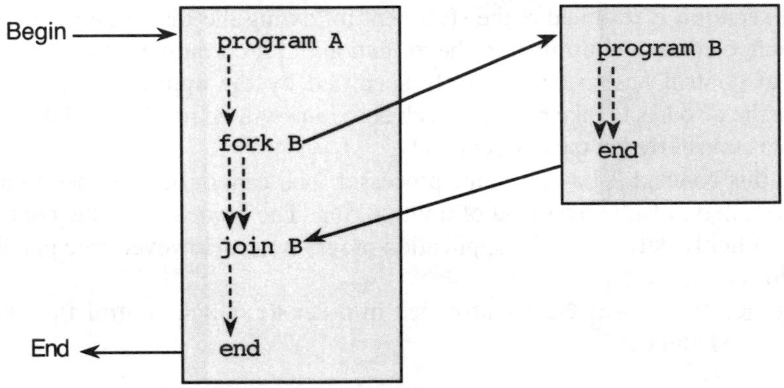

Figure 4.2 Fork and join

In order to start a different program and wait for its termination, the two Unix calls can be embedded in the C language in the following way (from [Kernighan, Pike 84]):

```
int status;
if (fork() == 0) execlp ("program_B",...);   /* Child Proc */
...                                          /* Parent Proc */
wait(&status);
```

The call to the `fork` operation returns the process number of the child process to the parent process (here `fork()` is not equal to 0); however, `fork` returns the value 0 to the child process. In this way, the child process immediately executes the `execlp` operation and not the parent's program, while the parent process executes the instructions following the `fork` operation in parallel to the child process. The parent process can wait for the termination of the child process with the `wait` operation; the return parameter contains the termination status of the child process.

4.3 ParBegin and ParEnd

Blocks of parallel code are defined with `parbegin` and `parend` (often also called `cobegin` and `coend`) in a manner analogously to the sequential `begin` and `end`; however, the instructions in the block should be carried out simultaneously. This concept is implemented for example in the robot programming language AL [Mujtaba, Goldman 81]. A parallel program in AL may control several robots and coordinate their movements with semaphores (see Chapter 7). The `par` operator in Algol68 has a similar function. It allows the creation of parallel processes which are also synchronized with semaphores.

As an analogy to railway signal posts, semaphores allow the controlled reservation and return of system resources. Requests which may not be satisfied at the moment result in a blocking of the caller, which will be released at a later time. Synchronization through semaphores is rather primitive and somewhat non-obvious. Furthermore, there are no high level synchronization and communication concepts available for the `parbegin/parend` concept, to support parallel programming.

Due to the restrictions mentioned, this concept of a parallel statement block has no application in modern parallel programming languages.

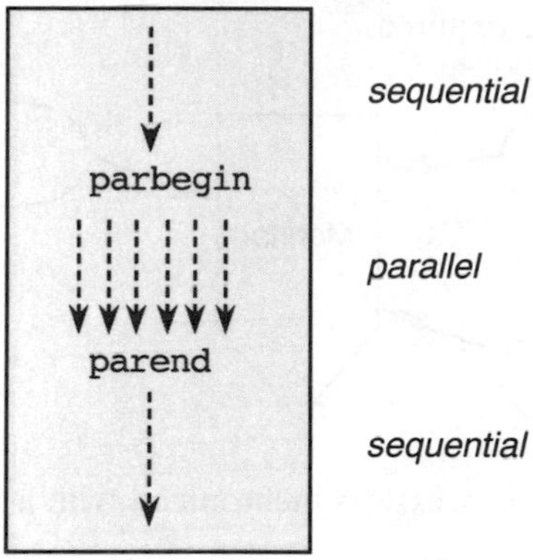

Figure 4.3 Parallel statement block

4.4 Processes

Processes are declared similarly to procedures and are started with a specific instruction. If several copies of a process need to be executed, then that process type must be started with multiple calls possibly having different parameters (similar to procedure parameters). The synchronization between processes executing in parallel may be controlled through the concepts of semaphores or monitors with condition variables [Hoare 74] (see Chapter 7). Monitors, as compared to semaphores, allow a much safer synchronization at a higher level of abstraction. All shared data are encapsulated together with the data access operations and the waiting lists (conditions) into one unit: *the monitor*. Only one process is allowed to operate inside a monitor at one time. This eliminates a number of synchronization problems right from the start. Blocking and release of processes inside a monitor are handled via explicit operations on condition waiting lists.

The explicit synchronization of parallel processes exacts not only an additional control cost, but is also extremely susceptible to error. This comes from the considerable amount of time required to become accustomed to this method of expressing parallel execution. If several processes need to access shared memory, the so called 'critical regions' must be protected with a synchronization construct. This means that only one of the processes is allowed to enter its critical region, where it is allowed to work on shared data. Common errors are the uncontrolled entrance to or exit from a critical region (e.g. forgetting the synchronization operations), as well as mistakes in handling waiting (blocked) processes. These mistakes can lead to inconsistent (corrupted) data in the first case or to 'deadlock', the blocking of several processes or the entire system, in the second case.

Communication and synchronization are accomplished in systems with shared memory ('tightly coupled') via monitors with conditions. In systems without shared memory ('loosely coupled'), the concepts shown in the following section for sending and receiving of messages are required.

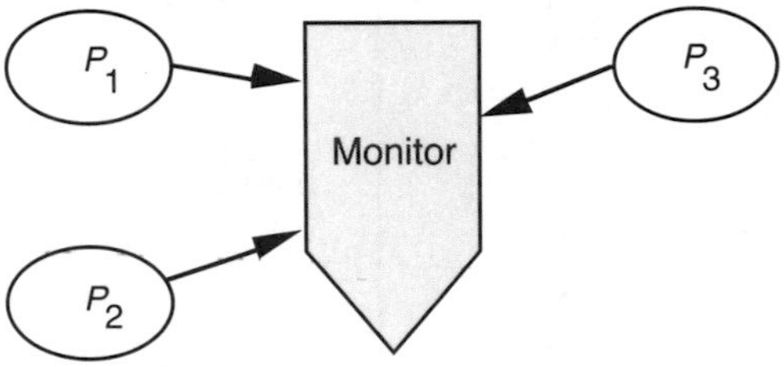

Figure 4.4 Processes synchronized with a monitor

4.5 Remote Procedure Call

In order to extend the process concept to a parallel computer system without shared memory, the communication between processes located on different processors has to be carried out by message passing. However, message passing may also be implemented on a MIMD system with shared memory (being more comfortable, but causing more overhead).

The programming system is divided into multiple parallel processes, where each process takes on the roll of either a client or a server. Each server basically consists of an endless loop in which it waits for the next computational request, carries out the request, and if necessary returns a result. Every server can also become a client by using the services of another server. Each client confers tasks on one or more appropriately configured server processes.

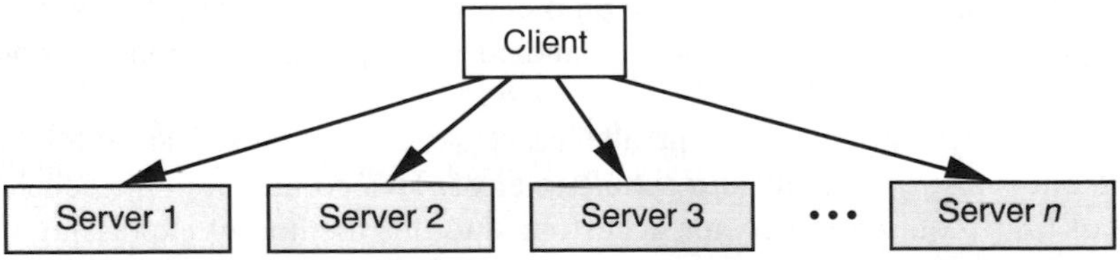

Figure 4.5 Client with multiple servers

This type of parallel task distribution is implemented with the 'remote procedure call' (RPC) mechanism (see Figure 4.6). The processing throughput naturally increases considerably if the client can continue processing in parallel, instead of having to wait for the result from the server at each request. However, problems may arise from this attempt to achieve higher efficiency through better utilization of the parallel hardware. Now, return parameters are no longer available immediately after the execution of a server operation. Here, a remote procedure call resembles just a 'task deposit' operation. Returning the results after the calculation by the server requires another explicit data exchange in the opposite direction (from server to client). Problems with the 'remote procedure call' include the application of error tolerant protocols for resetting or maybe restarting of the client after a server failure.

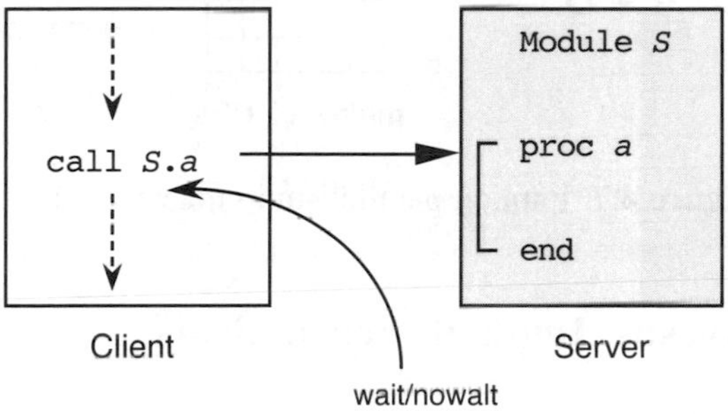

Figure 4.6 Remote procedure call

4.6 Implicit Parallelism

All parallel concepts covered so far use special, *explicit* language constructs for controlling the parallel execution. Much more elegant, however, are programming languages that do not require any language constructs for parallelism, but nevertheless allow parallel processing. Such programming languages are called languages with *implicit* parallelism.

The implicit representation of parallel execution is by far the most elegant form of parallel programming. The programmer, however, is much more limited in controlling the parallel processors which are executing his program. Enough procedural information ('knowledge') must be present to enable efficient parallelization since this has to be done by an 'intelligent' compiler without (or only with limited) interaction with the application programmer. This problem becomes especially clear with declarative languages like Lisp (functional) or Prolog (logic). The declarative representation of knowledge or problems to be solved (for example a set of complex mathematical formulas) may unequivocally specify a solution. However, it may be quite difficult to convert this knowledge into an imperative parallel program, e.g. generating a program to solve the formula and separate the problem into parallel sub-problems (performing the actual parallelization).

The implicit parallelism of vector expressions, for example from the programming languages FP (Functional Programming [Backus 78], see Section 17.2) or APL (A Programming Language [Iverson 62]), can be directly extracted. However, in APL the indispensable high level control structures are lacking.

As shown in Figure 4.7, the mathematical notation of a matrix addition contains implicit parallelism that can (in this case) quite easily be converted to a parallel computer architecture through automatic parallelization (see parallelism at the expression level in Section 2.2).

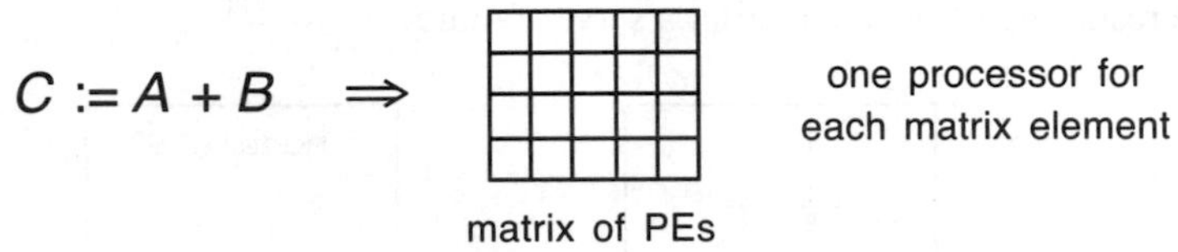

Figure 4.7 Implicit parallelism in matrix operations

4.7 Explicit versus Implicit Parallelism

Explicit Parallelism	Implicit Parallelism
• Programmer has total control over parallel activities	• Programmer is freed from the control complexities of parallel processes
• Efficient program execution (depends on the programmer, requires special knowledge)	• Often inefficient program execution
• Difficult, error prone programming	• Simple programming, less error prone
• Mostly procedural programming languages (exception *Lisp)	• Mostly non-procedural programming languages or parallelizing/vectorizing compiler for procedural programming languages (e.g. Fortran)

Figure 4.8 Comparison of implicit and explicit parallelism

A summary of the advantages and disadvantages of explicit and implicit parallelism is presented in Figure 4.8 . Implicit parallelism relieves the programmer since he does not have to handle a number of control problems. The programming actually occurs at a higher level of abstraction; for this reason implicit parallelism is often found in higher, non-procedural languages. In contrast, explicit parallelism gives the programmer considerably more flexibility that, when used correctly, can lead to better processor utilization and higher performance. This advantage is paid for with more complicated and more error prone programming methods.

CHAPTER 5

Network Structures

Every parallel computer contains a set of processors and one or more memory modules. These functional units must be connected with one another by some type of network structure, in order to build one system. All high level communication concepts, like shared memory (real or virtual) or the exchange of messages, will be mapped onto the network structure available in a parallel computer system. Depending on the duties of the computer system, the network structure must fulfil different criteria. For one, the network structure should have a sufficiently high connectivity. This means that a connection between any two processors (or between a processor and a memory module) can be constructed without having to use too many intermediate stations. Next, the network should be capable of providing a sufficient number of simultaneous connections, thereby minimizing restrictions on the parallel execution due to the network structure. On the other hand, there are a number of limitations constraining the physical construction of the network. For example, the number of connection lines per processor is limited, as is the bandwidth (transmission speed) of the network.

The following types of costs are defined for a parallel system with n PEs (processing elements):

Costs:
a) Number of connections per PE
(Production costs)

b) Average distance between the PEs
(Operating costs)

It follows from the observations above that the number of connections per PE should be kept moderately low, while the distance (the shortest connection between two given PEs) should be as short as possible. The connection structure should be extendible (*scalable*) from smaller to larger networks.

Network structures are divided into three major classes, which will be discussed in the following sections:

- Bus networks
- Switching networks
- Point to point networks

5.1 Bus Networks

The bus is already known as a network structure for the construction of a von Neumann computer. Just as a bus connects the functional units of a sequential computer, it can also connect the processors and memory modules of a parallel computer system (see Figure 5.1).

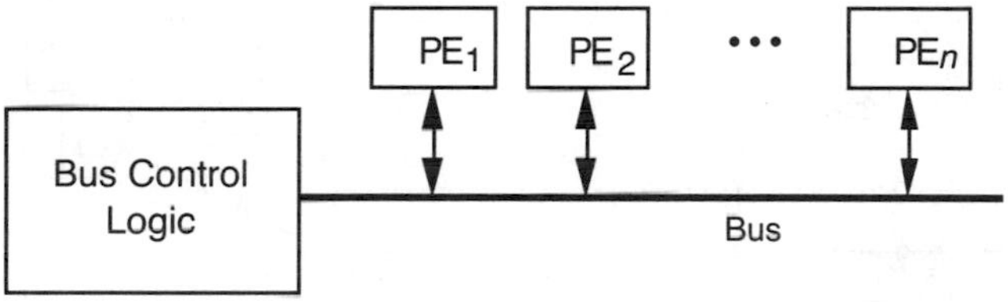

Figure 5.1 Bus network

The number of connections per PE is always one, which is optimal. The distance between two PEs is also constant at 2 (not 1, since each connection must go from a PE to the bus and back to a PE: $PE_i \rightarrow Bus \rightarrow PE_j$). This is almost optimal as well. The disadvantages of a bus come from the fact that only one connection can exist at a time. Parallel reading of the same address of a memory module is possible, but parallel writing is not. Neither parallel reading from different memory locations nor parallel writing to them is possible. Multiple processor pairs can in no way exchange information independent of each other. Therefore, parallel problems requiring the exchange of information between multiple pairs of processors cannot be carried out in parallel. The bus controller must provide for a sequentialization of simultaneous bus requests.

When increasing the number of PEs in the system, the bus network bandwidth remains fixed. This serious disadvantage restricts the scalability of bus architectures. Therefore bus networks become unusable for parallel computers with more than about ten processors.

5.2 Switching Networks

Switching networks are dynamic connection structures with active elements. Varying connection patterns can be engaged during the run time of a program. The dynamic networks explained here are crossbar switch, delta networks, Clos networks, and 'fat trees'.

Crossbar Switch

Each PE has n crosspoints, building connections to all other PEs including itself. Actually connections are not necessary on the identity diagonal, however, they are usually included to facilitate general data exchange operations. Therefore the total network with n PEs has n^2 crosspoints. Every possible set of connections between all PEs can be arranged (any 'permutation of PE connections' can be specified, see Section 2.3), which means collision free, fully parallel information exchanges can be performed. The considerable disadvantage of a crossbar switch is its cost of construction. Networks with quadratic order costs can only be realized for a very small number of processors. Even with just 100 processors, 10,000 crosspoints are required.

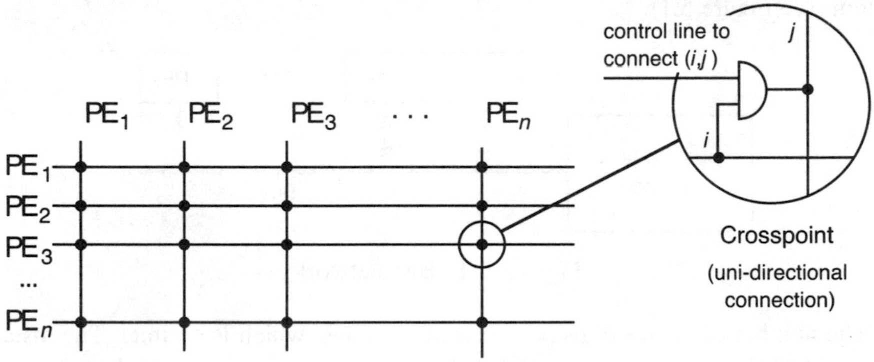

Figure 5.2 Full crossbar switch

Delta Networks

Delta networks were developed in order to reduce the n^2 costs of crossbar switches. In the simplest case (see Figure 5.3), two data connection bundles can by means of a control function f either be crossed or passed straight through.

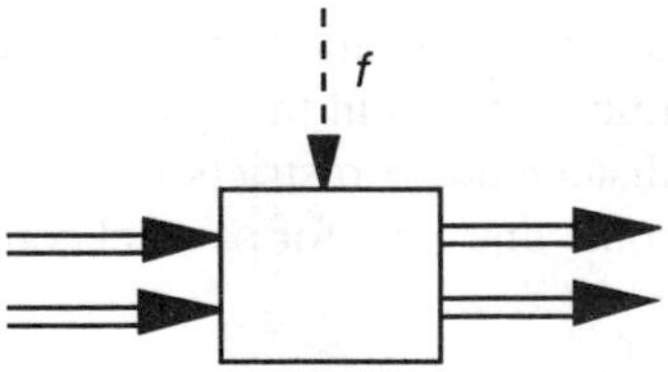

Figure 5.3 Delta network

Figure 5.4 shows the function inside the 'black box' of a delta network. If a zero is present on the control line, the two incoming connections (or connection bundles) will be switched straight through. If a one is present, the connections are crossed.

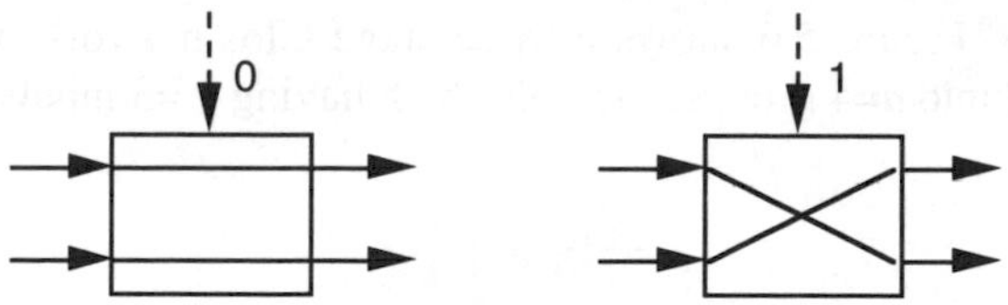

Figure 5.4 Delta network switches

Large networks can be constructed on this simple basis. Figure 5.5 shows a three level delta network which connects eight inputs with eight outputs. Each box is a basic switch from Figure 5.4.

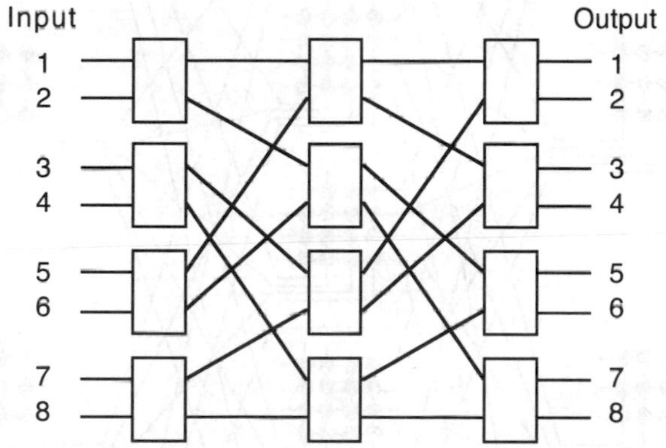

Figure 5.5 8 × 8 delta network

The advantage of delta networks is their relatively small cost in comparison to crossbar switches. A delta network with n inputs and n outputs needs only $\frac{1}{2}n * \log(n)$ basic delta switches (black boxes). The most important disadvantage is that not all of the possible connection permutations may be executed in a single step. The network can become blocked, which must be dealt with by special programming concepts. A blocking in a network leads to a considerably longer execution time for the parallel program, since a reconfiguration of the network and a new connection set-up are required. This situation is comparable to the telephone network.

Clos Networks

Clos attempted to combine the best characteristics of crossbar switches and delta networks in Clos networks [Clos 53], [Gonauser, Mrva 89]. The requirement for this network is that every possible permutation of connections be supported, which means blocking cannot occur. On the other hand, the costs (total number of crosspoints) should be minimal. This is achieved through the cost minimizing construction of a multiple stage delta network where the elements of each stage consist of small, simple crossbar switches. Figure 5.6 shows a three stage Clos network with N=12 inputs, which are divided into a=4 groups, each of which having m=3 inputs.

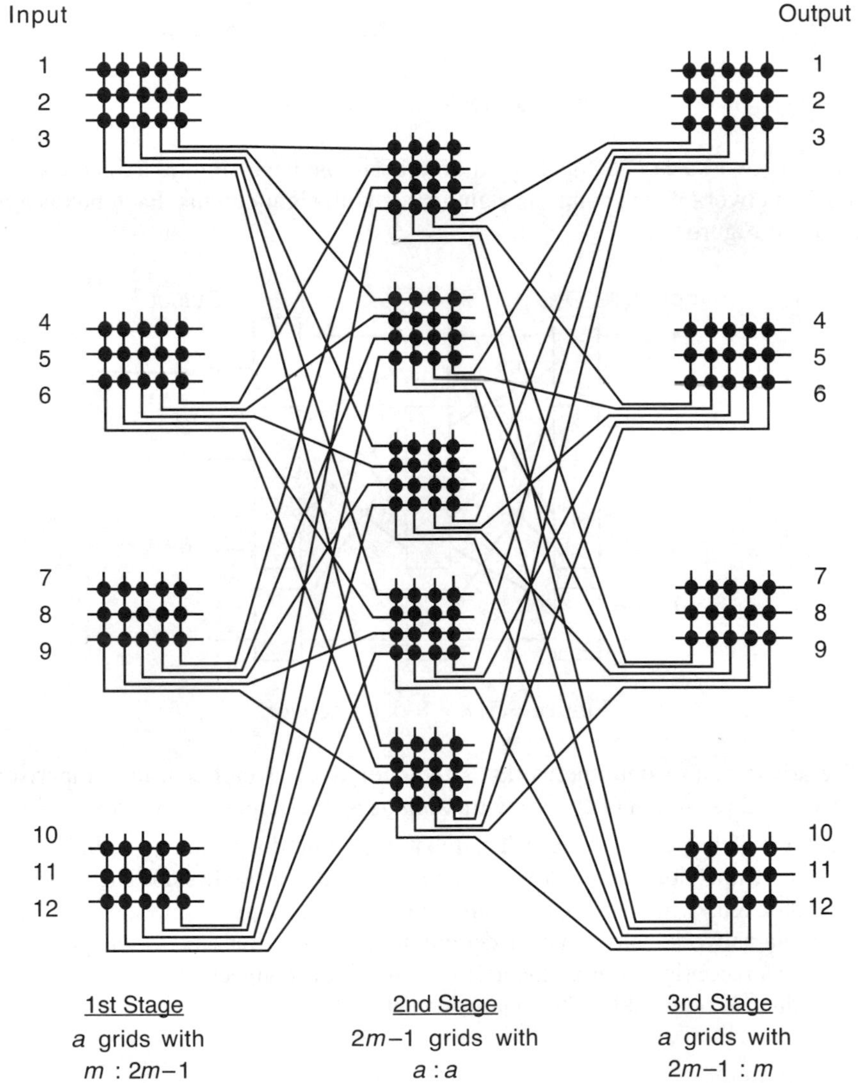

Figure 5.6 Three level Clos network for N = 12 (with a=4, m=3)

The first stage of this three stage Clos network is implemented via a small crossbar switches, each of which having m inputs and $2*m-1$ outputs ($N = a*m$). The second stage constitutes $2*m-1$ crossbar switches with a inputs and a outputs. Finally, the third stage has once again a crossbar switches, but in this case with $2*m-1$ inputs and m outputs. The selectable parameter for the configuration of a three stage Clos network is m (directly specifying the size of the sub-networks in the first and third stages). It is easy to prove that the total number of crosspoints in a three stage Clos network is close to minimum, if

$$m \approx \sqrt{\frac{N}{2}}$$

(for $N \geq 24$, since only for large values of N is a Clos network more favourable than a full crossbar network).

The total number of crosspoints, C, in a three stage Clos network comes to:

$(2*a)$ crossbar switches with $m : (2*m-1)$ [stages 1 and 3] and
$(2*m-1)$ crossbar switches with $a : a$ [stage 2]

$$\begin{aligned} C &= m*(2*m-1)*a + a^2*(2*m-1) + (2*m-1)*m*a \\ &= m*(2*m-1)*2*a + a^2*(2*m-1) \\ &= (2*m-1)*(a^2 + 2*m*a) \end{aligned}$$

$$\Rightarrow \quad C = (2*m-1)*(\frac{N^2}{m^2} + 2*N)$$

(for $N = a*m$)

For the optimal choice of m, the cost for a three-stage Clos network is about:

$C \approx \sqrt{32} * N^{3/2}$
(this is in contrast to costs of approximately N^2 for a full crossbar switch)

Example:

For a three stage Clos network with 1,000 inputs and outputs:

$$m \approx \sqrt{\frac{1{,}000}{2}} \approx 22.4$$

Selecting the following approximations:

$$m = 20 \quad \Rightarrow \quad a = 50 \;\; (= \frac{N}{m})$$

The total number of crosspoints comes to:

$$\begin{aligned} C &= 39 * (\frac{1{,}000{,}000}{400} + 2{,}000) \\ &= 175{,}500 \end{aligned}$$

This number of required crosspoints is considerably smaller than that which would be required by a full crossbar switch:

$$C_{CB} = N^2 = 1{,}000{,}000$$

The Clos network saves more than 82% of the crosspoints compared to a full crossbar switch.

A Clos network is a 'multiple stage crossbar switch', where the reduced number of crosspoints is traded against higher delay when carrying out the communication (the data must pass through the individual stages of the Clos network). The sizes of the crossbar sub-networks are suitably selected to ensure that blocking does not occur.

Fat Tree Networks

The 'fat tree' is a new development in the area of tree-fashioned connection structures [Leiserson 85]. This network is scalable in both the number of processors and the number of parallel communications. The processors are the leaves of a complete binary tree, while the inner nodes are switches. The number of processors therefore is a power of two ($N = 2^m$) and the number of switches is N–1. The higher a switch is placed in the tree structure, the more connections are routed through it (though not necessarily twice as many for each tree level).

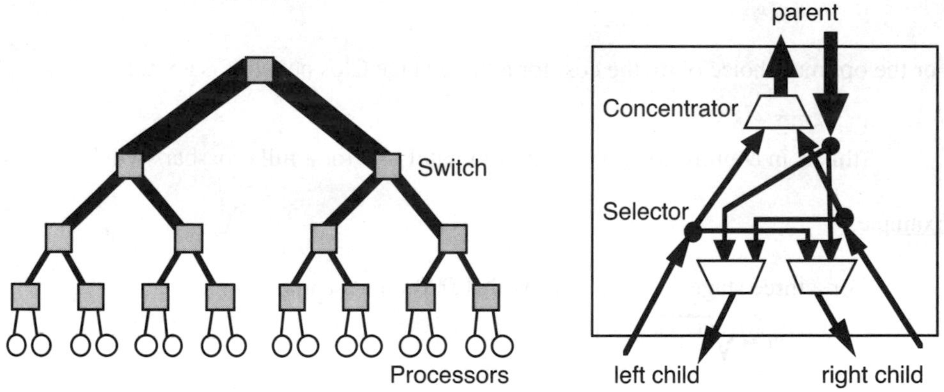

Figure 5.7 Fat-tree network and single switch in detail

It has been proven in [Leiserson 85] that for any kind of communication network, a fat tree simulating this network can be constructed using the same amount of communication hardware, while being slower only by a poly-logarithmic factor. This means that the fat tree is an almost optimal network structure. This property makes it an excellent choice for the use in parallel computer systems. The network structure of the Connection Machine CM-5 from Thinking Machines Co. is based on a fat tree.

5.3 Point to Point Networks

Static point to point networks are described in this section. All connections are assumed to be bi-directional, if not stated otherwise. The following abbreviations are used in the description of the connection structures:

n	=	Number of PEs in the network
V	=	Connections for each PE
A	=	Maximum distance between two PEs

Ring

The ring structure has only two connections per PE (a very positive characteristic). However, it requires in the worst cast n/2 steps for an information exchange (a very negative characteristic), when a PEs wants to communicate with its most distant PE.

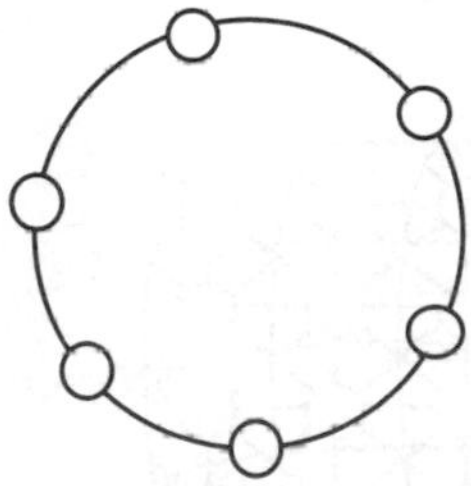

$V = 2$
$A = \frac{n}{2}$

Figure 5.8 Ring

Complete Graph

The opposite of a ring is a complete graph. Its optimal connectivity (each PE is directly connected to every other PE) is paid for by the enormous number of connections, $n-1$, per PE.

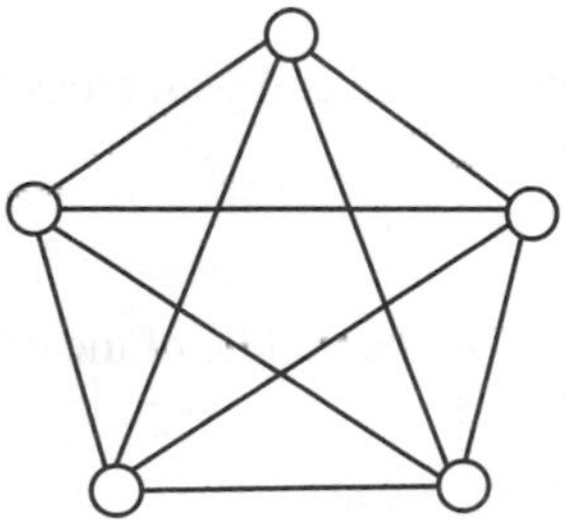

$V = n-1$
$A = 1$

Figure 5.9 Complete graph

Grid and Torus

The various grids and their closed forms, the tori, are very popular types of network. Figure 5.10 shows the differences between 4 way and 8 way nearest neighbor connections. All of the square grids have a maximum distance on the order of the square root of the number of PEs. The maximum distance is cut in half through the doubling of the number of connections in the 8 way nearest neighbor grids. The same effect is achieved by implementing a torus without increasing the number of connections per PE.

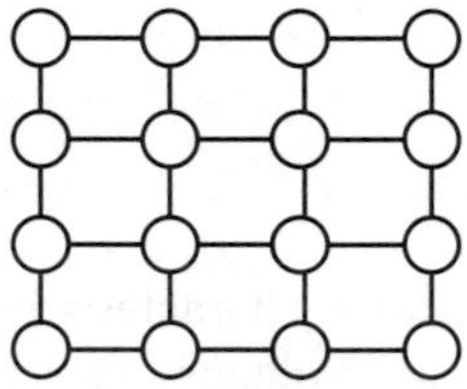

Square Grid
(4-way nearest neighbor)

$V = 4$
$A = 2*\sqrt{n} - 2 \approx 2 * \sqrt{n}$

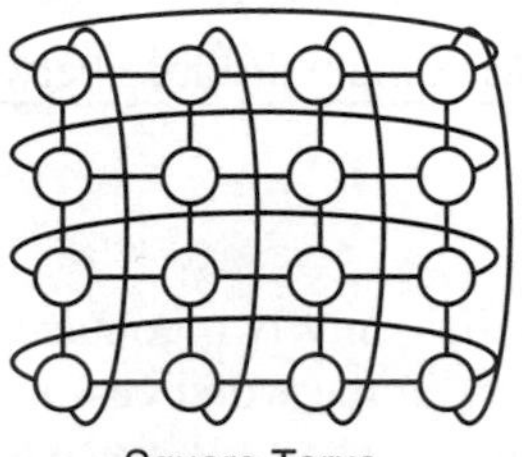

Square Torus
(4-way nearest neighbor)

$V = 4$
$A = \sqrt{n}$

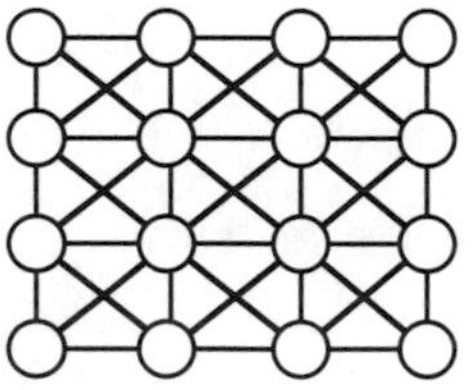

Square Grid
(8-way nearest neighbor)

$V = 8$
$A = \sqrt{n} - 1 \approx \sqrt{n}$

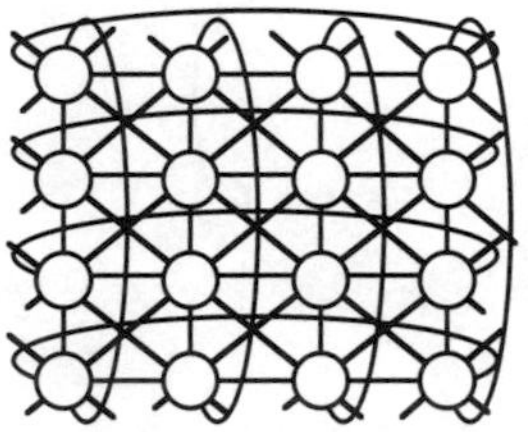

Square Torus
(8-way nearest neighbor)
(Fig. without diagonal border connections)

$V = 8$
$A = \frac{\sqrt{n}}{2}$

Figure 5.10 Square grids and tori

Hexagonal Grid

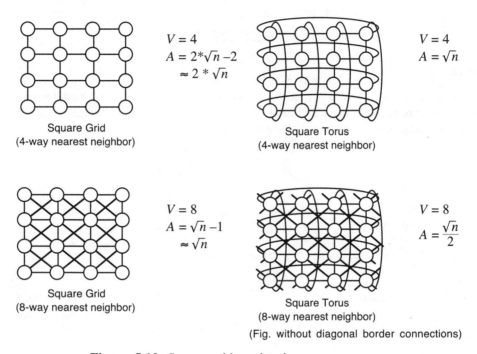

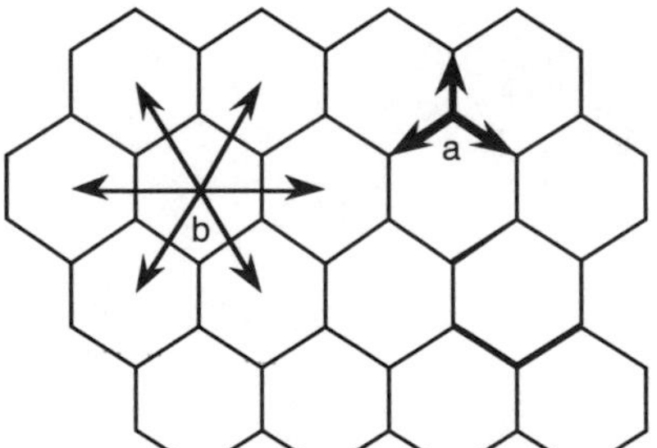

a) PEs on the cell wall crossings
$V = 3$
$A \approx 2 * \sqrt{n}$

b) PEs in the middle of the cells
$V = 6$
$A \approx \frac{3}{2} * \sqrt{n}$

Figure 5.11 Hexagonal grid

The hexagonal grid is just a modification of the square grid and is also two-dimensional. Depending on whether the PEs are placed on the cell wall crossings or in the middle of each cell, there are three or six connections per PE, respectively. Since the hexagonal grid is also a two-dimensional structure, the maximum distance remains in the order of the square root of n.

Cube

The transition from two dimensions to three dimensions results in the cubic grid. PEs are placed in a cubical arrangement in space and require 6 connections to their neighboring PEs. The maximum distance is reduced to the cube root of n.

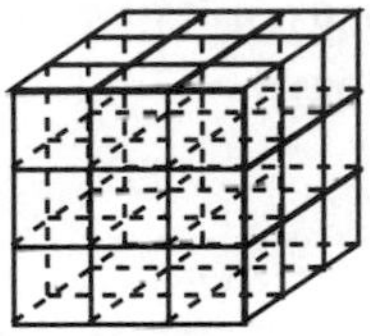

$$V = 6$$
$$A = 3 * \sqrt[3]{n} - 3$$
$$\approx 3 * \sqrt[3]{n}$$

Figure 5.12 Cubic grid

Hypercube

A hypercube of dimension *zero* is a single element (see Figure 5.13, left). A hypercube of dimension i+1 is constructed from two hypercubes of dimension i by connecting corresponding elements. For example in Figure 5.13, a cube (a hypercube of dimension 3) is made of two squares (hypercubes of dimension 2) by connecting each element of the 'front' square with the appropriate element of the 'back' square.

Each PE requires $\log_2(n)$ connections to neighboring PEs, which is not a constant as was the case in the earlier grid structures. However, in return, the maximum distance is reduced to the same logarithmic value. The hypercube is therefore a universal network structure with a small logarithmic maximum distance and a not too high logarithmic number of connections per PE.

$$n = 2^m$$
$$V = \log_2 n$$
$$A = \log_2 n$$

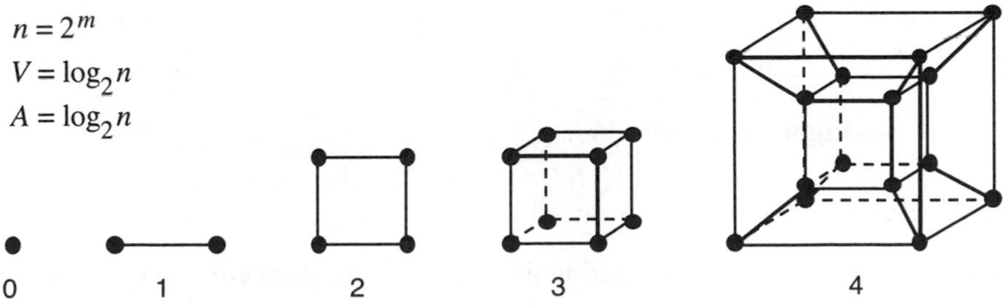

Figure 5.13 Hypercubes of dimensions zero through four

Binary Tree

Tree structures are further networks with logarithmic maximum distances. Only 3 connections per PE are required to achieve logarithmic maximum distances in the binary tree. The disadvantage of the tree structure is the 'root bottleneck', which restricts the simultaneous exchange of information between two sub-trees in a manner similar to the restriction imposed by a bus structure. One possible remedy for this are the fat trees, as discussed in Section 5.2 .

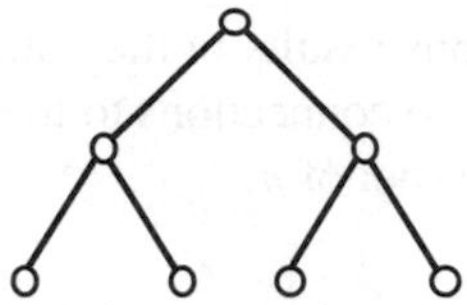

$$n = 2^m - 1$$

$$V = 3$$

$$A = 2 * \log_2 (n+1) - 2 \approx 2 * \log_2 n$$

Figure 5.14 Binary tree

Quadtree

In a quadtree each node has 4 children, which can be useful among other things for algorithms that partition images into quadrants. The maximum distance between two PEs in a tree is always double the height of the tree since in the worst case the connection between two leaves must go over the root. This equals approximately $\log_4(n)$ for a quadtree.

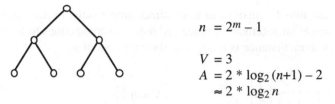

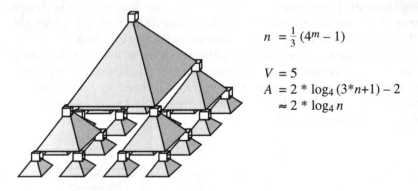

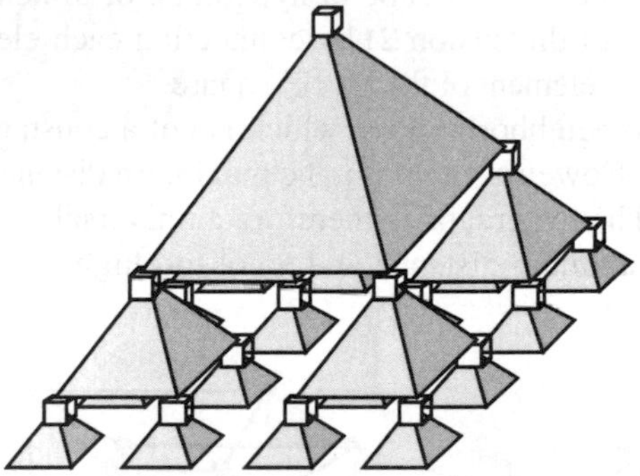

$$n = \frac{1}{3}(4^m - 1)$$

$$V = 5$$

$$A = 2 * \log_4 (3*n+1) - 2 \approx 2 * \log_4 n$$

Figure 5.15 Quadtree

Shuffle-Exchange

Another network structure with logarithmic measure is the shuffle-exchange. It consists of two separate connection types, the unidirectional 'shuffle' and the bi-directional 'exchange'.

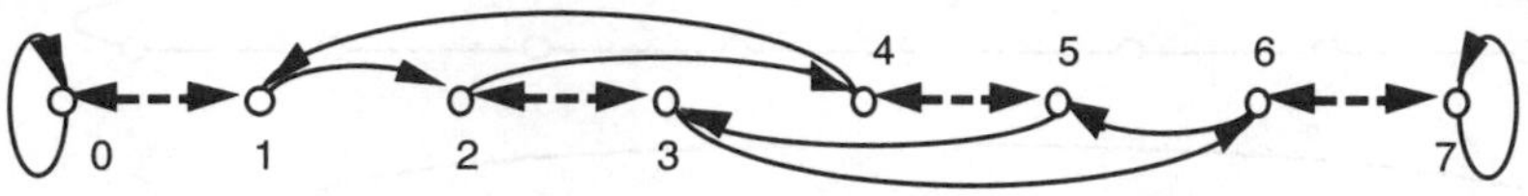

$n = 2^m$

$V = 3$ (uni-directional connections)
$A = 2 * \log n$

Figure 5.16 Shuffle-exchange

The two separate connection types can be easily represented with the help of operations on the binary representations of the PE numbers:

shuffle	$(p_m, \ldots, p_1) = (p_{m-1}, \ldots, p_1, p_m)$	*Left rotation*
exchange	$(p_m, \ldots, p_1) = (p_m, \ldots, p_2, \overline{p_1})$	*Negation of the low order bit*

The shuffle portion connects each PE to the PE whose number (in binary notation) is equivalent to the original PE's number rotated left by one bit. The first and last elements are connected to themselves; however, the other PEs are connected in cycles. The exchange portion negates the low order bit of the PE's number, which means that each even numbered PE is connected to the odd numbered neighbor to its right (and vice versa).

<u>Example of the application of the Shuffle and Exchange Operations:</u>

i) $001 \xrightarrow{\text{sh.}} 010 \xrightarrow{\text{sh.}} 100 \xrightarrow{\text{sh.}} 001$

ii) $011 \xrightarrow{\text{ex.}} 010 \xrightarrow{\text{ex.}} 011$

Plus-Minus 2^i Network (PM2I)

The last of the network structures presented here is somewhat more complex. It consists of $n = 2^m$ network nodes (PEs) connected by $2*m - 1$ different structures, which are designated as PM_{+0}, PM_{-0}, PM_{+1}, PM_{-1}, PM_{+2}, PM_{-2}, ... , PM_{m-1}. The following definition describes the connections that make up each of the PM structures:

$$PM_{+i}(j) = (j + 2^i) \bmod n$$
$$PM_{-i}(j) = (j - 2^i) \bmod n$$

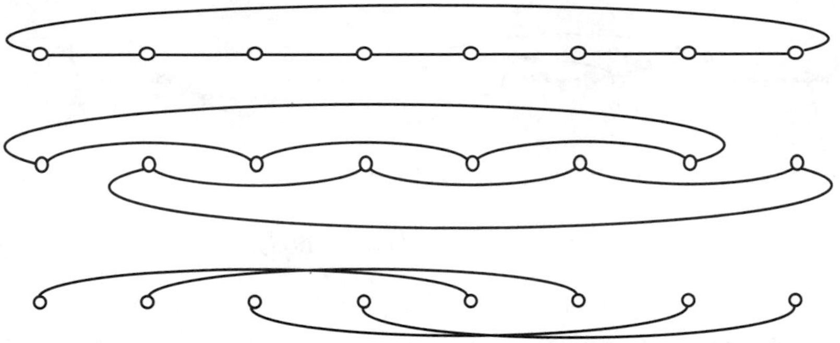

$V = 2 * \log n - 1$ (uni-directional connections)
$A = \log n - 1$

Figure 5.17 PM2I

When 2 is raised to the power of the index of a given uni-directional structure, the result is the distance to the next neighbor contained in the structure. With PM $_{+0}$ the distance is $+2^0$, or $+1$. With PM $_{-0}$ the corresponding distance is $-2^0 = -1$. The distance between the PM $_{+2}$ nodes is already $+2^2 = +4$, and in contrast -4 for the PM $_{-2}$ structure. Due to the closure of the structure, the positive and negative directions of the structure with the largest index (m–1) are identical:

$$\text{PM}_{+(m-1)} \equiv \text{PM}_{-(m-1)}$$

The two structures being identical explains why there is a total of only $2*m - 1$ structures in a PM2I network and not $2*m$. Figure 5.17 shows the PM2I network for $n = 8$ PEs. PM $_{+0}$ and PM $_{-0}$ connect each node with its right or left neighbor respectively and form together a bi-directional ring. PM $_{+1}$ and PM $_{-1}$ are two separate uni-directional graphs that are each made up of two structures which each connect 4 PEs. They are shown together above forming two bi-directional rings. Each PE has the PE on the other side of the PEs to its right and left as neighbors where the modulo function closes the rings. In the last structure PM $_{+2}$ is identical to PM $_{-2}$. Each PE is connected with the PE at a distance of 4 (modulo 8).

5.4 Comparison of Networks

As mentioned above, a valid comparison of networks solely on the basis of the values of V (number of connections per PE) and A (maximum distance between PEs) is not possible. A comparison among networks or an applicability analysis for a specific network can only be carried out accurately in light of the parallel application under consideration. Depending on the application, one network structure may be better suited than another. If the algorithm for solving a given problem requires a particular network, which may have 'poor' V and A values, the physical structure of this network will in general provide better results than attempting to fit the problem to a different network with 'good' values.

However, since building a special computer system for each particular problem is too expensive, a more general solution must be found. Every parallel computer has only one (or two, in some cases) network structures, which however may be quite versatile or even dynamically reconfigurable. All of the algorithms implemented on this computer have to make do with this network structure or a part of it. The value or utility of a network depends on how well *on average* it can be applied to the most frequently presented parallel problems. For example, the parallel computer system MasPar MP-2 (see Section 11.1) has two different networks at its disposal: a grid structure and a three-stage Clos network, which offers a high level of global connectivity. Algorithms which require a grid structure can use the fast local network directly, whereas algorithms requiring other structures can be implemented via routing on the global Clos network with a certain loss of efficiency. Other parallel computers such as the 'Distributed Array Processor' (DAP, see Section 11.1) have exclusively a square grid, which restricts their applicability. Only problems that can be solved with a local connection structure may be computed efficiently on such an architecture (e.g. numerical algorithms or image processing).

Net 1 simulates ↓ Net 2 →	Grid (2-D)	PM2I	Shuffle-Exchange	Hypercube
Grid (2-D)	—	$\approx \sqrt{n}/2$	$\approx \sqrt{n}$	$\sqrt{n}$
PM2I	1	—	$\approx \log_2 n$	2
Shuffle-Exchange	$\approx 2 \cdot \log_2 n$	$\approx 2 \cdot \log_2 n$	—	$\log_2 n + 1$
Hypercube	$\log_2 n$	$\log_2 n$	$\log_2 n$	—

Figure 5.18 Network comparison according to Siegel

The just mentioned simulation of various networks on another network was investigated by Siegel [Siegel 79]. The shuffle-exchange and hypercube proved to be superior as 'universal networks' for the efficient emulation of a variety of different network structures. Use of a physical grid is only efficient, when a grid structure is actually required by the parallel application, since a grid is not suited for the simulation of other networks. However, the emulation of networks as being discussed here, may be automatically performed by a compiler only if the network structure of the host computer system *and* the network structure required by the application program are both known. Unfortunately, this is rarely the case: most often, neighborhood relationships, used for data exchange between processors, are given by complicated arithmetic expressions, deviate slightly from the 'standard' or are even computed at run time. From this information, it is impossible to reconstruct the desired network structure automatically. Then a data exchange may only be performed by a general and possibly less efficient routing algorithm, which cannot take any a priori information about the application program into account.

The table in Figure 5.18 gives the number of required simulation (transfer) steps in relation to the number (n) of PEs.

Exercises I

1. Construct a sequence of basic parallel operations for the vector product (cross product) of two vectors. For this task, the 'storage' of intermediate results must be provided for.
$((a_x, a_y, a_z), (b_x, b_y, b_z)) \mapsto \ldots \mapsto (a_y b_z - a_z b_y,\ a_z b_x - a_x b_z,\ a_x b_y - a_y b_x)$

2. Develop a simple Petri net for the synchronization of three parallel processes.

3. Develop an extended Petri net, which performs the following calculation:
$$z := \begin{cases} x + 2 & \text{if } y > 0 \\ 2 * x & \text{if } y = 0 \end{cases}$$

4. Develop an extended Petri net, which performs the following calculation:
$z := x \text{ div } y$

   The places for x, y, and z contain non-negative values and are only allowed to occur once. The extended Petri net should have specified places for *Start*, *Finish* and *Error*. In the case of 'division by zero', both the places *Finish* and *Error* should be marked.

5. Develop an extended Petri net, which performs the following calculation:
$z := x \bmod y$

   The places for x, y, and z contain non-negative values and are only allowed to occur once. The extended Petri net should have specified places for *Start*, *Finish*, and *Error*. If y is equal to zero, both the places *Finish* and *Error* should be marked.

6. Produce an extended Petri net that adds integer numbers (positive *and* negative). The sign of a number should be handled with an extra place.

7. a) Construct a four-stage delta network with 16 inputs and 16 outputs by using elementary switches ('black boxes').

b) How many stages are required for a delta network with n inputs and n outputs (assume n is a power of 2, $n = 2^m$) ?

c) How many elementary switches ('black boxes') are required for a delta network with n inputs and n outputs (assume n is a power of 2, $n = 2^m$) ?

8. a) Prove that a shuffle-exchange network never requires more than $2 * \log n - 1$ steps for a data exchange between two nodes.

b) What is the similarity between a delta network and a shuffle-exchange network?

c) What is the similarity between a hypercube and a PM2I network?

9. Give the (approximate) optimal values for m and a in a three level Clos network with $N = 16{,}384$.

10. The total number of interconnections in a three level Clos network is approximately optimal when m is selected as follows:

$$m \approx \sqrt{\frac{N}{2}}$$

Prove this rule.

11. A Clos network only becomes more favourable than a full crossbar switch for $N \geq 24$. Prove this bound using the approximation rule of problem 10.

PART II

Asynchronous Parallelism

A distinction is made between the two large classes of parallel processing: asynchronous and synchronous parallelism. In 'classical' asynchronous parallelism, the problem to be solved is partitioned into sub-problems in the form of processes that can be distributed among a group of autonomous processors. This means that an asynchronous parallel program contains multiple threads of control. If the sub-problems are not totally independent, the processes must exchange information among themselves and therefore must be mutually synchronized. The individual processes mostly carry out large sub-problems, since a splitting of the problem into too small units, like arithmetic expressions, would lead to large synchronization costs in comparison to the gains of parallelism. For this reason, asynchronous parallelism is often characterized as 'coarse-grained parallelism'.

CHAPTER 6

Structure of a MIMD System

The most general model of a MIMD computer (multiple instruction, multiple data) is shown in Figure 6.1. The processors (PE) are autonomous computer systems that can carry out different programs independently of one another. Depending on the configuration, the processors may have their own local memory or may use a shared, global memory bank which is reached over a network structure. The difference between tightly coupled MIMD computers with shared memory and loosely coupled MIMD computers with exclusively local memory has already been dealt with in Chapter 2. In contrast to MIMD computers with shared memory, where a bus system is normally used, MIMD computers without shared memory often use complex network structures. However since the bus structure is only suited for use with a limited number of processors, most MIMD computers with many processors do not have physically shared memory. For them, the concept of 'virtual shared memory' (also called 'shared virtual memory', see [Li, Hudak 89]) can be applied to simulate a shared memory area by data exchange protocols between the PEs.

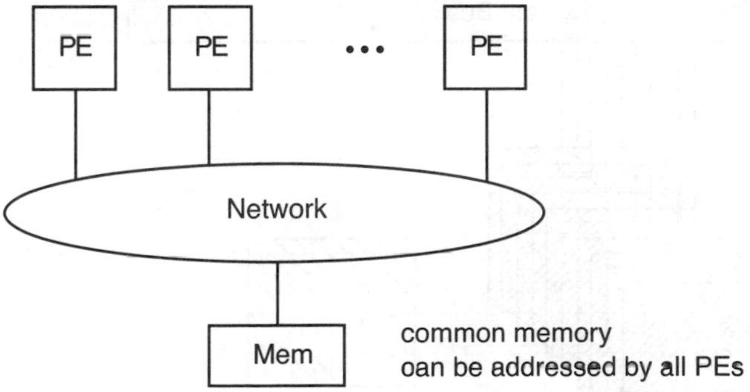

Figure 6.1 MIMD computational model with global memory

The processors function asynchronously independently of one another. In order to exchange information, they have to be synchronized. The software structure of a MIMD program reflects this hardware structure. A program is divided into individual processes that run asynchronously in parallel and must be synchronized for data exchanges using special mechanisms. The ideal mapping would be *1 Process : 1 Processor*, which is normally not possible in practice, due to the limited number of available processors. The general mapping is *n Processes : 1 Processor*. This means that a processor has to execute multiple processes in a time-sharing fashion. In order to implement time-sharing, each processor must have a scheduler with the associated extra control costs.

The Sequent Symmetry together with the Intel iPSC Hypercube and Paragon are presented as typical representatives of the MIMD class of parallel computers. Further information on the organization and hardware structure of parallel computer systems can be found in [Hwang, Briggs 84] and [Almasi, Gottlieb 89].

6.1 MIMD Computer Systems

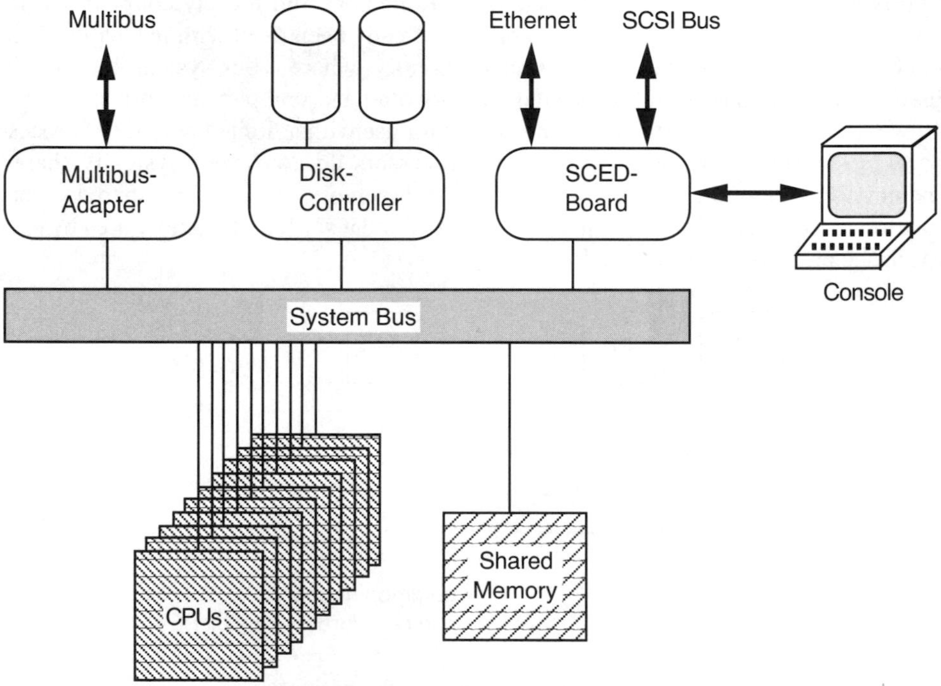

Figure 6.2 Block diagram of Sequent Symmetry

In this section, the MIMD computer systems Sequent Symmetry (bus connection structure), Intel Hypercube (hypercube network) and Intel Paragon (two-dimensional grid) will be briefly discussed.

Sequent Symmetry

The Sequent Symmetry MIMD computer is a good example of the tight coupling of processors and shared global memory accessed over a central bus (see Figure 6.2). All CPUs, the shared memory, and the peripherals communicate over this system bus. Up to 30 processors of type 80486 with high clock rate may be connected.

A bus does not allow parallelism in the data exchanges, since only two devices can communicate over it at one time. For this reason, the bus restricts the upward scalability of this parallel computer. The old model of the Sequent Symmetry, using processors of type 80386, was very soon passed by single-processor workstations with higher computing power. Furthermore these do not even require the costly parallelization of programs.

Intel iPSC Hypercube

The Intel Scientific Computer (iSC) line consists of three generations: iPSC/1 (Intel Personal Supercomputer), iPSC/2 and iPSC/860 (see [Trew, Wilson 91]), that are based on the 80286, 80386, and i860 CPUs respectively. A precursor to the Intel architecture was the Cosmic Cube, developed at CalTech, Pasadena.

Up to 128 powerful processors can be put together in a iPSC/860 Hypercube. This network structure allows a much higher level of parallelism during data exchanges between processors than is possible with a bus or ring structure.

This system architecture has no shared memory. The processors are only 'loosely' coupled over the network and must use time-consuming message-passing procedures in order to exchange data. Process synchronization mechanisms that are based on shared memory such as semaphores and monitors can only be implemented locally on individual processors, but not between different processor nodes.

Intel Paragon

Paragon XP/S is Intel's latest parallel computer system. It evolved from the 'Touchstone Delta' project and contains i860 XP processors. Paragon can have up to 512 nodes, with each node containing two i860 XP processors. One processor of each node is assigned to arithmetic/logic tasks, while the other processor is dedicated to handling data exchanges. The interconnection structure of the Paragon is much simpler than that of the iPSC Hypercube: the nodes are connected by a two-dimensional grid. Whole columns of nodes may be dynamically configured for users (compute nodes), system services (service nodes), or the connection of peripheral devices (I/O nodes).

6.2 Process States

A process is an individual program segment that executes asynchronously in parallel to other processes. Since there are in general multiple processes executing on any given processor, a portion of the processor's computation time is provided to each process in a time-sliced fashion. At the end of its time-slice, the currently executing process changes from state *Running* to state *Ready* and waits there in a queue for its next activation (process context switch). For this, all process control data (program counter, registers, data addresses, etc.) of a process must be stored in its process control block (PCB), so it can be retrieved later. Newly arriving processes are placed immediately in queue *Ready*, while terminating processes are removed from state *Running* in order to free the processor for other waiting processes. Processes that must wait a considerable time for the occurrence of a condition, such as the availability of a system resource or synchronization with another process, should not unnecessarily burden the processor with time-consuming back and forth switching between the states *Ready* and *Running*. Instead, they are placed in state *Blocked* and wait there in a queue specific to the condition they are waiting for. Only when this condition occurs will the blocked process be placed in queue *Ready* and be allowed to contend again for the processor. The operating system component which carries out these procedures on the individual processes is known as a *scheduler*.

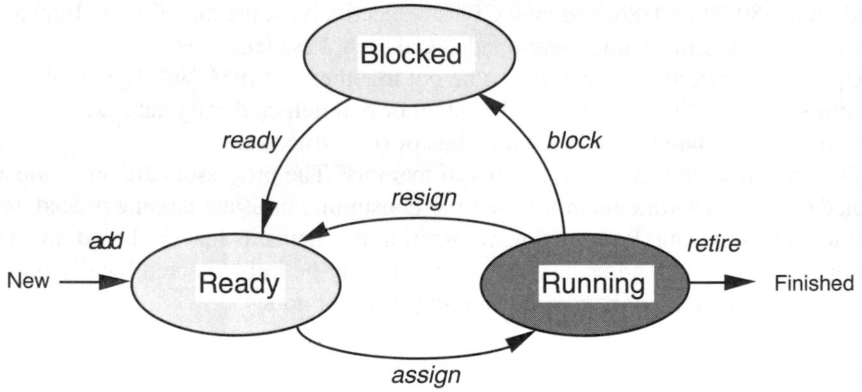

Figure 6.3 Process model

For each processor there exists such a scheduler, which controls the execution sequence of the processes for this processor. More complex procedures, which will be described later, control scheduling among different processors (for example moving processes from a heavily loaded processor to a more lightly loaded processor) in order to achieve higher system efficiency. In this model with identical processors, the mapping of processes onto processors is transparent to (meaning: not controllable by) the programmer. See [Goscinski 91] for details on operating systems for distributed computer systems.

CHAPTER 7

Synchronization and Communication in MIMD Systems

In Sections 4.4 and 4.5, the parallel concepts of processes and communication via remote procedure calls were introduced. These will be used as the basis for this and the following chapters. The parallel execution of processes presents two problems:

1. Two processes need to exchange data with one another.
   (Communication)

2. If shared memory is used, the simultaneous access of multiple processors to the same memory area must be avoided.
   (Synchronization in order to avoid incorrect data or blockings, see Chapter 8)

Since processes work independently of one another most of the time, data exchange between a pair of processes is the central problem of MIMD programming. The two processes participating in a data exchange operation are being executed asynchronously and possibly on different processors. In order to exchange data, they must first synchronize for that purpose, because an exchange can only take place when both partners are ready. The second problem occurs, among other places, in the solution of the first. If the exchange between two processors is carried out via a shared memory area (this occurs also when a processor has to execute more than one process), then the access (reading or writing) must be sequentialized. Otherwise erroneous data or deadlock can result (e.g. when reading erroneous data before a synchronization operation).

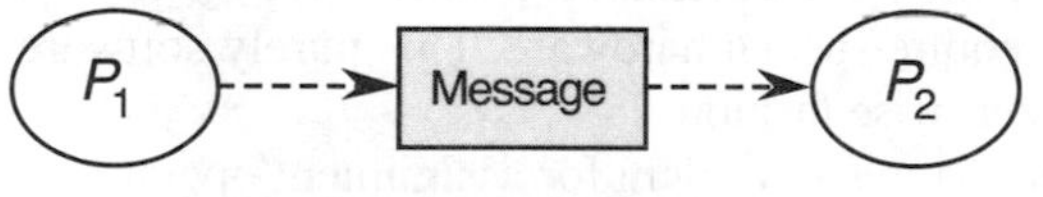

Figure 7.1 Message passing

First the simple case is considered: two processes need to communicate and are running on the same processor. For this case there exist a large number of solutions which are applied at various levels of abstraction. The more complicated case of communication between processors is dealt with subsequently. All synchronization operations may be described and analyzed by using Petri nets, as shown in Chapter 3.

A good example to help visualize this class of problems is the railway problem (see Figure 7.2). Two railways run circular routes, each on its own track, but there is a small single-track section that both have to share. Here it is obvious that one has to avoid both trains entering this 'critical section' at the same time in order to avoid a collision. Figure 7.2 very closely resembles the Petri net approach of Figure 3.8. This is not just a coincidence: the two tracks may be interpreted as parallel processes, with each train representing the current state or program counter of a process. While each train can stay in the 'uncritical section' of its track without interacting with the other train, precautions have to be taken (a *synchronization* has to take place) to stop (*block*) a train (*process*) that wants to pass through the single-track section while the other train (*process*) is currently running there. Only a single train (*process*) at a time may run in the critical section. The synchronization mechanism is symbolized by a traffic light; different approaches will be discussed in the following sections.

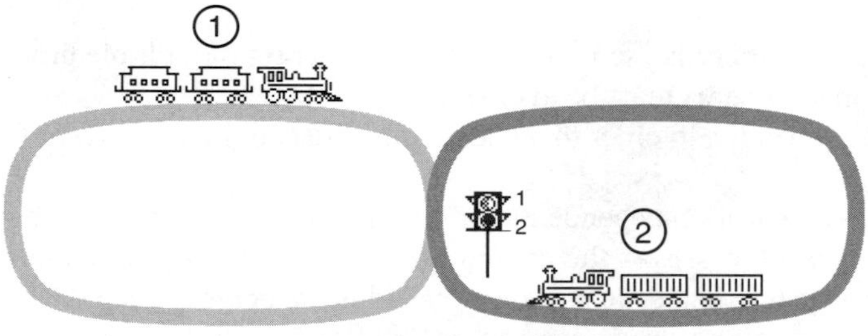

Figure 7.2 Railway problem

7.1 Software Solution

Ben-Ari [Ben-Ari 82] and Peterson and Silberschatz [Peterson, Silberschatz 85] describe a solution for the synchronization problem for systems with shared memory areas that does not require special hardware. This purely software solution will be approached here in a step-wise fashion.

Parallel execution is *not* a problem for assignment operations of a *single* variable: because in order to write data to a common memory location, a processor has to allocate the bus (or whatever network structure is present). The bus control logic prevents the bus from being allocated by two different processors – so one of the processes has to wait. In a single-processor system this is identical to the prevention of simultaneous bus allocation by a processor and a DMA unit (direct memory access). For processes on different physical processors this is even more obvious. Regarding the second part of this problem, a process context switch (e.g. due to expiration of the time-slice) cannot occur in the middle of a single assignment operation. That is, assignments of a simple (one word) variable from several parallel processes are mutually exclusive and automatically sequentialized simply by the design of all multiple-processor computer systems (indivisible, *atomic* operation).

The problem, therefore, is to protect statement sections with access of common data (*critical sections*) from interference with other processes. Since a statement section may be arbitrarily long, another process might be working on the same common data between any two statements.

In the following, two parallel processes both want to access a shared memory area. The operations on the data (reading and writing) are not important here and will be represented as *<critical section>*. Instructions not associated with the synchronization of the processes (not involved with accessing the shared memory area) will be represented as *<other instructions>*. The two processes P_1 and P_2 are started subsequently in the main program and execute thereafter in parallel:

```
...
start(P1);
start(P2);
...
```

First Attempt

The idea for synchronization investigated here is the use of a synchronization variable. Both processes can access the common variable `turn`; reading or writing of this variable is understood to be an atomic (indivisible) operation.

Declaration: `var turn: 1..2;`
Initialization: `turn:=1;`

P_1	P_2
loop	**loop**
while turn≠1 **do** (*nothing*) **end**;	**while** turn≠2 **do** (*nothing*) **end**;
<critical section>	*<critical section>*
turn:=2;	turn:=1;
<other instructions>	*<other instructions>*
end	**end**

Analysis:

- This solution guarantees that only one process may enter a critical section at a time.
- However, there is a big drawback: alternating access to the critical section is forced.

⟹ Restriction on parallelism

Both processes wait before entering the critical section in a ‘busy wait’ loop until the synchronization variable `turn` has the value of their process number. Thereafter the critical section is executed and the synchronization variable is set to the number of the other process. The functionality of this synchronization is such that after process P_1 exits the critical section, process P_2 must pass through its critical section, before P_1 is allowed to re-enter the critical section. However, this restriction is unjustifiable, since it might be important for P_1, for example, to place information in the shared memory area several times, which P_2 could then read all at once.

Second Attempt

The synchronization variable is now replaced with an array with two boolean elements, one for each process. Before entering the critical section, each process sets its array element to `true` and upon exiting the critical section resets the element to `false`. Through this procedure each process marks its presence in the critical section. Before entering the critical section each process waits in a ‘busy wait’ loop (`while`...`do` *(*nothing*)* `end`), until the other process has left its critical section.

```
Declaration:     var flag: array [1..2] of BOOLEAN;
Initialization:  flag[1]:=false; flag[2]:=false;
```

P_1	P_2
loop	**loop**
while flag[2] **do** *(*nothing*)* **end;**	**while** flag[1] **do** *(*nothing*)* **end;**
flag[1]:=**true;**	flag[2]:=**true;**
<critical section>	*<critical section>*
flag[1]:=**false;**	flag[2]:=**false;**
<other instructions>	*<other instructions>*
end	**end**

Analysis:

- In spite of the entrance check (`while` loop), under certain circumstances both processes can be in their critical sections at the same time.

⟹ Incorrect !!

Apparently it does not work quite that simply. If both processes execute the test in the `while` loop at the same time, they can both leave the loop. Then they will both enter their critical sections simultaneously, which is exactly the case to be avoided.

Third Attempt

Since the testing in the second attempt was not tight enough, in this attempt the processes will be modified such that they set their flags *before* the first test in the `while` loop occurs. The test and wait will be included in the critical section, so to speak.

```
Declaration:    var flag: array [1..2] of BOOLEAN;
Initialization: flag[1]:=false; flag[2]:=false;
```

***P*₁**

```
loop
  flag[1]:=true;
  while flag[2] do (*nothing*) end;
    <critical section>
  flag[1]:=false;
    <other instructions>
end
```

***P*₂**

```
loop
  flag[2]:=true;
  while flag[1] do (*nothing*) end;
    <critical section>
  flag[2]:=false;
    <other instructions>
end
```

Analysis:

- The processes are now secured against more than one of them entering its critical section at a time.
- However, if both processes set their flags simultaneously, a blocking will occur (in this case both processes are waiting in their `while` loops for ever).

⟹ Incorrect !!

The desired condition of mutual exclusion was achieved; however, if each process sets its flag to `true` and then each waits in its `while` loop for the other process to terminate its critical section and to reset its flag, then a blocking results. Neither of the processes can leave its loop; the parallel system is blocked!

Fourth Attempt

The fourth attempt brings the most complex solution for the synchronization problem, but is at last correct. The algorithm is taken from [Peterson G. 81] and is almost identical to Dekker's algorithm (see [Ben-Ari 82]), which is the first known solution to this problem. Here, both the simple synchronization variable `turn` and the flag array `flag` are applied. First a process shows that it is ready to enter the critical section by setting its flag. Then it sets the variable `turn` to the process number of the *other* process, and afterwards waits as long as the other process has its flag set *and* the `turn` variable contains the number of the other process. Upon exiting the critical section, each process resets its flag variable.

```
Declaration:    var turn: 1..2;
                    flag: array [1..2] of BOOLEAN;
Initialization: turn:=1; (* either one *)
                flag[1]:=false; flag[2]:=false;
```

P_1

```
loop
 flag[1]:=true;
 turn:=2;
 while flag[2] and (turn=2) do
 (*nothing*) end;
    <critical section>
 flag[1]:=false;
    <other instructions>
end
```

P_2

```
loop
 flag[2]:=true;
 turn:=1;
 while flag[1] and (turn=1) do
 (*nothing*) end;
    <critical section>
 flag[2]:=false;
    <other instructions>
end
```

Analysis:

- The processes are secured against more than one of them entering its critical section at a time.
- Blockings cannot occur.

⟹ Correct

The extra test in the wait condition of the `while` loop helps to avoid a blocking. Waiting only occurs when the other process has set its flag and actually is in the critical section or in its 'busy wait' loop. As soon as the process that first got the chance to enter the critical section leaves it, this process resets its flag and the other process can leave its 'busy wait' loop and enter the critical section.

This solution only works for two processes. There are other algorithms, however, such as the one from Eisenberg and McGuire [Eisenberg, McGuire 72], which solve the synchronization problem for an arbitrary number of processes. Unfortunately, there is one disadvantage in all of these solutions: since most of the time there will not be a processor available for each process, a considerable loss of performance occurs in the 'busy wait' loops. The algorithms of Peterson and Dekker and of Eisenberg and McGuire are quite complicated and are not used in practice (see the hardware solution in the following section).

7.2 Hardware Solution

Although a purely software solution to the synchronization problem of parallel processes is possible, as shown in the last section, it is quite complicated. For this reason, most computers implement a hardware solution. In a single-processor system, which executes processes in time-sharing mode, this may be achieved by disabling all interrupts. Since time interrupts are thereby inhibited, no process context switch can take place and the executing process can carry out the critical operations unhindered. Much more appropriate, however, is the 'test-and-set' operation discussed here. It is not at all an 'exotic' operation, since it is most valuable for implementing a multitasking operating system. Versions of test-and-set are included in the instruction sets of the microprocessors 68020 (TAS *test and set*, CAS *compare and swap*) and 80286 (XCHG *exchange*).

The test-and-set operation is a very simple hardware solution. It carries out the two steps:

1. Reading a boolean variable and
2. Setting this variable to `true`

```
procedure test_and_set
(var lock: BOOLEAN): BOOLEAN;
var mem: BOOLEAN;
begin_atomic (* indivisible *)
  mem  := lock;
  lock := true;
  return(mem)
end_atomic; (* indivisible *)
```

These two steps must be carried out one after the other as an *indivisible* operation, in order to prohibit another process from accessing the variable between the steps. Test-and-set is known as an *atomic operation* and is often implemented as a member of the CPU instruction set that is carried out in a single instruction cycle. For example, for the instructions TAS and CAS of the 68020 processor, this is achieved by activating the signal RMC (read–modify–write cycle). During this activation, no other unit may have access to the bus or request an interrupt.

Using the test-and-set hardware operation, a solution for an arbitrary number of processors becomes fairly easy. Resetting the variable to `false` can be done as a regular instruction and does not require special hardware support.

Each process waits in a 'busy wait' loop until the synchronization variable `lock` becomes `false`. With the first successful check via a `test_and_set`, it is immediately set to `true`. The successful process enters the critical section alone. Upon exiting the critical section, it resets the variable to `false` and the next waiting process can allocate the critical section with a `test_and_set`.

```
           var  lock: BOOLEAN;
Initialization: lock:=false;

                $P_i$

loop
  while test_and_set(lock) do (*nothing*) end;
    <critical section>
  lock:=false;
    <other instructions>
end.
```

The solution of the synchronization problem is now very easy and general; however, this solution is still very inefficient due to the use of a 'busy wait' loop. Much of the CPU time is wasted in these loops, while the processes are waiting to enter the critical section. The higher level synchronization concepts introduced in the following section are aimed at replacing the wait loop with much more efficient queues.

7.3 Semaphores

Semaphores were introduced by Dijkstra in 1965 and are based on the signalling mechanisms in railroad traffic [Dijkstra 65]. There had already been implementations of semaphores in operation systems years earlier, though they were not known by this name. In the simplest case, a semaphore can only take on two states: free or occupied. The operations for setting and resetting a signal (for example, in order to cross a section with just a single track for both directions) are called P and V, after the Dutch words for 'passing through' and 'leaving from' a critical section. These original terms are kept here, in order to avoid confusion with the monitor operations 'wait' and 'signal', which will be introduced in Section 7.4 . Semaphores may be used to restrict access to critical sections, but also more generally for the reservation and return of system resources (e.g. printer, terminal). Semaphores are a much more efficient synchronization concept than simple 'busy wait' loops.

Application

P_i

```
...
P(sema);
      <critical section>
V(sema);
...
```

The application of a semaphore is conceptually simple: each process 'brackets' its critical sections with a P and V pair of semaphore operations. It is critical that every process that accesses a given piece of shared memory use the *same* semaphore variable to control access to the memory! So the semaphore belongs to the shared data and *not* to a single process.

Implementation

The data structure for a semaphore is a record containing the semaphore value and a queue of processes, which are waiting for the release of the resource (for example, a memory region) controlled by the semaphore. In the simplest case, the semaphore value is of type boolean and the semaphore is called a 'boolean semaphore'. On the other hand, the semaphore value can also be of type integer (as shown here), in which case the semaphore is known as a 'general semaphore'.

```
type Semaphore = record
                       value: INTEGER;
                       L:     List_of_ProcID;
                     end;
var S: Semaphore;
```

Naturally, the P and V operations must be implemented as atomic (indivisible) operations, since multiple processes have to access common semaphore data.

Initialization of a Semaphore:

`S.L`	←	*empty list*
`S.value`	←	*number of P operations allowed to pass non-blocked without the occurrence of a V operation (e.g. 1 for critical sections)*

While a simple semaphore, for example to protect a critical section, is always initialized to one, there are also cases where a higher (or even lower) initialization value makes sense. If the value is higher than one, it indicates the number of P operations that can occur (without a V operation in between) before a calling process becomes blocked by the semaphore. If a process is blocked by a semaphore, it must wait for the next V operation by another process.

```
procedure P (var S: Semaphore);
begin
  S.value := S.value-1;
  if S.value < 0 then
    putlast(S.L, actproc); (* add this process to queue S.L *)
    block(actproc)         (* and put it in state 'blocked' *)
  end
end P;
```

The P operation reduces the semaphore value by one and checks whether it has become less than zero, which indicates that the semaphore and the associated resource are occupied. If so, the calling process is placed at the end of the semaphore's queue and is blocked.

```
procedure V (var S: Semaphore);
var Pnew: ProcID;
begin
  S.value := S.value+1;
  if S.value ≤ 0 then
    getfirst(S.L, Pnew);         (* remove process P from S.L   *)
    ready(Pnew)                  (* and put it in state 'ready' *)
  end
end V;
```

The V operation increases the semaphore value by one and checks whether it is still less than or equal to zero, which indicates that there are still processes waiting in the semaphore queue. If so, the next waiting process is removed from the semaphore queue and appended to the queue of processes in state *Ready*.

How are P and V implemented as atomic operations *themselves*?

- Software solution (see Section 7.1):
  A *short* 'busy wait' loop is used with the short P or V operation as the critical section. The 'busy wait' loop is naturally an inefficient operation; however, the critical section now contains just the three or four elementary instructions of a P or V semaphore operation. This means that if a waiting period occurs at all, it will be quite short.

- Hardware solution (see Section 7.2):
  A *short* 'busy wait' loop is used for the test-and-set command before the beginning of the P or V operation. Even with the hardware solution, it is not possible to avoid a short 'busy wait', which might occur. However, the point made above is just as true here: due to the short length of the 'critical section', specifically the P or V operation itself, only a negligible loss of efficiency will occur.

However, a problem does occur when a process loses its time-slice *while executing* these 'four elementary instructions'. Then the other processes that want to execute a semaphore operation will use up their entire time-slice in a 'busy wait' until the original process gets another time-slice and finishes the semaphore operation. As described in the following section, this problem becomes much worse when it occurs at the level of queues instead of 'busy wait' loops.

The Convoy Phenomenon

The 'convoy phenomenon' occurred in older operating systems due to an unfortunate conjunction of the scheduling strategy implementation and lock (semaphore) operations [Blasgen, Gray, Mitoma, Price 79]. In analogy to a traffic jam on a highway, processes can be thrown into a queuing hold-up when there are many processes P_1 to P_n present that often use a particular semaphore (*high traffic lock*). This problem only occurs when many more processes than processors are present in a system and pre-emptive scheduling with FIFO (first in, first out) is used. Pre-emptive means that the scheduler can transfer processes that have occupied a semaphore from state *Running* to state *Ready*. FIFO means that processes waiting for a semaphore are released from the queue in the order of their requests.

If a process P_1 happens to lose its time-slice during the execution of its critical operation, or in other words, while 'owning' the 'high traffic' semaphore, then none of the processes P_2 to P_n can acquire this semaphore. The probability of this happening is rather small, but not zero. This means that *at some* non-reproducible point in time it will occur. The loss of the time-slice by a process owning the high traffic semaphore leads to processes P_2 through P_n (a large number of processes that only wanted to carry out a short operation) being placed in the queue of the high traffic semaphore. Under this condition, the performance of the whole computer system is drastically reduced. Only when P_1 becomes reactivated with a new time-slice and releases the semaphore can the next process P_2 continue execution. However, a process context switch is very costly in comparison to an arithmetic instruction or a semaphore operation, and P_1 will very soon thereafter need the high traffic semaphore again to carry out a critical operation. So, with a high probability, process P_1 will be placed once more in the queue of the high traffic semaphore during the very same time-slice. A traffic jam has occurred (also known as 'lock thrashing') which is very unlikely to resolve itself. Most of the CPU time is used for useless process context switches (between states *Running* and *Blocked*).

The convoy phenomenon does not occur in modern operating systems. Measures that can be taken against this problem are, for example:

- Changing the dispatcher
  Knowledge of the 'high traffic' semaphore

- Changing the scheduling strategy
  Avoid FIFO, and instead use a 'busy wait' loop or release all processes when a V operation occurs, which then must once again carry out the P operation (equivalent to putting P in a while loop)

- Avoid 'high traffic locks' in general

- Reduce the operations required for a context switch

The end of this section dealing with semaphores presents a number of situations where they are typically applied. The programming language used in the examples here and in the following section is Modula-P [Bräunl, Hinkel, von Puttkamer 86]. Modula-P is an extension of Modula-2 along the lines of the process concept and will be dealt with in more detail in Section 9.7. The language serves here just as a notation for the synchronization concepts.

The Producer–Consumer Problem

Two processes that are exchanging data over a common buffer area must be synchronized. One process generates data and places it in the buffer, while the other reads the data and processes it further. The use of semaphores avoids overwriting of unprocessed data (in case the producer is faster than the consumer), as well as reading the same data a second time (in case the consumer is faster than the producer).

This example uses two boolean semaphores to control access to a single buffer area. One semaphore indicates whether the buffer is empty; the other indicates whether the buffer is full.

Declaration and Initialization:

```
var   empty: semaphore [1];
      full : semaphore [0];

process Producer;              process Consumer;
begin                          begin
  loop                           loop
    <generate data>                P(full);
    P(empty);                        <empty buffer>
      <fill buffer>                V(empty);
    V(full);                       <process data>
  end;                           end;
end process Producer;          end process Consumer;
```

Before starting the processes, the semaphore `empty` is initialized to one and the semaphore `full` is initialized to zero, which indicates that the buffer is *empty*. The producer immediately generates new data and tests with a P operation on semaphore `empty` whether the buffer is empty (or waits until it is emptied by the consumer process). If the buffer is empty (as it is in the beginning), the producer fills the buffer (this is the critical section) and signals with a V operation on semaphore `full` that the buffer is full and can be read by the consumer (which might already be waiting for it). The consumer on the other hand first checks/waits on the buffer to become full via a P operation on semaphore `full`. If the buffer is full (or when it becomes full), the consumer reads the data from the buffer (its critical section), carries out a V operation on semaphore `empty` (signalling that the producer can refill the buffer), and may now further process the data just read.

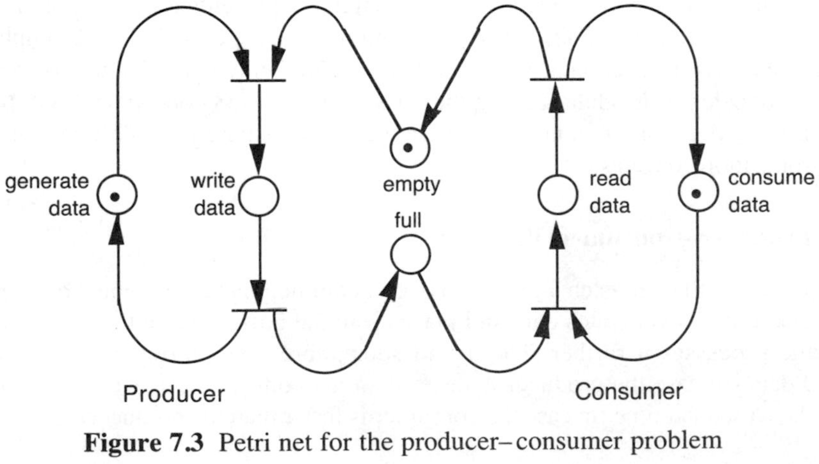

Figure 7.3 Petri net for the producer–consumer problem

Figure 7.3 explains the synchronization problem by using a simple Petri net. Each of the two processes describes a cycle, corresponding to the endless `loop` in the program. Each cycle comprises two states, which are represented by Petri net places (drawn as circles in the figure). A P operation on one of the semaphores `empty` or `full` is represented by an incoming arc to a transition (drawn as a bar in the figure), while a V operation is represented by an outgoing arc. For example, when the upper transition of the producer process fires, the token in semaphore place `empty` disappears and will therefore block this process (or any other additional producer, not pictured here) in the next iteration. This will last until the consumer executes the V operation, which here corresponds to the firing of the upper transition of the consumer. This transition has an outgoing arc to place `empty` and will therefore reproduce this semaphore token.

The Bounded Buffer Problem

In the example just presented, the producer and consumer processes could more or less work independently in parallel. However, the single buffer space presented a restriction on the achievable parallelism: e.g., it is possible that some parts of the data require longer for processing than other parts for both the producer and the consumer. This could average out, but with the use of just one buffer space the delays would add up. To resolve this problem, a larger but still bounded buffer could be used. In the example shown here, the buffer contains *n* memory elements. This requires a boolean semaphore to protect the critical section and two general semaphores to indicate how much of the buffer is occupied.

Declaration and Initialization:

```
var critical: semaphore[1];
    free    : semaphore[n];       (* n buffer spaces are available *)
    occupied: semaphore[0];

process Producer;
begin
  loop
    <generate data>
    P(free);
      P(critical);
        <write data in buffer>
      V(critical);
    V(occupied);
  end;
end process Producer;

process Consumer;
begin
  loop
    P(occupied);
      P(critical);
        <read data from buffer>
      V(critical);
    V(free);
    <process data>
  end;
end process Consumer;
```

The semaphore `free` is initialized to *n* and `occupied` is initialized to 0, which indicates that the buffer has *n* free elements. The semaphore `critical` is initialized to one in order to allow just one process to enter a critical section at a time. The read and write operations of the processes are enclosed by P and V operations on the semaphore for the critical section. This is required since here the buffer can have both free and occupied elements at the same time, while the previously presented producer–consumer problem had only a single buffer element, which was either full or empty. In analogy to the producer–consumer problem, the producer first generates data, then carries out a P operation on the `free` semaphore, writes the data into the buffer, and finally executes a V operation on the `occupied` semaphore. In the same way, the consumer begins with a P operation on the `occupied` semaphore (for it can only continue if there is data in the buffer), then reads data from the buffer, carries out a V operation on the `free` semaphore (by reading from the buffer, at least one buffer element becomes free), and finally processes the data it read. The semantics has been slightly changed to handle multiple elements in the buffer with two general semaphores, instead of handling a single buffer element with two boolean semaphores, as presented earlier. The numbers of free and occupied buffer elements are incremented or decremented within the semaphores `free` and `occupied`, according to whether a P or V operation is applied to them.

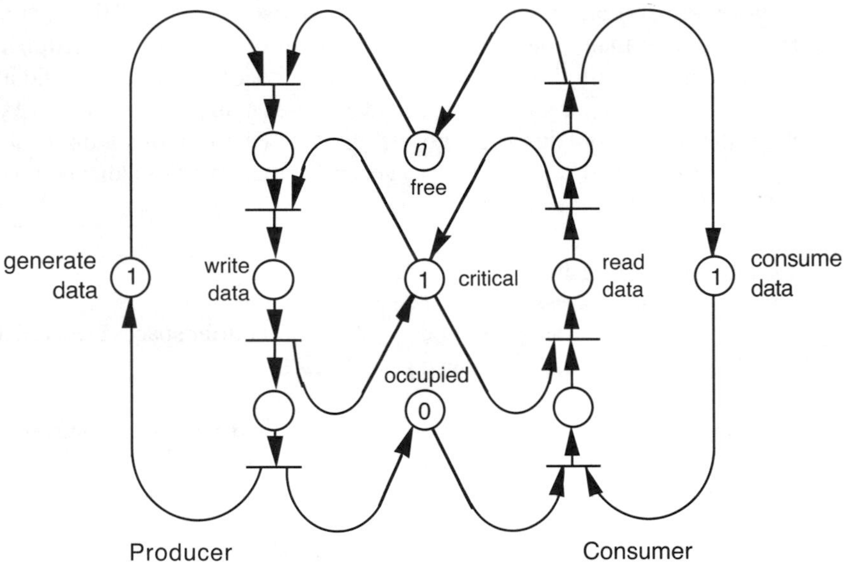

Figure 7.4 Extended Petri net for the bounded buffer problem

This synchronization mechanism is shown as an extended Petri net in Figure 7.4 . This Petri net evolves from the simpler net in Figure 7.3 by replacing both boolean semaphores by general semaphores, represented in extended Petri nets by places (circles) with an arbitrary number of tokens. The additional (boolean) semaphore `critical` is required for synchronization of multiple producers and consumers. The counter `occupied` represents the number of currently filled buffer elements, while `free` represents the number of currently free buffer elements.

The Readers–Writers Problem

For many types of system resource, one group of processes requires exclusive access to the resource while a different group can access the resource simultaneously. This occurs, for example, when multiple processes wish to access a shared memory area, some just reading and others writing. While multiple processes can read from a shared memory block simultaneously, only one process at a time may be allowed write-access to this area. During the write-access, no other process can be allowed to read from the memory area in order to avoid inconsistent data (see Section 8.1). When using a trivial solution with just one semaphore, only one reader could obtain access. This would be a loss of obtainable parallelism. The solution to the so-called 'readers–writers problem' presented here allows the maximum possible parallelism according to [Courtois, Heymans, Parnas 71].

```
Declaration:    var  count:      semaphore[1];
                     r_w:        semaphore[1];   (* reading or writing *)
                     readcount:  INTEGER;

Initialization: readcount:=0;
```

```
process Reader;
begin
 loop
   P(count);
    if readcount=0 then P(r_w)
    end;
    readcount := readcount + 1;
   V(count);

    <read data from buffer>

   P(count);
    readcount := readcount - 1;
    if readcount=0 then V(r_w)
    end;
   V(count);
   <process data>
 end; (* loop *)
end process Reader;
```

```
process Writer;
begin
  loop
     <generate data>
      P(r_w);

       <write data into buffer>

      V(r_w);
  end; (* loop *)
end process Writer;
```

Every reader must check before accessing the data whether it is the first process to read from the shared memory area. If so, `readcount` is equal to zero and the semaphore `r_w` is occupied for the readers. Other readers coming in increment the counter `readcount`, but do not execute a semaphore operation. The first writer trying to access the shared memory area will be blocked in the `P(r_w)` call. As the reader processes leave the critical area, the counter `readcount` is decremented. The last reader to exit carries out the V operation on the `r_w` semaphore. With this call, the waiting writer will gain exclusive access to the shared memory. Newly arriving readers and writers must wait until the exclusive access by the writing process is concluded.

The counter operations and the conditional semaphore operations create two extra critical regions, which must be protected with an additional semaphore (`count`).

With this solution, starvation of the writer processes might occur, given enough reader processes. With reader processes constantly coming into and leaving the critical region, the writer processes may never be allowed access. This can be avoided with a more complex solution, in which reader processes are no longer allowed to enter the critical region, as soon as the first writer process is waiting for access.

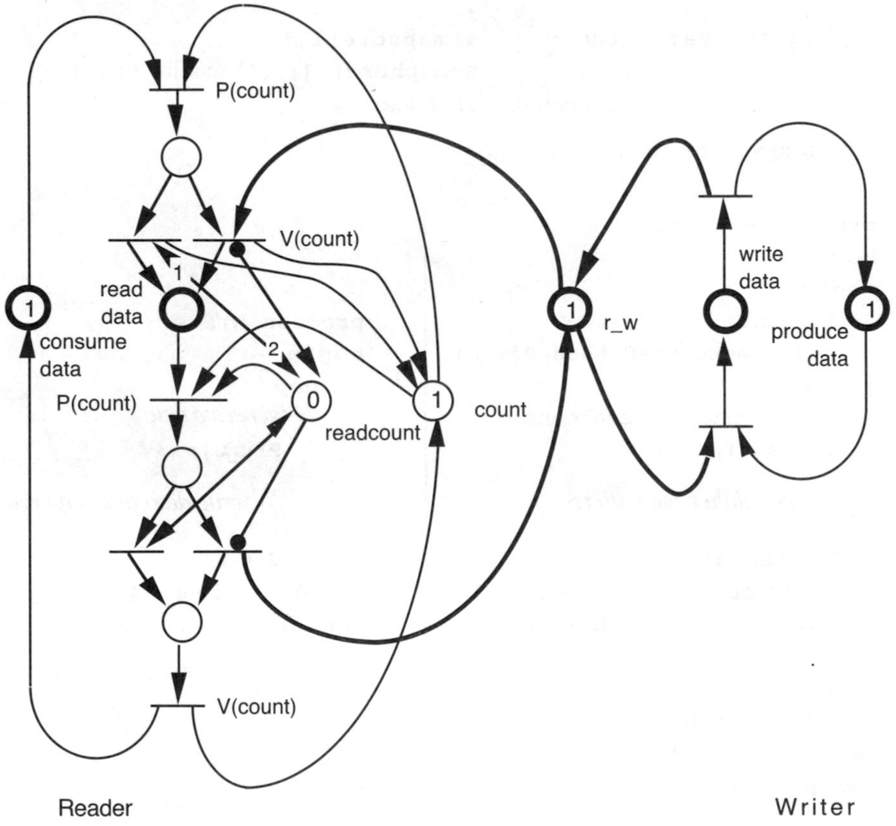

Figure 7.5 Extended Petri net for the readers–writers problem

As for the previous problems, Figure 7.5 displays the facts by using an extended Petri net. For clarity, only a *single* reader and a *single* writer are pictured. The connections of the central semaphore `r_w` are drawn in bold face and connections back and forth between the same place and transition are drawn as double arcs (or double arcs with negation) for readability. If there are multiple readers, they share the *same* Petri net places `count`, `readcount`, and `r_w`; multiple writers share the *same* place `r_w`.

After occupying the semaphore `count` (removing the token) by the first reader process, a case selection is performed by using an inhibitory arc. It depends on the value of the variable `readcount`, which may be zero or larger than zero (representing whether this process is the first reader, or there are already other readers working on common data). Only when `readcount` is equal to zero will firing of the corresponding transition also execute a P operation on the central semaphore `r_w` (removing the token). In both cases, firing the corresponding transition decrements the variable `readcount` by one (if `readcount > 0` holds, the arc weights stipulate subtraction of 1 and addition of 2, so overall 1 is added). Now, the reader process may execute its operation on common data. When it wants to leave the critical section, first it has to occupy the semaphore `count` and then decrement the counter `readcount` by one. Only if `readcount` is then equal to zero (so that this is the last active reader process) is the V operation on semaphore `r_w` performed (recreating the token in `r_w`), before semaphore `count` is released (producing the token in `count`).

The behaviour of the writer process, however, is much simpler. The token of the semaphore place `r_w` is removed via an incoming arc before each access (executing a P operation), and the token is recreated via an outgoing arc after each access (executing a V operation).

In database systems a different type of semaphore is introduced in addition to the type presented in this section. This other type is that of a 'shared' semaphore (see [Gray, Reuter 92]). A 'shared' semaphore can either be used in *shared* mode by multiple processes or in *exclusive* mode by just one process. This means that the readers–writers problem described above can be trivially solved using shared semaphores. Shared semaphores are therefore the more general semaphore model. However, they can be implemented, as shown above, by using exclusive semaphores.

Finally, one should note that semaphores are a very simple type of process synchronization, but also represent a large source of errors. This extends from forgetting P or V operations to exception handling in processes. If an error or exception occurs in a process that has acquired a semaphore and the process terminates, the entire process system could block under certain conditions, due to the failure to release the semaphore. Only in operating systems with expensive, so-called 'functional recovery' can a measure of error tolerance be achieved. These systems attempt to release the semaphores held by terminating processes. Semaphores are a tool of system programming and should be replaced whenever possible by higher level concepts like monitors, as presented in the following section.

7.4 Monitors

Monitors were introduced in 1974/75 by Hoare and Brinch Hansen as a further synchronization concept for parallel processes [Hoare 74], [Brinch Hansen 75]. A monitor is an abstract data type, which means that it exists at a higher level of abstraction than the semaphores discussed earlier. Every monitor comprises both the data to be protected as well as the corresponding access and synchronization mechanisms. These access and synchronization mechanisms are know as 'entries' and 'conditions'.

Application

P_1	P_2
...	...
`Buffer:WriteData(x)`	`Buffer:ReadData(x)`
...	...

Calls are mutually exclusive,
they will be synchronized.

The use of monitors is much simpler than that of semaphores. The processes to be synchronized simply call monitor entries with the appropriate parameters, which are essentially special procedure calls. Particularly important is that problems with 'forgotten P or V operations' can never occur. The set-up of monitor entries with their corresponding conditions is not so simple, as the following example shows. A stack buffer (see Figure 7.6), which can be written to or read from by any number of processes, is to be managed.

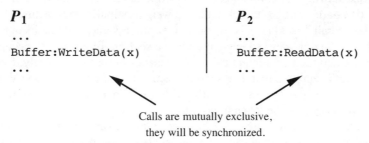

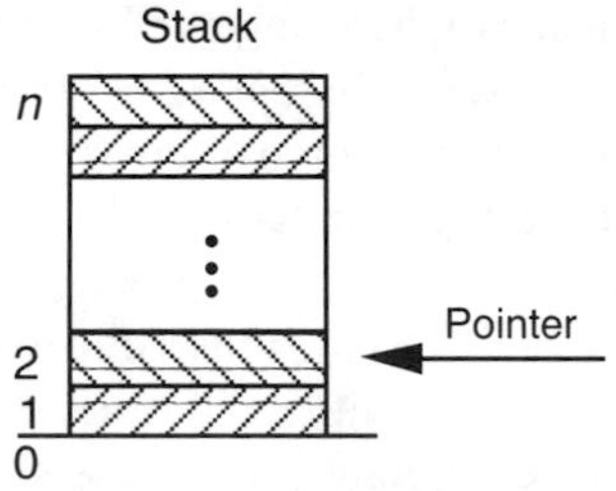

Figure 7.6 Stack

Inside a monitor, the monitor data is first defined. This data has the following characteristics:

- static
  monitor data retains its value between calls to the monitor entries
  (as opposed to procedure data).

- local
  monitor data can only be accessed via calls to the monitor entries (analogously to local procedure data).

The declaration of entries ('monitor procedures') comes next. These are the only parts of a monitor that are exported and can be called by processes with both value and result (`VAR`) parameters. Since they access shared data, they are mutually exclusive during their execution and the required synchronization is provided by the operating system. This means that as long as a process stays inside a monitor entry call, all of the other processes wishing to call an entry in the same monitor must wait. The initialization section is found at the end of the monitor and is carried out exactly once at the start-up of the entire program system and even before any of the processes are started (so before the main program initialization).

Conditions are queues, similar to the queues in semaphores, but they do not have a counter like semaphores do. Three operations are defined on conditions, and will be explained further in the implementation section below:

- `wait (Cond)`
  The calling process blocks itself and waits until another process performs a `signal` operation on this condition.

- `signal (Cond)`
  All of the processes waiting in this condition are reactivated and request access to the monitor again. (Another variation is to activate *only one* process: the next one waiting in line.)

- `status (Cond)`
  This function returns the number of processes waiting for this particular condition to occur (that is, the number of processes being blocked in this condition).

The following is a program example for the management of a stack buffer in the Modula-P language. In this example two conditions called `free` and `occupied` are declared. The processes enqueued are waiting for the corresponding conditions. For entry `WriteData` holds that if the expression `Pointer=n` is true, then the stack is full and the calling process must wait until a place in the buffer is free. This waiting must occur inside a `while` loop, since otherwise with multiple waiting processes another process may have slipped in first and used up the free space already (in case `signal` has been implemented to reactivate *all* processes waiting in a condition). Operations on the monitor data (writing parameter `a`) follow. Finally, a signal on condition `occupied` activates any processes that might be waiting in entry `ReadData`.

The entry `ReadData` is constructed similarly. If the stack is empty, a process must wait for condition `occupied`, before data can be read from the stack. At the end, a signal on condition `free` is given to activate any processes waiting in the `WriteData` entry. Since signals are costly operations, they are enclosed in an `if` check and are only carried out when the possibility actually exists that there are processes waiting (for example, the condition `Pointer=1` for the signal on 'occupied' indicates that the pointer was zero beforehand and the buffer was completely empty).

```
monitor Buffer;
var   Stack: array [1..n] of Datarecord;
      Pointer: 0..n;
      free, occupied: condition;

entry WriteData (a: Datarecord);
begin
  while Pointer=n do            (* Stack full *)
    wait(free)
  end;
  inc(Pointer);
  Stack[Pointer]:=a;
  if Pointer=1 then signal(occupied) end;
end WriteData;

entry ReadData (var a: Datarecord);
begin
  while Pointer=0 do            (* Stack empty *)
    wait(occupied)
  end;
  a:=Stack[Pointer];
  dec(Pointer);
  if Pointer=n-1 then signal(free) end;
end ReadData;

begin                           (* Monitor Initialization *)
  Pointer:=0
end monitor Buffer;
```

Implementation

Monitors are generally implemented with the help of semaphores. An implementation according to [Nehmer 85] is shown in the following six steps.

1) A boolean semaphore is declared for each monitor declared.
   `var MSema: semaphore[1];`

2) Entries are transformed into procedures, where each procedure is enclosed by P and V operations on the monitor semaphore. This guarantees that only one process can actually carry out the instructions of an entry at a time.

```
procedure xyz(...);
begin
  P(MSema);
   <Instructions>
  V(MSema)
end xyz;
```

3) The monitor initialization is converted into a procedure and a call to it is placed at the very beginning of the main program.

4) Implementation of the `wait` operation
The calling process is added to the condition queue and blocked. Then the monitor semaphore is released (so another process can enter the monitor) and the next process in state *Ready* is loaded for execution. The parallel constant `actproc` indicates the number of the currently active processes.

```
procedure wait(var Cond: condition; var MSema: semaphore);
begin
  PutLast(Cond,actproc);  (* add ProcID to the condition queue *)
  block(actproc);         (* add ProcID to the blocked list *)
  V(MSema);               (* release the monitor semaphore *)
  assign;                 (* load the next ready process *)
end wait;
```

5) Implementation of the `signal` operation

a) Version that only frees only one waiting process:

In this version, the `wait` operation must always be inside an `if` selection, since otherwise a process might wait for a condition that is already valid. The next process waiting in the condition is removed and a P operation for *this* process is carried out on the monitor semaphore (not for the process *calling* the signal operation, hence the awkward expression of the P operation).

```
procedure signal(var Cond: condition; var MSema: semaphore);
var NewProc: Proc_ID;
begin
  if status(Cond) > 0 then
    GetFirst(Cond, NewProc);
    PutFirst(MSema.L, NewProc); }  P operation for NewProc
    dec(MSema.Value)            }
  end
end signal;
```

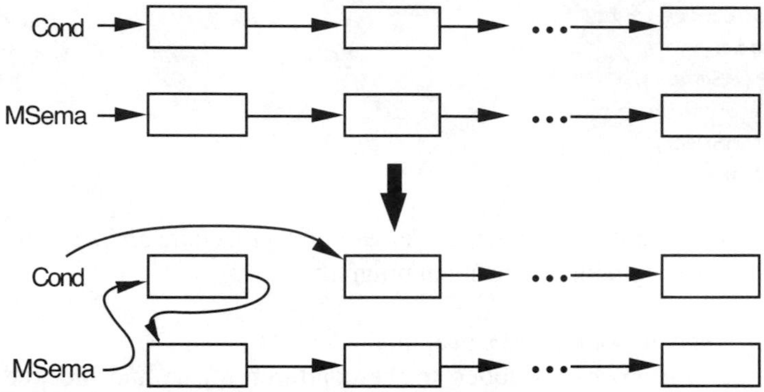

Figure 7.7 Signal version (a)

b) Version that frees all the waiting processes (as in Modula-P):

In this variation, the `wait` operation must always be inside a `while` loop, since otherwise the condition could be invalidated by another process that has also been freed.

```
procedure signal(var Cond: condition; var MSema: semaphore);
begin    (* here, the status check is not necessary *)
  append(MSema.L,Cond);   (* list concatenation *)
  MSema.Value := MSema.Value - status(Cond);
  Cond := nil
end signal;
```

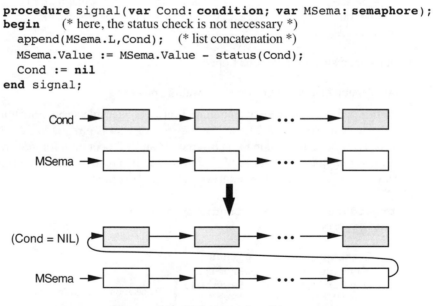

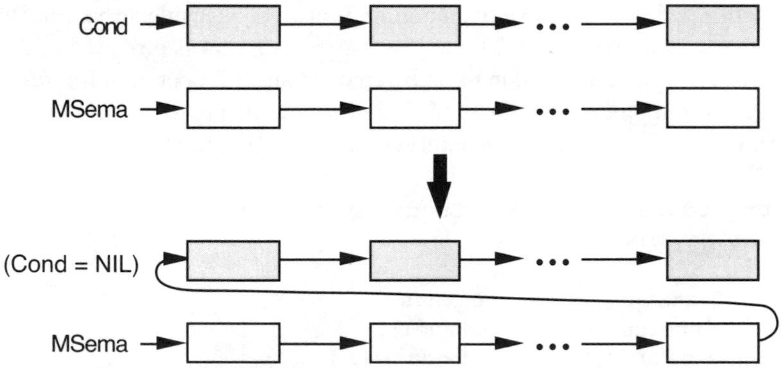

Figure 7.8 Signal version (b)

6) Implementation of the `status` operation
This function returns the length of a condition queue.

```
procedure status(Cond: condition): CARDINAL;
begin
  return length(Cond)
end status;
```

7.5 Message Passing and Remote Procedure Call

All of the synchronization mechanisms dealt with up to this point can only be used when the processors have shared memory available. In distributed systems, message passing is the only way to synchronize two processes with one another or exchange data. On the other hand, the concepts of message passing and the remote procedure call mechanisms built thereupon are also suited for systems with shared memory. These procedures are very comfortable, but incur higher processing costs for control problems. For details on message passing through distributed computer systems see [Tanenbaum 89] and [Black 87].

Processes that perform a remote procedure call are designated as 'clients' (they are *customers* of a service provided by another process), while the called processes are designated as 'servers' (they are *offering* a service to other processes).

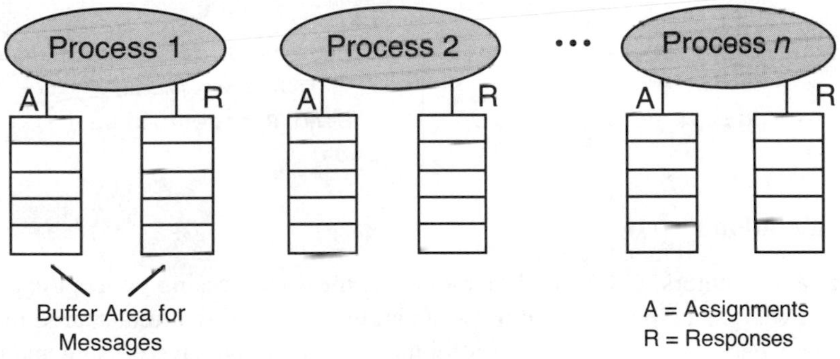

Figure 7.9 Processes with message buffers

Figure 7.9 shows a simple model for assignment handling via message passing between processes, according to [Nehmer 85]. Since a process may be a server as well as a client, each maintains two different buffers for incoming messages, 'A' for assignments (processing requests) and 'R' for responses.

The following operations are defined for message passing:

- Send an Assignment
  `Send_A     (Destination, Message)`
- Receive an Assignment
  `Receive_A (var Sender; var Message)`

- Send a Response
  `Send_R    (Destination, Message)`
- Receive a Response
  `Receive_R (var Sender; var Message)`

Of course, one could also get by on just two operations, one for sending and one for receiving messages. The operations selected here allow for differentiation between received assignments and received responses. This allows the selection of a more flexible service priority scheme. Otherwise a process waiting on a response could be blocked by a just received assignment.

Application

The client process P_C sends its assignment to the server process P_S. It can then handle other work until it finally waits for the response from the server. The server processes the assignments from different clients in an infinite loop. Each assignment is read in, carried out, and the result is returned to the sender.

P_C	P_S
`...`	**loop**
`Send_A(to_server,assignment);`	`Receive_A(client,assignment);`
`...`	*<process assignment>*
`Receive_R(from_server,result)`	`Send_R(client,result);`
	end;

Implementation

On parallel computers with shared memory, the message passing concept can be implemented with the help of a monitor. On a parallel computer without shared memory, an additional decentralized network control module with a message passing and routing protocols is required. These will not be handled further here. The following is just a short implementation sketch of the message management required in any case within just *one* computing node of a distributed system or for an entire system with an arbitrary number of processors and shared memory.

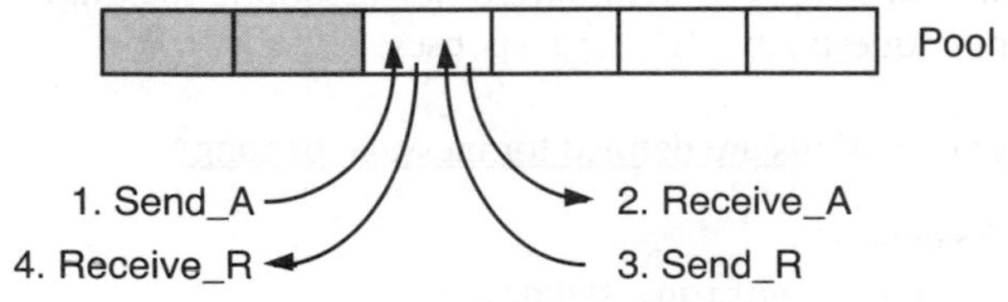

Figure 7.10 Message pool

As shown in Figure 7.10, all of the messages are managed in a global pool. The parallel constant `actproc` returns the appropriate process number for each process.

Implementation sketch adapted from [Nehmer 85]:

```
type   PoolElem =  record
                     free: BOOLEAN;
                     from: 1..numberProcs;
                     info: Message;
                   end;
       queue    =  record
                     contents: 1..max;
                     next    : pointer to queue
                   end;

monitor Messages;
var  Pool            : array [1..max] of Message;
                         (* global message pool *)
     pfree           : CONDITION;
                         (* queue, if the pool is completely filled *)
     Afull, Rfull    : array [1..numberProcs] of CONDITION;
                         (* queues for every process for incoming messages *)
     queueA, queueR: array [1..numberProcs] of queue;
                         (* local message pools for every process *)

entry Send_A (dest: 1..numberProcs; as: Message);
var  id: 1..max;
begin
  while not GetFreeElem(id) do wait(pfree);
  with pool[id] do
    free := false;
    from := actproc;
    info := as;
  end;
  append(queueA[dest],id);  (* add element position to assignment queue *)
  signal(Afull[dest]);
end Send_A;

entry Receive_A (var sender: 1..numberProcs; var as: Message);
var  id: 1..max;
begin
  while empty(queueA[actproc]) do wait(Afull[actproc]) end;
  id     := head(queueA[actproc]);
  sender := pool[id].from;
  as     := pool[id].info;    (* pool[id] not yet released*)
end Receive_A;
```

```
entry Send_R (dest: 1..numberProcs; re: Message);
var  id: 1..max;
begin
  id := head(queueA[actproc]);
  tail(queueA[actproc]);   (* remove first element (head) of queue *)
  pool[id].from := actproc;
  pool[id].info := re;
  append(queueR[dest],id];    (* Enter pool position in response queue *)
  signal(Rfull[dest])
end Send_R;

entry Receive_R (var sender: 1..numberProcs; var re: Message);
var  id: 1..max;
begin
  while empty(queueR[actproc]) do wait(Rfull[actproc]) end;
  id := head(queueR[actproc]);
  tail(queueR[actproc]);   (* remove first element (head) of queue *)
  with pool[id] do
    sender := from;
    re     := info;
    free   := true;      (* set pool element free *)
  end;
  signal(pfree);      (* free pool element available *)
end Receive_R;
```

The characteristics of MIMD systems without shared memory is only briefly dealt with here. For more detailed information on distributed computer systems refer to [Mullender 89] and [Coulouris, Dollimore 88].

CHAPTER 8

Problems with Asynchronous Parallelism

As shown in the previous chapters, asynchronous parallel programming is rather complicated and therefore error prone. Forgetting a P or V operation or using the wrong semaphore are typical errors with heavy consequences for program execution. With monitors there exists the danger of incorrectly using the condition variables or the wait and signal operations. In general the following problems can occur through programming errors during process synchronization:

a) Inconsistent Data

b) System Lockup (Deadlock / Livelock)

The results of these problems and ways to avoid them will be dealt with more closely in the following sections. The problem of load balancing is handled subsequently, where the emphasis is on achieving an efficient loading of all processors.

8.1 Inconsistent Data

A data element, or a relation between data, is inconsistent after the execution of a parallel operation if and only if it does not have the value that it would have received from sequential processing of the operation. Without adequate concurrency control mechanisms (e.g. locking), erroneous data may easily occur during execution of parallel processes. There are three basic classes of problem [Date 86]:

- lost update problem
- inconsistent analysis problem
- uncommitted dependency problem

Lost Update Problem

This problem shall be made clear by the following example. Mr. Miller's salary comes to $1000. Process 1 should raise the salary by $50. Process 2, which executes in parallel to process 1, should increase the salary by 10%. Depending on the sequence of execution and the interleave of the execution of the two processes, the system yields varying results. Naturally not all of them can be correct.

Figure 8.1 lists all four possible results for this example. All results may be found, in general, by systematically trying all interleaving execution orders of the processes involved.

Before: salary[Miller] = $1000

P_1	P_2
...	...
`x := salary[Miller];`	`y := salary[Miller];`
`x := x+50;`	`y := 1.1*y;`
`salary[Miller] := x;`	`salary[Miller] := y;`
...	...

After:

salary[Miller] = ? { $1050, $1100, $1150, $1155 } according to memory access interleave of the parallel processes

Figure 8.1 Lost update problem

<u>The value 1050 can occur in the following way:</u>

Both processes carry out their first instruction at the same time, which means both x and y contain the original value of 1000. Then P_2 carries out the rest of its instructions and sets the salary temporarily to 1.1 * 1000 = 1100. However, P_1 then carries out the remainder of its instructions and sets Miller's salary to its final value of 1000 + 50, or 1050. The intermediate result from P_2 is not taken into account and therefore overwritten.

According to the original intentions of the two transactions (which were not specified here) there is exactly one correct execution order, i.e. P_1 has to be completed before P_2 can start. This sequential execution then gives the correct result (here: $1155).

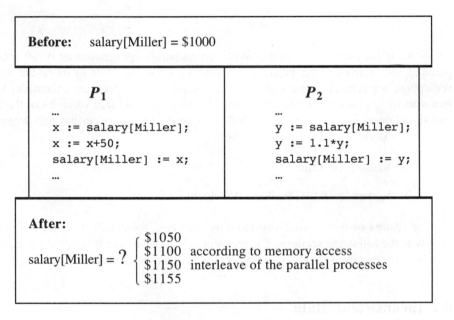

All other values are erroneous, which results from an incorrect interleaving of the memory accesses by the processes. These errors are 'time-dependent errors'. Since they depend on a large number of uncontrollable parameters, such as the number of processors available, the system load, and others, these errors are particularly insidious. Time-dependent errors are as a rule *not reproducible*, which means that they cannot always be found through systematic testing (see [Beizer 90] for general techniques on testing) !

Inconsistent Analysis Problem

A typical example of this problem is a money transfer at a bank. The sum of the two accounts involved is identical before and after the transaction. However, a different process, which reads (analyzes) the current account balances during execution of the money transfer, may receive erroneous data (see example in Figure 8.2).

Before: account[A] = $2000
account[B] = $1000 *Sum(A,B) = $3000*

P_1	P_2

...
`x := account[A];`
`x := x-400;`
`account[A] := x;`
 	
`x := account[B];`
`x := x+400;`
`account[B] := x;`
...
	...
	`a := account[A];`
	`b := account[B];`
	`sum := a+b;`
	...

After: account[A] = $1600
account[B] = $1400 *Sum(A,B) = $3000*

sum = ? { $2600, $3000, $3400 } according to the interleaving memory accesses of the parallel processes

Figure 8.2 Inconsistent analysis problem

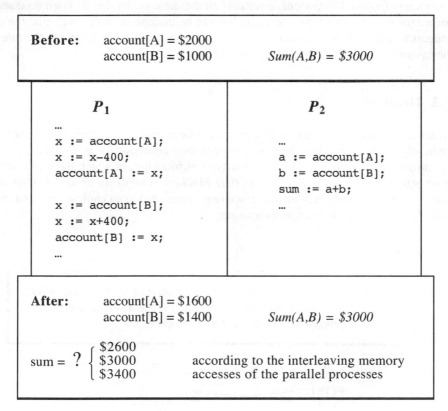

While process P_1 is executing the money transfer, the relation between the two data elements (account balances) is incorrect for a short period of time. The analyzing process P_2 receives erroneous data, if it reads one or both of the variables' contents (account balances) at just the wrong moment.

Uncommitted Dependency Problem

The possibility of uncommitted transactions is a typical database problem. Since a transaction may succeed or fail (see below), the changes of global data made by a transaction are only valid with the proviso of the transaction's successful termination. If transaction A changes global data, transaction B then reads this data, and transaction A subsequently fails, then transaction B has been using invalid data.

In database systems, transactions are implemented as 'atomic operations' (a quite non-trivial task, as these problem classes document [Date 86]). A transaction will either succeed or fail (due to an exception of some reason). A successful transaction will always be completely executed (*commit*), while a failing transaction has to be cancelled completely (*rollback*). Any changes made on the database by this ill-fated transaction before the occurrence of the exception have to be undone in such a way that the data appears as if the whole transaction had never been executed. By following the rules of the transaction concept, inconsistent data are avoided.

8.2 Deadlocks

Deadlock describes the situation in a parallel system where a number of processes permanently block each other. This may happen as a consequence of incorrect process synchronization. A livelock is a specific type of blocking, in which the processes remain active (so they are not in process state *Blocked*, as holds for deadlocks) but carry out only unproductive operations (e.g. waiting operations) in an endless loop and therefore cannot continue with useful processing.

Definition

> A group of processes waiting for the occurrence of conditions which can only be brought about by the waiting processes themselves (mutual dependence) is said to be deadlocked.

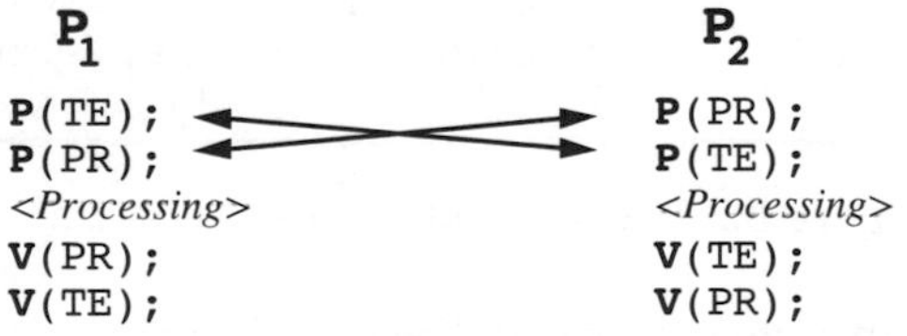

Figure 8.3 Danger of deadlock

Deadlocks occur, for example, when all of the processes are blocked in a semaphore or condition queue. The following example shows the occurrence of deadlock with the use of semaphores. Both processes require both the terminal (TE) and printer (PR) resources, but the requests in the form of P operations occur in a different order. P_1 first requests the terminal and then the printer, but P_2 tries to acquire the resources in the opposite order. Although each process appears harmless when considered alone, deadlock can occur through the interplay of the two. This does not always take place. It occurs only when P_1 has already taken the terminal and P_2 has already taken the printer. Then P_1 waits in its P operation for the printer, which P_2 already has and will only release after also gaining control of the terminal, which is held by P_1. The two processes find themselves in reciprocal dependence, from which they cannot free themselves. Deadlock has occurred.

The following conditions must be met before (unresolvable) deadlock can occur (according to [Coffman, Elphick, Shoshani 71]):

1. Resources can only be used exclusively.
   mutual exclusion

2. Processes have resources allocated while requesting new ones.
   incremental request

3. Resources cannot be forcibly taken from processes.
   no preemption

4. A circular chain of processes exists in which each process has a resource that is requested by the next process in the chain.
   circular wait

A large number of algorithms to recognize and avoid deadlocks exist, which are based on these four points and attempt to break one of the deadlock conditions. The following are examples thereof, but will not be treated any further here:

- Breaking down condition 3:
  When deadlock occurs, the resources already allocated to the processes can be forcibly deallocated. In order to support this, costly algorithms are required to recognize when deadlock has occurred and restart the process (or processes) which have to be set back.

- Breaking down condition 2:
  Every process must request all required resources at one time. This procedure sets down a request protocol which all of the processes must recognize. Requesting multiple resources must be implemented as an *atomic operation*, which means, for example, protecting the operation(s) with a semaphore for a critical section. If a process determines that it needs more resources, then it must first

release all of the resources allocated up to that point. Only then can all of the required resources (previously held plus new ones) be requested.

If all of the processes recognize this protocol, deadlock can never occur. However, this protocol results in higher management costs for obtaining and releasing resources. Another drawback is that implementing the enforcement of the protocol for all processes is quite difficult, and resources may be occupied considerably longer than necessary.

Other methods for deadlock avoidance may be found in [Habermann 76].

8.3 Load Balancing

Another large problem area in asynchronous parallel programming, although without the drastic consequences of the earlier mentioned problem areas, is load balancing. Considerable loss of performance, which one is trying to avoid through the use of a parallel computer, can occur due to unfavourable distribution of processes among the available processors. Loss of performance is a general problem in computing, but especially when using a powerful parallel computer system it shall be avoided.

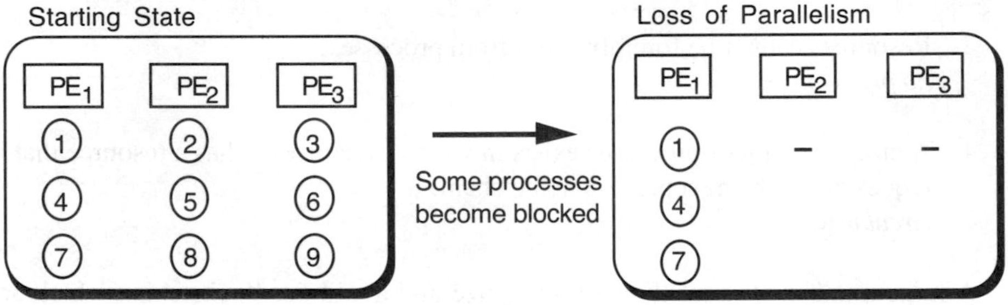

Figure 8.4 Example for unbalanced load

In a simple scheduling model, a static distribution of processes among the processors is used. This means that at run time, processes are not moved from heavily loaded processors, to which they were originally assigned, to more lightly loaded processors. As the example in Figure 8.4 shows, this procedure can lead to very inefficient loading.

In the beginning, nine processes are evenly distributed among the three available processors. During execution of the parallel program all of the processes on processors 2 and 3 might become blocked in waiting queues and all of the processes on processor 1 might remain active. The performance of the parallel computer has been reduced to that of a single-processor system, even though further parallel processing would be possible.

In order to avoid such inefficiencies, extended scheduling models have been developed [Hwang, DeGroot 89]. These allow dynamic distribution of processes on processors at run time (dynamic load balancing) by reshuffling already assigned processes depending on the local processor load in relation to a threshold. One distinguishes between three principle methods for controlling the central operation of 'process migration':

i)	Receiver Initiative:	Processors with little load request more processes. Well suited for heavy system load.
ii)	Sender Initiative:	Processors with heavy loads attempt to hand processes to other processors. Well suited for light system load.
iii)	Hybrid Method:	Switching between sender and receiver initiative depending on global system load.

Advantages and Disadvantages of Load Balancing Methods

+ Higher processor usage is achieved without giving up any possible parallelism.

+/− Circular 'process migration', the continually passing of the *same* process between processors, must be avoided by using suitable parallel algorithms and bounding values.

− Considerable administrative costs arise from determining the processor load as well as from determining the total system load.

− Moving a process to a more lightly loaded processor (process migration) is an expensive operation and should be performed only on longer-running processes. Unfortunately, the total run time of a process cannot be determined without additional information.

− All of the methods of load balancing are engaged too late, namely when the load balance has already been considerably disrupted. However, 'forward-looking balancing' is not possible without additional information concerning the run time behaviour of the individual processes.

− Under heavy parallel system load, all forms of load balancing are pointless, since at that point only the lack of processing power can be balanced and the administrative costs of load balancing lead to an unnecessary overhead, which in addition reduces system performance.

CHAPTER 9

MIMD Programming Languages

Only procedural, parallel programming languages for MIMD systems will be dealt with in this chapter. Non-procedural parallel languages (functional and logic languages) are treated in Chapter 17. The individual languages are only briefly introduced. The most important concepts are discussed and further explained with programming examples. A summary of articles on MIMD programming languages can be found in [Gehani, McGettrick 88].

9.1 Concurrent Pascal

Developed by: Per Brinch Hansen, 1975
Concurrent Pascal [Brinch Hansen 75], [Brinch Hansen 77] is, as the name implies, a parallel extension of Wirth's sequential programming language, Pascal. It is one of the earliest parallel programming languages.

The most important parallel concepts of Concurrent Pascal are:

- the introduction of the process concept
  (declaration of `process` types and corresponding variables, the processes)
- the synchronization of parallel processes via monitors with conditions
  (here called `queue`)
- the introduction of classes
  (abstract data types)

The concepts of Concurrent Pascal are not dealt with further here, instead the reader is referred to Section 9.7 on Modula-P. This language contains similar parallel extensions with Modula-2 as the base language.

9.2 Communicating Sequential Processes

Developed by: C. A. R. Hoare, 1978

Several years after developing the monitor concept together with Brinch Hansen, Hoare introduced his own parallel programming language, CSP [Hoare 78], [Hoare 85]. Although there exist compilers for CSP, it is often considered to be only a design notation and not a real programming language – in contrast to the language *occam* (see Section 9.3) that is based on CSP.

CSP is a somewhat cryptic language. A system consists of a number of parallel processes. Each is executed sequentially, and they communicate via data exchanges as necessary. Primitive input/output commands for message communication, a command for parallel execution, and the use of Dijkstra's 'guarded commands' are the fundamental concepts of CSP. Since all synchronization and communication between processes in CSP is handled via messages, there is no need for semaphores or monitors.

Parallel Language Constructs

`[P1 || P2]` Start parallel processes

`terminal ? number` Receive data from process `terminal`

`printer ! line` Send data to process `printer`

```
[ x=1 → m:=a []
  x=2 → m:=b ]
```

'guarded command'
{IF x=1 THEN m:=a ELSE IF x=2 THEN m:=b ELSE error}
This is a selection instruction, where each 'case' must be switched by a condition (*guard*), in which the programmer should assure that the following instruction will be correctly carried out.

```
*[ x=1 → m:=a []
   x=2 → m:=b ]
```

'repetitive command' (marked by '`*`')
The instruction sequence is carried out iteratively until none of the guards is satisfied.

Two final examples will conclude the discussion of CSP. The first example, from [Hoare 78], is an implementation of the bounded buffer problem with ten buffers (however, there is no test for overflow of the variables `in` and `out` !).

Bounded Buffer Program in CSP:

Producer call to the buffer:	`BB!p`	Write new data
Consumer call to the buffer:	`BB!more(); BB?p`	Read new data

```
BB::
buffer : (0..9) portion;
in, out: integer;  in:=0; out:=0;
  *[in  < out+10;  producer?buffer(in mod 10)
                   → in := in+1
   [] out < in;    consumer?more()
                   → consumer!buffer(out mod 10); out := out+1
   ]
```

After the declaration and initialization of the local data, a single repetitive (guarded) command follows, which constitutes an endless loop. Both guards comprise two parts, which have to be fulfilled together. Messages from the producer are only received if space is still available in the buffer (guard: `in < out+10`), otherwise the producer must wait. When there is available space, the supplied data record is accepted and the `in` pointer is incremented by one. The buffer is handled as a cyclic queue (modulo operation).

The consumer must request its data with the `more()` message. If at least one space in the buffer is occupied (`out < in`), the bounded buffer process sends the contents of the next buffer space to the consumer and increments the `out` pointer by one.

The bounded buffer process terminates when the queue is empty (`in = out`) and the producer has already terminated; only then is none of the guards satisfied.

<u>Program for Volume Control (1):</u>

Calls to volume control `VolCon`

from process `louder`	:	`VolCon!val`	Increase volume by `val` units
from process `softer`	:	`VolCon!val`	Decrease volume by `val` units
from process `off`	:	`VolCon!val`	Switch off system (ignore `val`)

```
VolCon::
active        : boolean;
volume, value: integer;
active := TRUE;
volume := 0;
amplifier!volume;
  *[ active; volume<100; louder?value
              →  volume := volume + value;
                 [volume>100 → volume:=100];
                 amplifier!volume;
   [] active; volume>0; softer?value
              →  volume := volume - value;
                 [volume<0 → volume:=0];
                 amplifier!volume;
   [] active; off?value
              →  [ amplifier!0 || active := FALSE ]
   ]
```

The example program for controlling the volume of a sophisticated amplifier system follows an idea of [Pountain, May 87] and is included in the sections on occam and Ada as well. Unfortunately CSP does not have the concept of a 'message name' or 'message class' ('entry' in Ada), but can only select incoming data by the name of the sender. (As a matter of fact, occam is pretty similar in this regard; incoming messages are differentiated by their 'channels', see Section 9.3 .) So the first version of the CSP program assumes that all three possible types of control message (`louder`, `softer` and `off`) come from different processes. This may be realistic, e.g. if each process represents a hardware button on the front panel. However, for this solution it is not possible for one process to send both messages for increasing and decreasing the volume (e.g. a hardware control knob or a software module for enhancing passages of soft music and softening passages of loud music).

As long as `VolCon` does not receive a message from `off`, the repetitive command continues receiving messages from proceses `louder` and `softer` for increasing or decreasing the volume. These messages are protected by guards, which enforce restrictions, such as the volume being below the maximum value before accepting a message to increase it. After a message has been accepted, the `volume` value is updated and sent to the amplifier.

<u>Program for Volume Control (2):</u>

Calls to volume control:

from process `user` :
- `VolCon!val` Increase / decrease volume (`val` may be positive or negative)
- `VolCon!0` Switch off system

```
VolCon::
active        : boolean;
volume, value: integer;
active := TRUE;
volume := 0;
amplifier!volume;
   *[ active; user?value
           →  [ value =  0 → [ amplifier!0 || active:=FALSE ]
              [] value <> 0 → volume := volume + value;
                              [       volume>100 → volume:=100
                              []      volume<  0 → volume:=  0 ];
                              amplifier!volume;
              ]
    ]
```

In order to allow a single process to send different messages to `VolCon`, the example program has to be changed considerably (see second version). Now it lacks a lot of the clarity and readability of the original version (see also implementation in Ada, Section 9.4).

9.3 occam

Developed by: Inmos Limited, 1984
The occam programming language is a direct commercial successor of CSP, and was developed by the Inmos company [Inmos 84]. The language was specially developed for networks of transputers. These consist of (in the old generation) powerful microprocessors, each having four communications channels for data exchange between the transputers. For the new transputer generation, which is much more powerful, the transparent construction of large networks is accomplished by special communication chips.

Parallel Language Constructs

`!` Sending data (see CSP, Section 9.2)

`?` Receiving data (see CSP, Section 9.2)

`SEQ` Sequential execution of statement blocks

Example:

```
SEQ
  keyboard ? char
  screen   ! char
```

Read a character from the keyboard process and then subsequently send it to the screen. The indentation of lines shown is a must.

`PAR` Parallel execution of statement blocks ('processes')

Example:

```
PAR
  SEQ
    keyboard1 ? char
    screen1   ! char
  SEQ
    keyboard2 ? char
    screen2   ! char
```

Here, two parallel processes, each containing two sequential statements, are executed in parallel. Note that the indentation here determines whether a statement is being executed sequentially or in parallel.

Parallel and sequential statements may also be 'replicated', which is a simple way of writing down a number of operations.

Example:

```
PAR i = 2 FOR 3
  screen[i| ! char
```

is equivalent to:

```
PAR
  screen[2] ! char
  screen[3] ! char
  screen[4] ! char
```

The first parameter of the replication specifies the initial value, while the second parameter specifies the number of replications.

`PRI` Optional setting of the priority of a process

`PLACED` Optional mapping of a process to a physical processor for the purpose of optimization

Example:

```
PLACED PAR
  PROCESSOR 1
    printer  (print.out)
  PROCESSOR 2
    terminal (term.in)
```

Processes `printer` and `terminal` are placed directly onto the physical processors 1 and 2, respectively.

`ALT` Selection of one from many possible processes, guarded by inputs.

Example:

```
ALT
  left_child ? char
    parent ! char
  right_child ? char
    parent ! char
```

This alternation models data transfer in a tree from the leaves to the root. The message of either left or right child, whichever is received first, will be relayed one node up the tree.

`CHAN` Declaration of communications channels between processors

Example:

```
CHAN OF INT my_channel :
```

A channel is used to handle data exchange between parallel processes. Data of the appropriate type (here integer) may be sent to and read from a channel.

`PROTOCOL` Specifying data types to be exchanged over a channel

`TIMER` Declaration of a clock,
e.g. for programming of periodic occurrences or time-outs

Most of the comments concerning CSP in Section 9.2 apply to occam as well. Higher programming language constructs are only partially present in occam; even the indentation of lines is a requirement! There are no dynamic data structures, and recursive programming within a process is not possible. Only in the latest version of the language (occam 3, see [Barrett 92]) are structured data types, modules, and libraries included. One of the biggest problems with large program systems in occam remains the finding of a suitable mapping of processes onto processors (building a *configuration* with construct `PLACED`), which is not sufficiently supported by the programming language and often will not be satisfactorily solved by the operating system on its own.

Program for Volume Control:
(adapted from [Pountain, May 87])

```
VAL max IS 100 :
VAL min IS 0 :
BOOL active :
INT volume, value :
SEQ
  active := TRUE
  volume := min
  amplifier!volume

  WHILE active
    ALT
      (volume<max) & louder?value
        SEQ
          volume := volume + value
          IF
            volume>max
              volume := max
          amplifier!volume

      (volume>min) & softer?value
        SEQ
          volume := volume - value
          IF
```

```
            volume<min
              volume := min
          amplifier!volume

      off?value
        PAR
          amplifier!min
          active := FALSE
```

This sample program contains the essential language constructs of occam. `SEQ` and `PAR` start sequential and parallel instruction sequences, respectively, while `ALT` selects between different incoming messages. In this way, messages such as `louder?value` can be controlled with a guard; `volume<max` must be true before the message will be accepted. The above program receives messages through channels called `louder`, `softer` and `off` from other processes or hardware components. These messages are used to adjust the `volume` variable, the value of which is then sent to the amplifier through channel `amplifier`.

9.4 Ada

Developed by: Jean Ichbiah for the US Department of Defense, 1979
The programming language Ada (see [United States Department of Defense 81] and [Sommerville, Morrison 87]) arose from an attempt by the US Department of Defense to reduce the increasing number of programming languages used there to one single language. Multiple research groups world-wide developed designs for this programming language project. From these, a commission selected one and called it 'Ada'. In order to meet the high demands of universality, Ada was naturally somewhat overloaded with a multitude of language concepts.

In Ada, communication for data exchange between processes (here called *tasks*) is performed via messages in an unbuffered manner (known as the 'rendezvous concept'). A short overview of the most important parallel language constructs follows and these are further illustrated by an example program at the end of the section.

Parallel Language Constructs

`task` Parallel process

`entry` 'Entry point' of a process; declaration of the names of message entrances, which can be called from other processes

`accept` Wait for the call to an entry from another process
Call of an entry with: task name, dot, entry name, parameters (if any)
Example: `controller.louder(5)`

`select` Selection instruction to wait on multiple entries (the first incoming message will be processed)

`when` Restricts selection process in `select` instruction. Only when the boolean condition evaluates to true can the specified branch be executed (compares to Dijkstra's 'guarded commands' in Section 9.2).

These language constructs are applied in the following sample program (the example from Section 9.3 adapted). In Ada, a task (process) comprises a specification part, declaring all of its entries, and a body, giving its statement part. Task `controller` consists of an endless loop surrounding a selection. The selection differentiates between three classes of incoming message (entry), namely `louder`, `softer` and `off`. All three of the routines can be called by the corresponding messages from other processes, where the calling process is blocked during the execution of the `accept` routine. In order to exchange data, input (`in`) and output (`out`, but not used here) data can be transferred as parameters. The first two `accept` instructions are protected by `when` guards. The corresponding `accept` instructions can only be carried out when the variable `volume` lies within the required range. The `accept` instruction for the `off` message class is instead always executable, since there is no guard.

<u>Program for Volume Control:</u>

Calls to volume control `controller` from *any* other process:

e.g.:
```
controller.louder(5);
controller.softer(2);
controller.off();
```
(for increasing volume by 5 units, decreasing volume by 2 units and switching off, respectively)

```
task controller is
  entry louder(value:in integer);
  entry softer(value:in integer);
  entry off();
end;

task body controller is
max: CONSTANT integer := 100;
min: CONSTANT integer :=   0;
volume: integer;
begin
  loop
    select
       when volume<max =>
       accept louder(value:in integer) do
```

```
            volume := volume + value;
            if volume>max then volume:=max end if;
            amplifier.entrance(volume);
         end louder;
      or
         when volume>min =>
         accept softer(value:in integer) do
            volume := volume - value;
            if volume<min then volume:=min end if;
            amplifier.entrance(volume);
         end softer;
      or
         accept off() do
            amplifier.entrance(min);
         end off;
      end select
   end loop
end controller;
```

For simplification, the endless loop in this example program does not have a termination condition. The program contains a 'single task', which means there exists only a single task (process) `controller` in the parallel program. It will be started automatically during the initialization phase of the Ada program. However, there are also the possibilities of defining 'task types' and declaring multiple tasks of the same type (see the following example). Even arrays or records may have a task type. Each task of a task type is started automatically when its declaration is initialized.

Example Program:

```
task type controller is
  entry louder(value:in integer);
  entry softer(value:in integer);
  entry off();
end controller;

c    : controller;
multi: array (1..10) of controller;
```

9.5 Sequent-C

Developed by: Sequent Computer Systems Incorporation, 1987
The 'Parallel Programming Library' [Sequent 87] was developed for the Sequent Symmetry parallel computer in order to extend several programming languages, among them C, by parallel library calls. These library routines can be called as procedures or

functions with return parameters. Very simple process control (comparable with `fork` and `wait` from Unix, see Section 4.2) and rudimentary synchronization of processes are made possible by this parallel library. It is coordinated with the system structure of the Sequent Symmetry (MIMD system with bus network and shared memory, see Section 6.1).

Parallel Library Functions

General Functions

`cpus_online()`	Returns the number of physical processors
`m_set_procs` (number)	Specifies the number of required processors
`m_fork` (func, arg_1,...,arg_n)	Duplicates a procedure and starts it in multiple processors (with identical parameter values)
`m_get_numprocs ()`	Returns the total number of actually started child (or sibling) processes
`m_get_myId ()`	For a child process: returns the child's process number For the parent process: returns zero
`m_kill_procs ()`	Deletes all child processes (Child processes end with a 'busy wait' loop and must therefore be explicitly stopped and deleted)

Semaphore Implementation

`s_init_lock` (sema)	Initialization of a semaphore
`s_lock` (sema)	P operation
`s_unlock` (sema)	V operation

The following example program illustrates some of these parallel library calls in context.

Sample Program Excerpt:

```
...
m_set_procs(3);         /* request 3 more processors              */
m_fork(parproc,a,b);    /* start the parallel child processes     */
m_kill_procs();         /* delete child processes after they
...                        terminate */

void parproc(a,b)       /* parallel procedure of child processes */
float a,b;
{...
  n=m_get_numprocs();   /* Get the number of all child processes */
  m=m_get_myId();       /* Get own process number                */
  ...
}
```

Figure 9.1 shows the execution of the four processes over time. After the child processes are started (via `m_fork`), the main process (P_1) also executes the parallel procedure. After termination, it waits on the termination of all of the child processes. These carry out their procedure with local data and may terminate at different points in time, where the earlier ending child processes wait on the others in a 'busy wait' loop. Child processes may access global data by reading or writing, but they themselves have to take care of synchronizing their activities (e.g. using semaphores). All of the child processes are deleted at the same time (with `m_kill_procs`) and the main process continues its program.

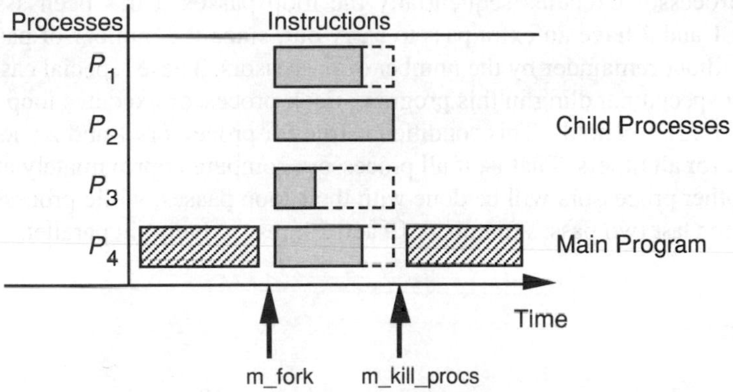

Figure 9.1 Execution of the sample program

If not enough processors are available in the hardware, or fewer than required are provided by the operating system, the assignment to be parallelized must be solved iteratively. In order to avoid the overhead of process starts and terminations, the loop for the iterative solution should be inside the parallel processing procedure (that is, inside the child processes).

<u>Example of Iteration inside Child Processes:</u>
(`N` loop passes)

```
void parproc(a,b)              /* child process */
float a,b;
{ int counter,id,pe;
  pe=m_get_numprocs();         /* Total number of child processes */
  id=m_get_myId();             /* Own process number */
  for (counter=id; counter<=N; counter+=pe)
  {  /* actual processing */ }
}
```

Assume `N=20` passes were required, but only `pe=6` processors were available. In this case the processors have the identifications numbers (`id`) 1 to 6. The example program executes in the following way:

Processor 1 carries out the following loop passes:	1,	7,	13,	19.
Processor 2 carries out the following loop passes:	2,	8,	14,	20.
Processor 3 carries out the following loop passes:	3,	9,	15.	
Processor 4 carries out the following loop passes:	4,	10,	16.	
Processor 5 carries out the following loop passes:	5,	11,	17.	
Processor 6 carries out the following loop passes:	6,	12,	18.	

Each processor executes sequentially the loop passes it has been assigned to. Processors 1 and 2 have an extra pass to carry out, since the number of passes is not divisible without remainder by the number of processors. These 'special cases' do *not* require any special handling in this program. Each processor executes loop passes, as long as `counter<=N` holds. This condition is true for processors 1 and 2 one loop pass longer than for all others. That is, if all processors compute approximately at the same speed, all other processors will be done with their loop passes, while processors 1 and 2 compute the last two passes (numbers 19 and 20, respectively) in parallel.

9.6 Linda

Developed by: Nicholas Carriero and David Gelernter, 1986

Parallel programming concepts can be almost completely independent of a programming language. Linda ([Ahuja, Carriero, Gelernter 86] and [Carriero, Gelernter 89]) is not exactly a parallel programming language, but more a compact set of language independent parallel concepts for MIMD systems. They can be embedded into different programming languages such as C, Fortran, Modula-2, etc. However, this ability to transfer parallel concepts is not restricted to Linda, but also holds for other parallel programming languages – all procedural programming languages are pretty similar, after all.

The concept of parallelism in Linda is a *content addressable* common data pool, known as the *tuple space*, which can be accessed by all processes (*active tuples*) simultaneously in order to read or write data (*passive tuples*). Tuples can consist of multiple data elements of any type. There are six basic operations for accessing the common tuple space in Linda.

Parallel Operations

`OUT` Write data into the tuple space
Generation of a passive tuple

`RD` Read data from the tuple space (without erasing it)

Parts of the tuple can be given values (see Figure 9.2), in which case only the matching tuples come into play. *Read a passive tuple*

`RDP` Read predicate (a boolean test operation of the data in the tuple space)
Test whether a suitable data tuple exists, without reading it

`IN` Read and erase a data element from the tuple space
Corresponds to the `RD` operation with final deletion of the data tuple
Removing a passive tuple

`INP` Read predicate
like `RDP` without reading the element, but with deletion

`EVAL` Start a new process, which will later use `OUT` to write its result into tuple space
Generate an active tuple

Termination of the program system:

If there are no more active tuples in the tuple space or all of the active tuples are blocked in read operations, the system terminates. In the latter case, the required data is not present and cannot be generated by the other processes. So, a deadlock situation is defined as a termination condition here.

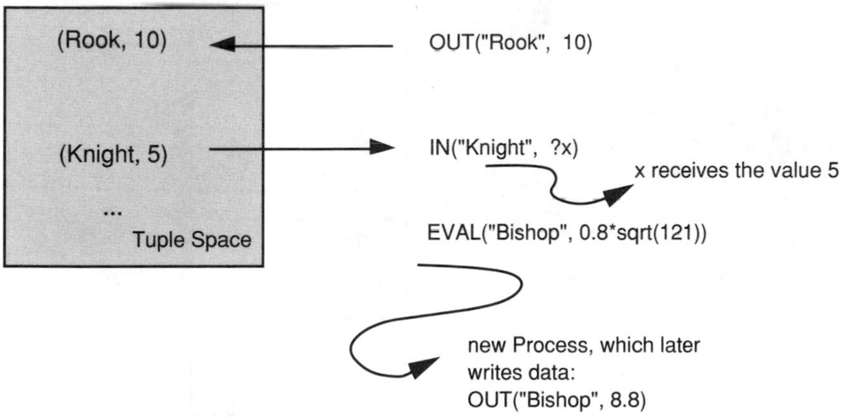

Figure 9.2 Linda's tuple space

Any number of processes can be started, which exchange data through a central data pool. These parallel accesses are synchronized by the base operating system required by Linda. The MIMD communication model chosen here creates some restrictions because an implementation of Linda on a MIMD system without shared memory is only possible with considerable communication costs. These costs for parallel overhead could under certain circumstances render the entire parallel application inefficient.

Figure 9.2 illustrates the interaction of operations in the tuple space, for what might be part of a chess program. In `RD/IN` operations, a variable may be used either as a value that has to match the corresponding component of a tuple in tuple space, or it may be used as a return variable, which is bound to take the component value from the tuple read. A variable used in the latter way has to be prefixed by a question mark '`?`', in order to distinguish these two cases.

<u>Example:</u>

```
x := 5;
RD("Knight", x);
              ↑
```

This process tries to read tuple `("Knight",5)`.

```
RD("Knight", ?x);
              ↑
```

This process tries to read any tuple of the form `("Knight", _)` and – when found – assigns the second component to `x`.

<u>Sample Tuple Space Operations:</u>

Operation	Tuple space
Start with empty tuple space	
`OUT("Knight",5);`	`("Knight",5)`

`OUT("Knight",7);`
`EVAL("Bishop",SQR(3));`
	`("Knight",5)`
	`("Knight",7)`
	`("Bishop",9)`

`RD("Knight",?x);`
`/* read arbitrary tuple, e.g. x=7) */`
	`("Knight",5)`
	`("Knight",7)`
	`("Bishop",9)`

`y := "Knight";` `IN(y, 5);`	`("Knight",7)` `("Bishop",9)`
`z := INP("Rook", ?x);` `/* z becomes FALSE */`	`("Knight",7)` `("Bishop",9)`
`IN("Rook", ?x);` `/* this process is` **`blocked`** `*/`	`("Knight",7)` `("Bishop",9)`

	`("Knight",7)`
	`("Bishop",9)`
	`("Rook",20)`

Other process:
`OUT("Rook",20)`

```
/* this process is released */      ("Knight",7)
/* x becomes 20 */                   ("Bishop",9)
```

When executing a read (`RD`) or input (`IN`) operation, three different cases can arise:

i) there is exactly one matching tuple in the tuple space
⇒ this tuple is read (or read and subsequently deleted (`IN`))

ii) there are two or more matching tuples in the tuple space
⇒ an arbitrary matching tuple is read (or read and subsequently deleted (`IN`))

iii) there is no matching tuple in the tuple space
⇒ this process is blocked until a matching tuple becomes available (i.e. is written into tuple space by some other process using '`OUT`'), or until the whole process system terminates

This blocking scheme may be used to easily implement 'conventional' synchronization mechanisms like semaphores. The following example shows the mutual exclusion of an arbitrary number of processes from a critical section (e.g. accessing shared variables). Here, `IN` corresponds to the semaphore operation `P`, and `OUT` corresponds to `V`.

<u>Initialization:</u> `OUT("sema");`

P_i

```
...
IN("sema");
   <critical section>
OUT("sema");
...
```

The final example is a prime number generator in C-Linda (slightly adapted from [Carriero, Gelernter 89]), which illustrates the functionality of Linda.

<u>Prime Number Generator in Linda:</u>

```
lmain()
{ int i, ok;
  for (i=2; i<=Limit; ++i) {
    EVAL("prime", i, is_prime(i));
  }
  for (i=2; i<=Limit; ++i) {
    RD("prime", i, ?ok);
    if (ok) printf("%d\n", i);
  }
}
```

```
is_prime(me)
int me;
{ int i, limit,ok;
  double sqrt();
  limit = sqrt((double) me);
  for (i=2; i<=limit; ++i) {
    RD("primes", i, ?ok);
    if (ok && (me%i == 0)) return 0;
  }
  return 1;
}
```

The Linda program starts at `lmain` and generates the prime numbers between 2 and `Limit`. First, a process is started for each number with the operation `EVAL`, which checks the primeness of the number with the function `is_prime`. After this, the results are read from the tuple space sequentially with the `RD` operation. If a result is not yet available, then the read operation waits until the corresponding tuple is calculated from the process that owns it. All of the resulting tuples have the string `prime` as their first data element, the integer value as second data element and the result 0 or 1 as third data element. Figure 9.3 illustrates a few of the data tuples generated by the program.

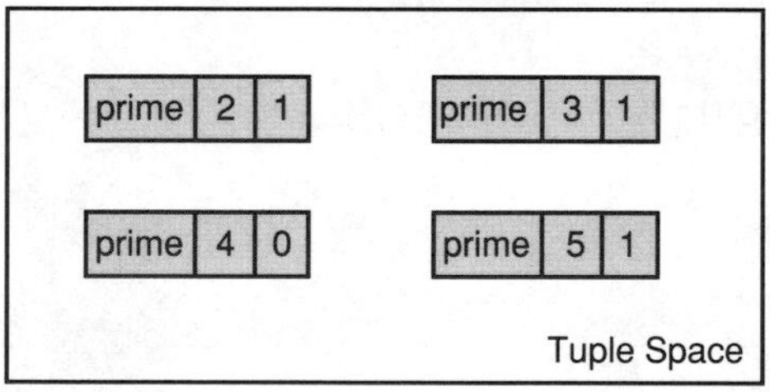

Figure 9.3 Data tuples from the prime number program

Function `is_prime` tests the primeness of its parameter value `me`. It does this by checking whether any of the previously found primes (tuple space entries with a '1' as last component), up to the square root of `me`, divides `me` without remainder. If so, `is_prime` returns 0 (no prime), otherwise 1 (prime).

Pros and Cons of Linda's Parallel Language Concepts

+ High level problem description
  Each process functions independent of the others and is only synchronized through data exchanges over the tuple space. The synchronization is transparent to the user.

+ Machine independence
  Linda requires a MIMD system with shared memory. However, there are no additional restricting assumptions, so Linda can be implemented for every parallel computer system of this class.

+ Language independence
  Linda presupposes no specific programming language model. However, the embeddings made so far are restricted to the very closely related procedural programming languages.

– Model is not well suited for MIMD systems without shared memory
  Relatively high (but application dependent) management costs arise on distributed systems, which is caused by the necessary propagation of tuple updates over the network.

– Understandability of Linda programs
  Even though the functions of the individual language constructs are easy to understand, the construction of a complete Linda program is not as easy. The implicit scheduling of the individual processes is sometimes difficult to grasp.

9.7 Modula-P

Developed by: Thomas Bräunl, 1986
Modula-P is an extension of Modula-2 to asynchronous parallelism [Bräunl, Hinkel, von Puttkamer 86] and has already been used in the previous chapters for coding program fragments. A number of concepts from Concurrent Pascal (see Section 9.1) are also included in Modula-P. In addition, Modula-P differentiates between different levels of process synchronization, which are expressed in the different module levels. A compiler for Modula-P is available as public domain software [Bräunl, Norz 92].

In Modula-P there are three types of module:

- Processor Modules
  The initialization of the whole process system is being started in the processor module. Communication procedures between different processors (or computer systems) via messages (remote procedure call) may be defined, if necessary.

- High Level Modules (regular modules)
  At this level, individual processes can be declared and started. Exception handling with restart points is available. Synchronization between processes on the same (physical) processor is handled via monitors and conditions. There is **no global data** whatsoever!

- Low Level Modules
  This lower processing level of a program is only required when real time programming or machine control (e.g. robot control) must be carried out via direct memory addressing. Interrupts can be declared and handled with interrupt service routines. Synchronization between processes on the same processing element may be handled via semaphores.

This three level hierarchy of a parallel program corresponds roughly to the division of the synchronization and communication concepts into their abstraction levels: messages, monitors, and semaphores.

Parallel Language Constructs

Interrupts can be declared at the beginning of a low level module as constants. If an interrupt occurs during program execution, execution is interrupted and the corresponding event (an interrupt service routine) is called.

```
INTERRUPT Ctrl_C = 2;
...
EVENT Ctrl_C;
BEGIN
  WriteString("Control-C intercepted");
END Ctrl_C;
```

A construct exists in Modula-P for microprocessor systems, which disables in a controlled way all interrupts and therefore all process context switches during an instruction sequence. When the instruction sequence finishes, the interrupts are reenabled. This bracketing is equivalent to a `BEGIN..END` block. The use of this construct is not possible on Unix systems (workstations) and multiprocessor systems.

```
DISABLE
  ... (* critical instructions *)
ENABLE
```

Synchronization via general semaphores is also a construct that can be applied within low level modules. Semaphores are declared as type `SEMAPHORE` with the initialization value given in brackets. Dijkstra's `P` and `V` operations are defined on semaphores (for details see the sample program in Chapter 10).

```
VAR protect: SEMAPHORE[1];
...
P(protect);
 ... (* critical section, e.g. accessing global data *)
V(protect);
```

In high level modules, parallel processes can be explicitly declared (similar to procedures) and started.

```
PROCESS abc(i: INTEGER);
BEGIN
  ... (* process instructions *)
END PROCESS abc;
...
START(abc(1));   (* starting process 'abc' twice with *)
START(abc(7));   (* different parameters              *)
```

The synchronization of processes in high level modules is handled via monitors with condition queues. Monitors are defined as a block encompassing both data and access operations. An access operation corresponds to a special procedure and is called `ENTRY`. Entries provide the only method for accessing the local data of a monitor. When calling a monitor entry from a process, the monitor's name with a colon is used as a prefix for the entry's name, which indicates that monitor calls mutually exclude one another. When one process occupies a monitor with a call to an entry, all the other processes wishing to enter the same monitor must wait. In order to avoid possible deadlocks, an entry is not allowed to call other monitor entries.

```
MONITOR sync;
VAR a: ARRAY[1..10] OF INTEGER;  (* monitor data *)
    j: INTEGER;

ENTRY read(i: INTEGER; VAR value: INTEGER);
BEGIN
  value := a[i];
END read;

ENTRY write(i,value: INTEGER);
BEGIN
  a[i] := value;
END write;

BEGIN (* monitor initialization *)
  FOR j:=1 TO 10 DO a[j]:=0 END
END MONITOR sync;
```

Call of a monitor entry from a process:

```
sync:read(10,v);
```

Conditions can be declared within a monitor as variables of type CONDITION. The operations WAIT, SIGNAL and STATUS (the number of waiting processes) are defined on them. Since all of the waiting processes are released in the implementation of SIGNAL, the WAIT operation must always be enclosed in a WHILE loop in order to avoid inconsistencies.

```
VAR full: CONDITION;
...
WHILE contents=0 DO WAIT(full);
...
SIGNAL(full);
```

For every process, an exception handler can be declared, which replaces the standard exception handler when an error occurs (e.g. division by zero). The cause of an error can be analyzed within the exception handler via the EXEPTNO variable and corresponding measures can be taken. The interrupted process can be continued with the RESUME operation or restarted with the RESTART operation. Exceptions can also be explicitly generated with the RAISE(<error_number>) procedure.

```
PROCESS abc(i: INTEGER);
VAR i: INTEGER;

EXCEPTION
  IF EXEPTNO = 8 THEN   (* Floating Point Exception *)
     i:=0;
     RESUME;
  END;
END EXCEPTION;

BEGIN
  ... (* process instructions *)
END PROCESS abc;
```

The communication between processes on different processing elements that do not have shared memory available takes place via message passing in remote procedure calls. The language construct is called COMMUNICATION. The connections are set up in the initialization section of the processor module using the INITCOM procedure and can be called from a process with the construct CALL, similar to a procedure call.

Multiple identical processes and communication servers may be stared by specifying the desired count as an additional parameter. Basic routines at operating system level take care of scheduling calls to multiple server processes.

```
COMMUNICATION pythagoras (x,y: REAL; VAR result: REAL);
VAR r: REAL;
BEGIN
```

```
  r := x*x + y*y;
  result := SQRT(r);
END COMMUNICATION pythagoras;
```

<u>Initialization of a communication at a remote processor or computer system:</u>
(e.g. at a remote workstation):

```
CONST vince = COMPUTER("sparc", "vincent");
              (* computer family and computer name *)
...
INITCOM(pythagoras, vince);
```

<u>Calling a communication:</u>

```
CALL vince:pythagoras(a,b,c);
```

CHAPTER 10

Coarse-Grained Parallel Algorithms

The cost of data exchange operations in MIMD computer systems is much higher than that of arithmetic/logic operations (which is *not* the case for SIMD computer systems). Performance considerations therefore indicate that it is a good idea to have each process compute somewhat longer passages locally between data exchange operations. This leads to so-called *coarse-grained* parallel algorithms, in contrast to the *fine-grained* parallel algorithms of SIMD systems. Since the processors that form a MIMD system are usually more powerful than the PEs of a SIMD system, they also require a larger area on the chip. This explains why MIMD systems usually have considerably fewer processors than SIMD systems. Algorithms for MIMD are developed on the basis of fewer but more powerful processors, while algorithms for SIMD are based on a large number of less powerful PEs (*massive parallelism*).

The description of the concepts presented in earlier chapters, of the process model and the synchronization mechanisms of semaphores and monitors with conditions, is supplemented at this point by a number of complete programs in Modula-P (see Section 9.7).

10.1 Bounded Buffer with Semaphores

The implementation presented here uses semaphores for process synchronization of the bounded buffer problem from Section 7.3 . Process `Producer` continuously generates new data (from 0 to 9 in an endless loop), while process `Consumer` continuously reads data and computes the cross sum of its input.

The program consists of two modules. The `PROCESSOR MODULE` is the main module in which the two processes are defined and started. The `LOWLEVEL MODULE` contains the synchronization software implemented as semaphores.

```
PROCESSOR MODULE bounded_buffer;
IMPLEMENTATION
IMPORT synch;

PROCESS Producer;
VAR i: INTEGER;
BEGIN
  i:=0;
  LOOP
    i:=(i+1) MOD 10;
    produce(i);
  END
END PROCESS Producer;

PROCESS Consumer;
VAR i,digitsum: INTEGER;
BEGIN
  digitsum:=0;
  LOOP
    consume(i);
    digitsum:=(digitsum+i) MOD 10; (* consume data *)
  END
END PROCESS Consumer;

BEGIN
  WriteString("Init Processor Module"); WriteLn;
  START(Producer);
  START(Consumer);
END PROCESSOR MODULE bounded_buffer.
```

```
LOWLEVEL MODULE synch;
EXPORT
  PROCEDURE produce(i: INTEGER);
  PROCEDURE consume(VAR i: INTEGER);

IMPLEMENTATION

CONST n=5;
VAR buf:       ARRAY [1..n] OF INTEGER;
    pos,z:     INTEGER;
    Critical: SEMAPHORE[1];
    Free:      SEMAPHORE[n];
    Occupied: SEMAPHORE[0];

```

```
PROCEDURE produce(i: INTEGER);
BEGIN
  P(Free);
  P(Critical);
    IF pos>=n THEN WriteString("Error in Producer");
                   WriteLn; HALT;
    END;
    pos:=pos+1;
    buf[pos]:=i;
    (* *) WriteString("Write Buf-Pos: "); WriteInt(pos,5);
    (* *) WriteInt(i,5); WriteLn;
  V(Critical);
  V(Occupied);
END produce;

PROCEDURE consume(VAR i: INTEGER);
BEGIN
    P(Occupied);
    P(Critical);
      IF pos<=0 THEN WriteString("Error in Consumer");
                     WriteLn; HALT;
      END;
     i:=buf[pos];
      (* *) WriteString("Read  Buf-Pos: "); WriteInt(pos,5);
      (* *) WriteInt(i,5); WriteLn;
     pos:=pos-1;
    V(Critical);
    V(Free);
END consume;

BEGIN
  WriteString("Init Synch"); WriteLn;
  pos:=0;
  FOR z:= 1 TO n DO buf[z]:=0 END;
END LOWLEVEL MODULE synch.
```

Sample Program Execution Semaphores:
(Executed on a Sequent Symmetry)

The read and write operations alternate with one another mostly since both the producer and consumer of the data require approximately the same computing time. As shown by even the first two calls in the sample execution shown below (see arrow), the read and write operations need not strictly alternate between one another (two write operations occurred in sequence here). Instead the parallelism is only restricted by the buffer size.

```
Init Synch
Init Processor Module
Write  Buf-Pos:     1    1
Write  Buf-Pos:     2    2
Read   Buf-Pos:     2    2
Write  Buf-Pos:     2    3
Read   Buf-Pos:     2    3
Write  Buf-Pos:     2    4
Read   Buf-Pos:     2    4
Write  Buf-Pos:     2    5
Read   Buf-Pos:     2    5
Write  Buf-Pos:     2    6
Read   Buf-Pos:     2    6
.....
```

10.2 Bounded Buffer with a Monitor

The same bounded buffer problem as in the previous section is implemented here with a monitor instead of semaphores. As before, process `Producer` continuously generates new data, while process `Consumer` continuously reads data and computes the cross sum. The program shown below consists of two modules. The `PROCESSOR MODULE` is as always the main module in which the processes are defined and started. The second (high level or *regular*) `MODULE` contains the synchronization code which is implemented as a monitor with two entries and two conditions.

```
PROCESSOR MODULE highlevel_buffer;
IMPLEMENTATION
IMPORT msynch;

PROCESS Producer;
VAR i: INTEGER;
BEGIN
  i:=0;
  LOOP
    i:=(i+1) MOD 10;   (* produce data *)
    Buffer:writebuf(i);
  END
END PROCESS Producer;

PROCESS Consumer;
VAR i,digitsum: INTEGER;
BEGIN
  digitsum:=0;
```

```
  LOOP
    Buffer:readbuf(i);
    digitsum:=(digitsum+i) MOD 10; (* consume data *)
  END
END PROCESS Consumer;

BEGIN
  WriteString("Init Processor Module"); WriteLn;
  START(Producer);
  START(Consumer);
END PROCESSOR MODULE highlevel_buffer.
```

```
MODULE monitor_buffer;

EXPORT MONITOR Buffer;
       ENTRY writebuf (a: INTEGER);
       ENTRY readbuf  (VAR a: INTEGER);

IMPLEMENTATION

MONITOR Buffer;
CONST max = 5;

VAR Stack:           ARRAY[1..max] OF INTEGER;
    SPointer:        INTEGER;
    Free, Occupied: CONDITION;

ENTRY writebuf(a: INTEGER);
BEGIN
  WHILE SPointer=max (* Buffer full *) DO WAIT(Free) END;
  inc(SPointer);
  Stack[SPointer] := a;
  IF SPointer=1 THEN SIGNAL(Occupied) END;
  (* *) WriteString("write "); WriteInt(SPointer,3);
  (* *) WriteInt(a,3); WriteLn;
END writebuf;

ENTRY readbuf(VAR a: INTEGER);
BEGIN
  WHILE SPointer=0  (*Buffer empty*)  DO WAIT(Occupied) END;
  a := Stack[SPointer];
  (* *) WriteString("read     "); WriteInt(SPointer,3);
  (* *) WriteInt(a,3); WriteLn;
  dec(SPointer);
  IF SPointer = max-1 THEN SIGNAL(Free) END;
END readbuf;
```

```

BEGIN (* Monitor Initialization *)
  WriteString("Init Monitor"); WriteLn;
  SPointer:=0;
END MONITOR Buffer;

BEGIN
  WriteString("Init High Level Module"); WriteLn;
END MODULE monitor_buffer.
```

Sample Program Execution Monitor:
(Executed on a Sequent Symmetry)

The read and write operations show up with the same probability in this example as well. However, on the fifth and sixth steps of this sample execution, two write operations occur in sequence (see arrow). The two processes can operate independently in parallel as long as the buffer size is not exceeded.

```
Init Monitor
Init High Level Module
Init Processor Module
write    1  1
read     1  1
write    1  2
read     1  2
write    1  3
write    2  4
read     2  4
write    2  5
read     2  5
write    2  6
read     2  6
write    2  7
read     2  7
write    2  8
read     2  8
.....
```

10.3 Assignment Distribution via Monitor

The following example algorithm from [Babb 89] uses the rectangle rule for approximating π. This algorithm is not well suited for comparing parallel programming languages, because – except for the summing of the rectangular areas – no communication between processes takes place.

$$\pi = \int_0^1 \frac{4}{1+x^2}\,dx$$

$$\approx \sum_{i=1}^{\text{interv.}} \frac{4}{1+((i-0.5)*\text{width})^2} * \text{width}$$

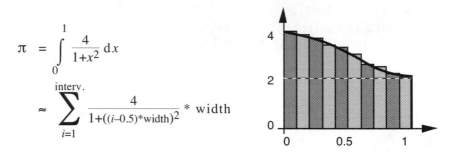

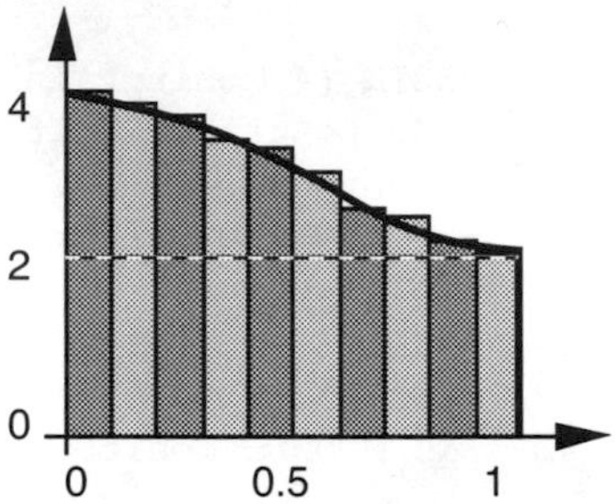

Figure 10.1 Approximation method for integral calculation

The *x*-axis in the range [0,1] is divided into as many intervals as required for accuracy. The task for each worker process comprises the calculation of several interval areas. The partial areas will be added up in the monitor, resulting in the desired approximation of π. According to the rectangle rule, the function's value is determined at the middle of each interval and multiplied by the interval width. The same problem is solved by a massively parallel algorithm for SIMD systems in Section 15.1 .

```
PROCESSOR MODULE pi_calc;
IMPLEMENTATION
CONST  intervals = 100;          (* number of intervals         *)
       width     =   1.0 / FLOAT(intervals); (* Int.-width   *)
       num_work  =   5;          (* number of worker processes *)

PROCEDURE f (x: REAL): REAL;
(* function to be integrated *)
BEGIN
  RETURN(4.0 / (1.0 + x*x))
END f;

MONITOR assignment;
VAR sum          : REAL;
    pos,answers: INTEGER;

ENTRY get_interval(VAR int: INTEGER);
BEGIN
  pos := pos+1;
  IF pos<=intervals THEN int := pos
                    ELSE int := -1     (* done *)
  END;
END get_interval;

ENTRY put_result(res: REAL);
BEGIN
  sum     := sum+res;
```

```
    IF answers = intervals THEN        (* print result *)
      WriteString("Pi = "); WriteReal(sum,10); WriteLn;
    END;
  END put_result;

  BEGIN (* monitor-init *)
    pos := 0;  answers := 0;
    sum := 0.0;
  END MONITOR assignment;

  PROCESS worker(id: INTEGER);
  VAR iv : INTEGER;
      res: REAL;
  BEGIN
    assignment:get_interval(iv); (* get 1. assignm. from mon. *)
    WHILE iv > 0 DO
      res := width * f( (FLOAT(iv)-0.5) * width );
      assignment:put_result(res);   (* put result to monitor *)
      assignment:get_interval(iv); (* get assignm. from mon.*)
    END
  END PROCESS worker;

  PROCEDURE start_procs;
  VAR i: INTEGER;
  BEGIN
    FOR i:= 1 TO num_work DO START(worker(i)) END
  END start_procs;

  BEGIN
    start_procs;
  END PROCESSOR MODULE pi_calc.
```

Each worker process gets its assignment by calling monitor entry `get_interval` inside a loop. After calculating the partial sum, the result is returned to the monitor by calling entry `put_result`, where it is added to the total sum. Since, for this simple problem, the assignments are equal at all times, the expensive entry calls for `get_interval` might have been saved. The intervals could have been more easily assigned to workers by employing the process parameter `id`, which is unused in the program above (see the example for Sequent-C in Section 9.5).

Exercises II

1. With respect to the parallel program fragment below with two parallel processes:

   a) Represent only the synchronization structure of this program as a Petri net!

   b) Is the resulting Petri net live?

   c) Is the resulting Petri net dead?

   d) Can deadlock occur in the process system below?

```
var critical: semaphore[1];
    k       : integer;
```

P_1

```
var a: integer;
...
loop
  P(critical)
    k:=a;
  V(critical);
end;
```

P_2

```
var x,y: integer;
...
loop
  P(critical)
    k:=x;
  V(critical);
  y:=2*x-1;
  P(critical)
    k:=y;
  V(critical);
end;
```

2. Explain which results were generated from which interleave of the memory accesses in Figure 8.1 .

3. Multiple identical processes need to access shared memory in a coarse-grained parallel MIMD system and should be synchronized with semaphores. A maximum of one process is allowed to access the shared data at any time.

a) With which value should the semaphore be initialized?

b) Complete the following program skeleton adding only the missing synchronization operations:

```
PROCESS work;
VAR s: SEMAPHORE[...];
BEGIN
  LOOP
    ......
    (* Accomplish work on shared data *)
    ......
  END;
END PROCESS work;
```

c) If the processes defined in part b) only read from the shared data, then these multiple processes could do so simultaneously. For reasons of efficiency, the maximum number of simultaneously reading processes shall be restricted to 5. How must the program segment for part b) be updated for this new synchronization requirement?

4. Multiple identical processes need to access shared memory in a coarse-grained parallel MIMD system and should be synchronized with semaphores. A maximum of one process is allowed to access the shared data at any time.
Complete the following program skeleton adding only the missing synchronization operations:

```
MONITOR work;
VAR space_free,
    element_present: CONDITION;
    d              : Shared_Data;

BEGIN
  ENTRY StoreData (e: Data_Element);
    WHILE "buffer full" DO  ............
     (* insert data element into shared memory *)
      .............................
```

```
  END StoreData ;

  ENTRY RetrieveData (VAR e: Data_Element);
    WHILE "buffer empty" DO  .............
    (* remove data element from shared memory *)
      .............
  END RetrieveData ;

BEGIN
  (* monitor initialization *)
END MONITOR work;
```

5. In a coarse-grained MIMD system `number_workers` copies of a 'worker' process are to be started. The procedure calls to be carried out are `f(1)` to `f(number_workers)`. They shall be equally distributed among the processes. Complete the Modula-P program below using the constants to accomplish this distribution. Assume the procedure `f` is given.

```
CONST number_workers =  10;
      number_jobs    = 256;

PROCESS Worker(nr: integer);
VAR i: INTEGER;
BEGIN
  ..........
END PROCESS Worker;

PROCEDURE Init;
VAR z: INTEGER;
BEGIN (* Initialization *)
  FOR z:=1 TO number_workers DO START( Worker(z) ) END;
END Init;
```

6. a) Translate the Petri net in Figure 3.8 into a process system in Modula-P, where only one semaphore is used.

b) Develop a variation of the Petri net in Figure 7.3 for the producer–consumer problem, which works with just one semaphore place (however, then only *one* producer and *one* consumer can be synchronized).

7. Find a solution to the readers–writers problem, where, beginning with the first request for access by a writer, no other readers are allowed to enter. After all of the readers have left the critical region, the writer is allowed exclusive access to the shared data.

8. The variable a has the value 500. How many different values can a take on after the unsynchronized execution of the following three processes?

Develop a general procedure to find all possible values of a variable (as well as the maximum number of values), which could arise through the interleave of unsynchronized processes.

P_1	P_2	P_3
`x := a;`	`y := a;`	`z := a;`
`x := 10*x;`	`y := y+1;`	`z := z-3;`
`a := x;`	`a := y;`	`a := z;`
`x := a;`	`y := y+5;`	`z := a;`
`x := 2*x;`	`a := y;`	`z := z-7;`
`a := x;`		`a := z;`

9. Implement the distribution of loop iterations shown in Section 9.5 (Sequent-C) also in Ada or Modula-P.

10. In several programming languages like Ada, there are communication constructs for exchanging messages. The semaphore operations P and V can be implemented by using exclusively message passing. The following program implements a boolean semaphore on which a P operation can be carried to start with. Further communications with 'P messages' are stored in the message buffer until a 'V message' comes in. The possibility of multiple V operations occurring in sequence is not taken care of here! These processes would be blocked until their corresponding P-messages are being received.

```
TASK BODY bool_semaphor IS
BEGIN
  LOOP
    ACCEPT  P
    ACCEPT  V
  END LOOP;
END bool_semaphor;
```

Complete the program below in pseudo-code, such that a general semaphore is implemented. Ten P operations should be allowed before the first V operation.

```
TASK BODY int_semaphor IS
counter: INTEGER;
BEGIN
```

```
LOOP
  SELECT
    WHEN ........ =>
    ACCEPT  P  DO
      ........
    END P;

    ACCEPT  V  DO
      ........
    END V;
  END SELECT;
END LOOP;
END int_semaphor;
```

11. Write a program in Sequent-C for the producer–consumer problem.

12. Write a program in Modula-P to solve the 'dining philosophers' problem (see the figure below): five philosophers sit at a round table. In between each pair there is one fork. Each philosopher goes through the states: Thinking → Hungry → Eating → Thinking. All of the philosophers are thinking at the beginning. If a philosopher becomes hungry, he must acquire the left and the right fork (if they are not already in use by a neighboring philosopher) in order to eat. Deadlock can easily occur when all of the philosophers first pick up their left fork and then must wait (possibly for ever) for the right fork.

The implementation should coordinate the 'access behaviour' of the philosophers such that deadlock cannot occur. One possible solution is first to check whether both the left and right forks are free. If so, the philosopher picks up both of the forks simultaneously and eats. If not, he must hungrily wait until both of the forks are free. The starvation of an individual philosopher, however, can still occur in this simple solution.

13. Solve the dining philosophers problem in problem 12 using a Petri net.

14. Write a program in Modula-P for the parallel control of a warehouse. Since multiple processes can access the database (wares) simultaneously, the access must be synchronized through a monitor.

The records 'stock' have the form: <item no.> <price> <number> .
The records 'budget' have the form: <account no.> <budget> .

Multiple identical stock handling processes should process requests of the following form:

- Withdrawal of stock with booking in the given account
- Arrival of stock
- Output of the current stock on hand

15. Write a program in Modula-P to calculate the fractal image according to the following complex iteration instructions:

a) $z_0 := 0$
$z_{i+1} := z_i^2 + c$

b) $z_0 := 0$
$z_{i+1} := z_i^3 + (c-1)\, z_i - c$

Calculate for a field of 100 × 100 pixels and select for example for part a), the Mandelbrot set, the area $[(-0.76 + 0.01i)\ ,\ (-0.74 + 0.03i)]$. The iteration should be stopped when $|\, z \,| > 2$ or when the maximum number of 200 steps has been carried out. Every pixel is colored according to its iteration number (in the simplest case 200 = black, otherwise white). Start five working processes, which reserve square areas of size 10 × 10 through a request monitor. Notice that if the border of a subregion completely converges (e.g. the maximum number of iterations for *every* border element), the entire contents of the surface converges and therefore no further processing is necessary.

PART III

Synchronous Parallelism

For synchronous parallelism, the processors used for a task are controlled by one central processor with a global clock, so they are not independent of one another. Therefore, a synchronous parallel program has only a single thread of control. This simplified model restricts generality; however, due to their simpler structure, these processors can be more highly integrated. In this way, computer systems can be constructed with considerably more processors than is possible with asynchronous parallelism. This results in the expression 'massive parallelism'. Synchronization between the processors occurs implicitly at each step and is no longer the responsibility of the programmer. The emphasis is placed on vector expressions (fine-grained parallelism). So-called 'data parallel' programming opens up a variety of new possibilities, but also requires new algorithmic concepts.

Structure of a SIMD System

As shown in Figure 11.1, the synchronous model of parallelism corresponds to the SIMD (single instruction, multiple data) computer. The central control processor is a common sequential computer (SISD: single instruction, single data), to which the peripherals are attached as usual. The parallel PEs do not execute their own program, instead they receive their commands from the control processor. Since the PEs do not have their own control logic (no instruction decoding unit, etc.), they are not complete stand-alone processors. These PEs are simple ALUs (arithmetic/logic units) with local memory and communication hardware. The restrictions of the SIMD model result from this simplification of the processor design. The PEs cannot execute different instructions in parallel. Each of them either carries out the same instruction transmitted from the control processor or is inactive. Every parallel selection (`if` instruction) must therefore be divided into two sub-steps. First, the `then` part of the instruction is carried out on all of the PEs for which the selection condition is fulfilled, while the other PEs are inactive. In the second step, the `else` part of the instruction is carried out by all of the PEs that were inactive before, and the first group of PEs is inactive. This sequentialization of the two parts of an `if` selection naturally causes considerable inefficiency. However, since the simple structured PEs of a SIMD computer can be more highly integrated, there exist SIMD systems with a much higher number of PEs than MIMD computers. The immense number of PEs (*massive parallelism*, meaning the employment of a thousand or more PEs) alone compensates for this inefficiency in suitable applications.

The PEs are connected to one another via a network that can have a 'fixed wiring' or a reconfigurable topology (see Chapter 5). This network allows fast, parallel data exchange between groups of PEs. Data can also be exchanged between the control processor and individual PEs (selective) or between the control processor and all active PEs (broadcast).

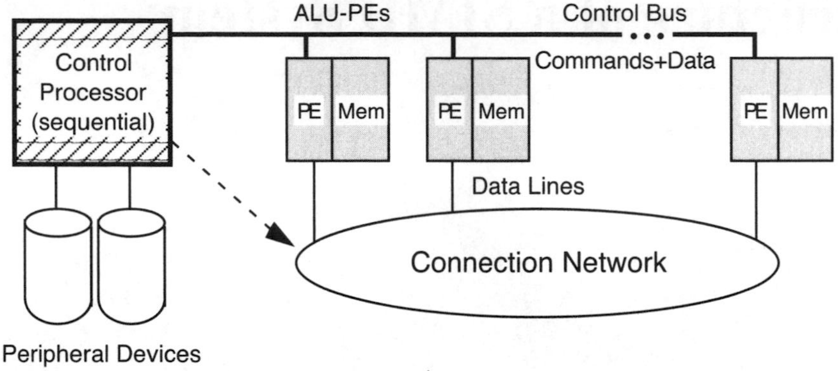

Figure 11.1 SIMD computer model

11.1 SIMD Computer Systems

The most important performance data of three typical SIMD computers is given below. The peak performance values by themselves are only of limited significance, since these values are never achieved in practical applications. These values only hold for very simple operations (e.g. dot product) and SIMD applications generally carry out much more complex computations. However, these figures are suitable for the comparison of SIMD systems with one another, if they refer to the same operations. The measures used here are MIPS (million instructions per second) and MFLOPS (million floating-point operations per second), where the corresponding operation length (e.g. 32-bit) and the operation types used for the measurement (e.g. addition only, average value or dot product) also have to be considered.

The capital letter 'K' denotes a factor of 1024, in contrast to 'k' which represents a factor of 1000 . The capital letter 'B' denotes the unit 'byte', while 'b' represents the unit 'bit' (one byte equals eight bits).

Connection Machine

Company:	Thinking Machines Corporation Cambridge, Massachusetts
Model:	CM-2
Processors:	65,536 PEs (1-bit processors) 2,048 floating-point coprocessors (64-bit, option)
Memory in each PE:	128 KB (maximum)
Peak Performance:	2,500 MIPS (32-bit operation) 10,000 MFLOPS (dot product, 32-bit) or 5,000 MFLOPS (dot product, 64-bit)

Interprocessor Connection:	global hypercube 0.32 GB/s 4-way reconfigurable nearest neighbor grid (implemented using the hypercube) 1.0 GB/s
Programming Languages:	CMLisp (initial extension of Lisp) *Lisp (based on Common Lisp) C* (based on C) CMFortran (patterned after Fortran 90) C/Paris (C with calls of assembly library routines)

The Connection Machine CM-2 is currently one of the best-known and highest-performance SIMD computer systems. It has the most processors, though each processor only has a 1-bit ALU. Groups of 32 PEs share a floating-point coprocessor, which provides a considerable performance advantage (in the GFLOPS range) over systems without arithmetic coprocessors. The CM-2 has two connection networks for the PEs: a global hypercube network for universal communication and a fast nearest neighbor grid that is implemented over the hypercube and can be flexibly configured. Each set of 16K PEs (16,384 PEs) receives instructions from an independent 'sequencer' (control processor). A fully equipped CM-2 consists of four SIMD computers that can be also be operated separately. Another feature of the Connection Machine CM-2 is hardware support for virtual processors (see Section 11.3). The application programmer can easily write programs using more processors than are physically present in the system.

Another very important point is the multiplicity of programming languages available for the Connection Machine. These range from assembly language through extended Fortran and C up to functional programming languages.

Thinking Machines' latest parallel computer system, the CM-5, is not a pure SIMD computer, but a combination of MIMD and SIMD systems (SPMD model, see Section 2.1).

MasPar

Company:	MasPar Computer Corporation Sunnyvale, California
Model:	MP-2216
Processors:	16,384 PEs (32-bit processors)
Memory in each PE:	64 KB (maximum)
Peak-Performance:	68,000 MIPS (32-bit operation) 6,300 MFLOPS (add./mult., 32-bit), or 2,400 MFLOPS (add./mult., 64-bit)

Interprocessor Connection:	3-stage Clos-network (router) 1.3 GB/s (set-up of 3 μs not taken into account) 8-way nearest neighbor torus grid (independent of the router) 20 GB/s
Programming Languages:	MPL (based on C) MPFortran (patterned after Fortran 90)

Since there are no arithmetic coprocessors available and all floating-point calculations have to be performed in software, the MasPar's high integer performance cannot be achieved in the floating-point area. Unlike the CM-2, there are two physically separate connection structures in the MasPar MP-2: a fast, local neighbor grid (with 8-way connectivity, but not configurable), and a global 3-stage router for arbitrary (random) interconnectivity. Virtual processors are not supported in the hardware, instead an 'intelligent compiler' is supposed to take over this task. The sequential control processor of the MP-2 is built in 'Harvard style', that is, unlike the 'von Neumann style', there are separate memories for programs and data.

Extensions of C and Fortran are available from MasPar as programming languages. However, a rudimentary management of virtual processes is only available in Fortran.

Distributed Array Processor (DAP)

Company:	Cambridge Parallel Processing Limited Reading, England A Division of Cambridge Management Co. Irvine, California (previously: Active Memory Technology AMT)
Model:	DAP 610C
Processors:	4,096 PEs (1-bit processors) 4,096 floating-point coprocessors (8-bit)
Memory in each PE:	128 KB
Peak-Performance:	40,000 MIPS (1-bit operation), or 20,000 MIPS (8-bit) 1,200 MFLOPS
Interprocessor Connection:	4-way nearest neighbor grid (**no** global network) 5.2 GB/s
Programming Language:	Fortran-Plus (patterned after Fortran 90)

With just 4K PEs, the DAP has a relatively small number of PEs. As in the Connection Machine CM-2, these are simple 1-bit ALUs. Each of them is, however, complemented by an 8-bit coprocessor for floating-point calculations. With these coprocessors, the DAP achieves a noticeable peak performance in the MFLOPS range. There is no universal connection network; a local neighbor grid is the exclusive connection structure. This grid is suitable for a number of applications, but it does not support universal connection structures. If an application requires complex connection structures, these can only be simulated on the grid with enormous communications costs and are difficult to program (about $\sqrt{n}$ steps are required for a single data exchange among n PEs; see Section 5.4 on the simulation of networks). A summary of massively parallel applications for the Distributed Array Processor can be found in [Parkinson, Litt 90].

Fortran-Plus, a parallel version of Fortran, patterned after the new Fortran 90 standard, is the single programming language offered. A variation of the C* language from the Connection Machine is in development; however, it remains to be seen how much of the functionality of C* will be implemented.

Comparison

In spite of the different structures of the SIMD systems presented here, some commonalties are recognizable. All of the companies manufacturing massively parallel computer systems offer (unfortunately incompatible) versions of parallel Fortran, which are all orientated on the new standard Fortran 90 (see Section 14.1). Presumably it is hoped to appeal to the traditional Fortran areas of engineering and the natural sciences. However, it should not be forgotten that the program packages already written in Fortran 77 cannot easily be automatically parallelized, and must therefore be rewritten in Fortran 90 (see Chapter 16).

All of the SIMD systems presented have at least a two-dimensional grid or torus as a fast connection structure between processors. This is only useful for certain classes of applications, such as image processing or solving numerical problems. But still, the use of a large percentage of SIMD computer systems in these areas explains the presence of this connection structure.

11.2 Data Parallelism

In contrast to MIMD systems, SIMD systems have just one single program at the central control processor, whose instructions are executed sequentially but with data parallelism (vector-parallel on the PEs). Programming is highly simplified by the fact that just one control flow exists and there are no independent processes running asynchronously.

Since all of the PEs execute 'in lock-step', so each step is synchronized, the requirement for expensive and error prone synchronization mechanisms, such as semaphores and monitors, does not exist. SIMD programs do not need these concepts. Of course, the PEs exchange data, but as explained later, data exchanges do not take place between just a pair of PEs. Instead a *collective* data exchange occurs between all of the PEs, or a subset thereof. While communication on some MIMD systems creates a bottleneck, it is highly parallel on SIMD computers. Using the local neighbor grids it has very small time requirements of the order of an arithmetic/logic instruction. This does not apply in full to the universal global connection structures of the SIMD systems, but even communications over these structures are carried out several orders of magnitude faster than communication on MIMD systems. What is more, in SIMD systems there are *thousands of PEs* participating in a *single* parallel data exchange operation, in contrast to only *one pair* of processors in a MIMD system.

While on classical von Neumann computers, just one active component (the CPU) carries out the calculations for a vast number of passive components (the memory cells), this situation is more balanced with data parallel SIMD computers. Every element of the large data blocks distributed among the PEs lies in the local memory of a PE. This means that all of the data elements can be seen as active computing components. This allows (and requires) a totally new programming style, in which operations are applied directly in parallel on the data elements. This direct parallel way of operating avoids, for example, the sequential iterative handling of array components: loading them into the CPU, processing them, and then writing them back to memory. Instead, all components can now be processed in parallel within a single step.

The data parallelism requires a paradigm shift from the von Neumann model, which programmers have been used to for decades. Data parallelism is fundamentally the simpler model, since problems with inherent parallelism can also be solved in this way, without having to take the artificial sequentialization restriction of the von Neumann model into account.

11.3 Virtual Processors

The SIMD computer systems presented in Section 11.1 all have an enormous number of PEs available. Nevertheless, it is still possible that even 65,536 processors might not be sufficient, for example, an image with $500 \times 500 = 250{,}000$ pixels needs to be processed and ideally one PE should be provided for each pixel. The mapping to the physically available processors can of course always be carried out by the application programmer. However, it is much more desirable to have this frequently required function handled by the programming environment of the parallel computer system itself.

When the number of PEs required by a program exceeds the number of PEs available, these virtual PEs should be provided transparently to the application programmer through a level of abstraction. The SIMD computer maps the virtual processors onto the available physical processors via either software or hardware. The concept of virtual processors is therefore an analogy to the concept of virtual memory.

If a program requires fewer virtual PEs than the available number of physical PEs, the superfluous physical PEs are simply switched off. They remain inactive and, because of the SIMD model, they cannot be used for other purposes. If a program needs more virtual PEs than physical PEs are available, the virtual PEs are mapped onto the physical PEs through iteration steps, as shown in the following example.

These iterations are carried out for every elementary operation (e.g. addition) or for instruction sequences in which no data exchanges occur. Some loss of parallelism occurs through temporally inactive PEs when the number of virtual PEs is not an exact multiple of the number of physical PEs. During every third step in the example below, PEs 501 to 1000 (corresponding to 50%) are inactive. This results in an up-front loss of 17% of the possible computational performance. No more than 83% of the theoretical maximum throughput of the physical PEs can be achieved.

Example of the Mapping of Virtual PEs:

Assume: 2500 virtual PEs are required by the application program
1000 physical PEs are available in hardware

Solution with iteration steps:

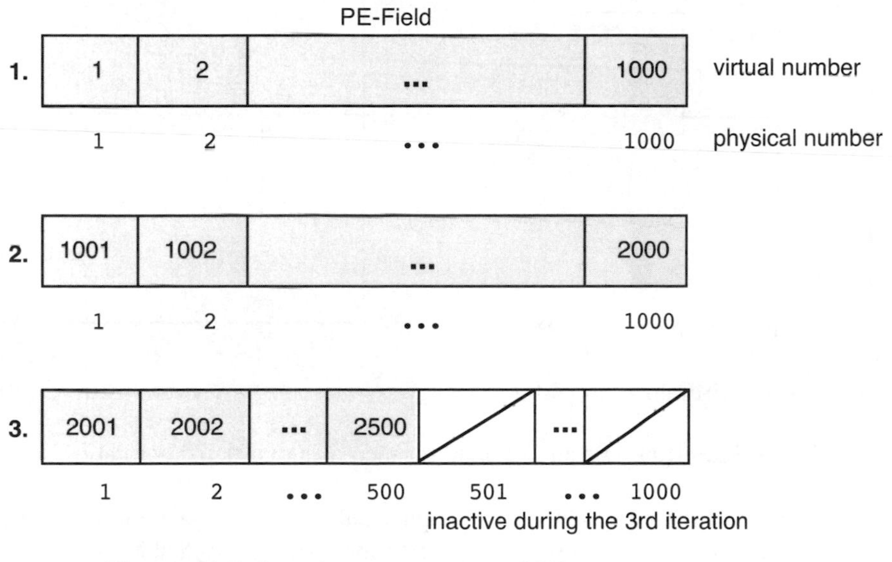

Figure 11.2 Iteration over groups of PEs

If the number of virtual PEs is denoted by v and the number of physical PEs is p, then the virtualization ratio R is defined as:

$$R = \frac{v}{p}$$

Figure 11.3 shows run time and PE load (the average number of *active physical* PEs) behaviour depending on the virtualization ratio for a hypothetical program with only vector instructions (no scalar commands or inactive PEs). See Chapter 18 for details on parallel speedup and scaleup.

Data exchange operations are complicated considerably by the complex interconnection structures emerging from the mapping and iteration required to support virtual PEs. For example, a simple virtual grid which is too large to fit in the physical grid of PEs requires a quite complex physical connection structure, which is actually just a local grid at its core, but requires connections to other physical PEs along its borders. The resulting complex physical structure slows down every data exchange operation. Since each data exchange will be executed in a loop (in each step but the last for as many virtual PEs as there are physical PEs available), this data must be placed into a buffer region. This buffer requires memory for all of the virtual PEs, so each physical PE has to reserve buffer space for all of its virtual PEs in the same way as it has to reserve memory space for all of its virtual PEs.

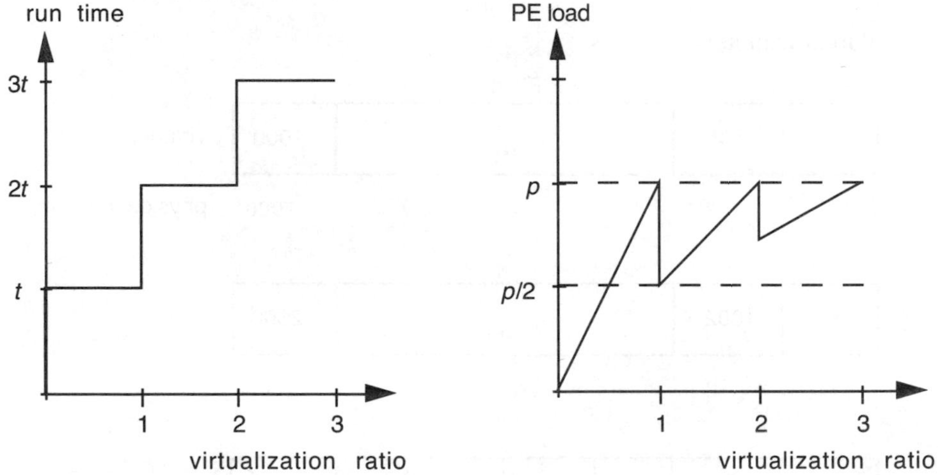

Figure 11.3 Run time and PE load for increasing virtualization ratio

The mapping of the virtual PEs onto the physical PEs should take place in such a way as to be *transparent* to the application programmer. This means that it can be implemented either through the support of special hardware or through software.

a) *Implementing virtual processors in hardware*
The Connection Machine CM-2 has hardware support for virtual PEs. The virtualization ratio R can be selected directly. The main memory of each PE is then automatically divided among the virtual PEs and every command is carried out once for each virtual PE, which means several times iteratively on the physical PEs.

This hardware solution offers a range of advantages. Efficient parallel processing is guaranteed and even system programs (e.g. compilers) can be much more easily implemented than would be the case without special hardware. The drawback comes from increased system overhead when the virtualization of the processors is not required. If the 64K PEs (still an impressive number) are sufficient, then the performance values can fall as much as 25% due to unnecessary virtual PE management.

b) *Implementing virtual processors in software*
A compiler providing virtual processors without hardware support has to perform the following tasks:

- get the numbers of virtual and physical PEs
and determine the virtualization ratio R

- allocate data for all *virtual PEs*
Example:

```
VECTOR i: INTEGER;   ➡   VECTOR i: ARRAY[1..R] OF INTEGER;
```

- generate explicit loops for vector statements
Example:

```
i := 2*i;            ➡   FOR step:=1 TO R DO
                               i[step] := 2 * i[step];
                           END;
```

- translate virtual PE addresses to physical PE addresses for data exchange operations

The MasPar MP-2 does not have special hardware for implementing virtual PEs, instead a software solution is recommended through an 'intelligent compiler'. Such a compiler generates special code for the application depending on whether virtualization is required or not: for applications where virtualization is required, special code is generated to map the virtual PEs onto the physical PEs, or if no virtualization is required, special code without the virtualization overhead and slow-down is generated. Even though the application programmer should not notice any difference between the hardware solution and the software solution (transparent mapping), system programming (e.g. developing a new compiler) is considerably more difficult with the software solution. The management overhead for the virtualization and thus the achieved efficiency is highly dependent upon the quality of the compiler.

Virtualization through software on the MasPar MP-2 is at present only implemented in MPFortran. No 'intelligent compiler' exists for MPL so far, so this task has to be assumed by the application programmer.

Communication in SIMD Systems

Since all instructions on a SIMD computer system are executed synchronously, synchronization between processors, as discussed earlier for MIMD systems, is not required. As already indicated in the last chapter, data exchange on a SIMD system is a 'collective function'. This means that individual data exchange between two processors does not occur, instead all of the active PEs take part in the data exchange. This could be all of the PEs in the system, or just a subset thereof. In any case, data exchange on a SIMD system is a significantly simpler and less expensive operation than on MIMD systems, since the connection set-up can be done much faster. In most cases, the network also has a higher connectivity and a larger bandwidth.

Figure 12.1 shows an example of data exchange. Every PE shifts the value of its local variable x one step to its neighbor to the right in the grid.

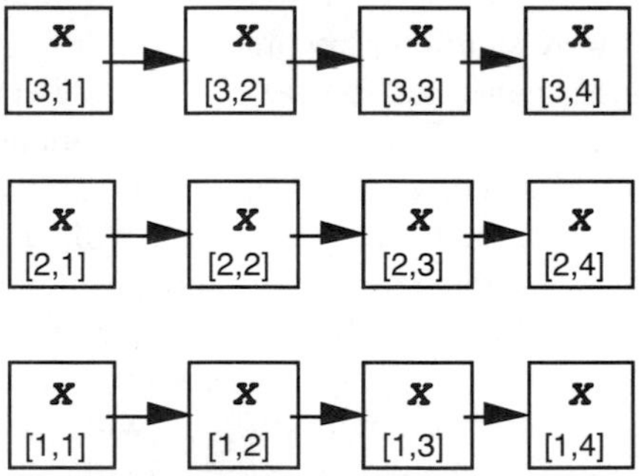

Figure 12.1 Data exchange on SIMD computer systems

Since most of the SIMD systems have a very fast, fixed point-to-point connection structure between processors, naturally the simple, regular structures can be easily mapped to the physical connection structure. Every deviation brings considerable loss of speed because each data exchange must be carried out through multiple steps, or (if available) over the slower universal connection structure.

12.1 SIMD Data Exchange

Data exchange on a SIMD computer system is performed *in parallel* between all active PEs. The 'pair-building' neighbor funtion between PEs may be *local* or *global*. Execution takes place in three steps:

1. Selection of a group of PEs
   (activation)

2. Choosing of an earlier defined direction in the connection structure or of a new dynamic neighbor function

3. Execution of the data transfer along the selected connection structure
   (pair-wise between all active PEs)

Such a data exchange is represented in the SIMD programming language Parallaxis [Bräunl 90] with the notation shown below. Other data parallel languages omit step 0 and include the 'neighbor function' as an arithmetic expression directly in step 2.

0. In advance: Definition of a connection structure

Example:

```
CONFIGURATION ring [0..11];
CONNECTION right: ring[i] ↔ ring[(i+1) mod 12].left;
```

The connection structure named `ring` has twelve elements, which are labelled from 0 to 11. There is a bi-directional connection with the symbolic names `right` and `left`. The connection to the right maps each PE onto the PE with the next higher identification number; PE 11 is mapped onto PE 0 with the modulo function. The corresponding rules apply to the connection to the left. The connection structure is therefore a closed ring.

1. Selection of a group of PEs

Example:

```
PARALLEL ring[3..8]
  ...
ENDPARALLEL
```

PEs are selected in this parallel instruction block. The block in this example activates the ring PEs 3 to 8; all of the others remain passive.

2.+3. *Execution of the parallel data transfer*
(inside of the parallel block)

Example:

```
PROPAGATE.right(x)
```

Each of the active PEs (numbers 3 to 8) carries out a clock-wise data transfer with its neighbor PE. In doing so, every PE first places the value of its local variable x on the connection line ('send') and then reads the new value of the local variable from its predecessor (see Figure 12.2). Due to the activation of only a portion of the ring, PE 3 has no predecessor and PE 8 has no successor. The same case can occur in open topologies, such as a linear list. In this case, PE 3 retains its 'old' value after the data exchange, because it does not receive a new value. The 'old' value of PE 8 is lost since there is no successor PE to accept it.

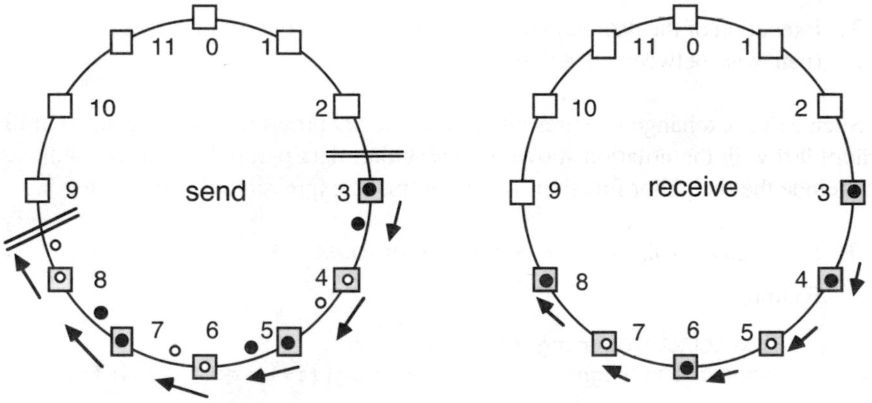

Figure 12.2 Sending and receiving data

The ring connection structure in Figure 12.2 can quite easily be mapped onto the most frequently available connection structure, the two-dimensional grid (see Figure 12.3). But even here special rules must be applied for several of the PEs in the physical structure. While the inner elements of the grid are connected one step in the second dimension (to the right), the right border elements of the grid must be connected to the leftmost element and one row higher, and the last ring element, number 11, must be connected back to the first element, number 0. Only the shaded PEs in Figure 12.3 of the physical grid are used.

For an apparently simple data transfer along the virtual ring structure, an expensive case decision on the physical grid must be carried out.

Example:

Virtual Structure:

```
PARALLEL ring [0..11]
  PROPAGATE.right(x)
ENDPARALLEL
```

is mapped to
Physical Grid:

```
PARALLEL grid [1..2],[1..4];
         grid [3],   [1]
  'grid[i,j] →  grid[i,j+1]'
ENDPARALLEL;
```

Case a: One step to the right

```
PARALLEL grid [1..2],[5]
  'grid[i,j] →  grid[i+1,1]'
ENDPARALLEL;
```

Case b: Go to beginning of next row

```
PARALLEL grid [3],[2]
  'grid[3,2] →  grid[1,1]'
ENDPARALLEL;
```

Case c: Return to the beginning

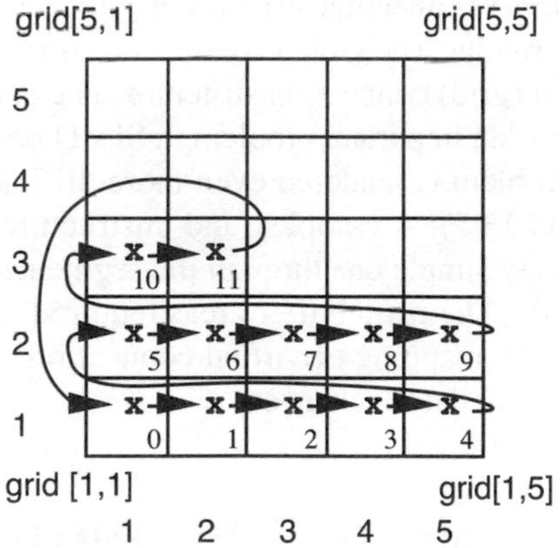

Figure 12.3 Mapping of a ring onto a grid

Since case selections must be implemented sequentially on a SIMD system, three physical data exchange operations are required for each virtual data exchange in this example. In addition, these assignments must be handled over a buffer region, otherwise local data might already be overwritten before it could reach the corresponding neighbor PE. Since the execution time of a data exchange does not depend on the number of participating PEs, every data exchange operation for the ring structure in this example takes three times as long as a simple data exchange in a grid structure!

As one can see from the example above, an automatic mapping of virtual connection structures onto a fixed physical structure (like the above grid) is exceedingly difficult to implement. As the complexity of the virtual structures increases, this task becomes even more difficult. Automatic mappings can therefore only be carried out for simple structures. Due to the increasing number of case selections and the simultaneously increasing processing time ($\sqrt{n}$ data exchange steps are required in general for n PEs; see Section 5.4), automatic mapping does not make sense for large complex structures. At this point, the global (universal) dynamic connection structure ('router') on a SIMD system is the better choice, if one is available. The destination address of a PE is specified for each physical PE. One can also interpret the general case of unstructured connections as a vector permutation (see Figure 12.4).

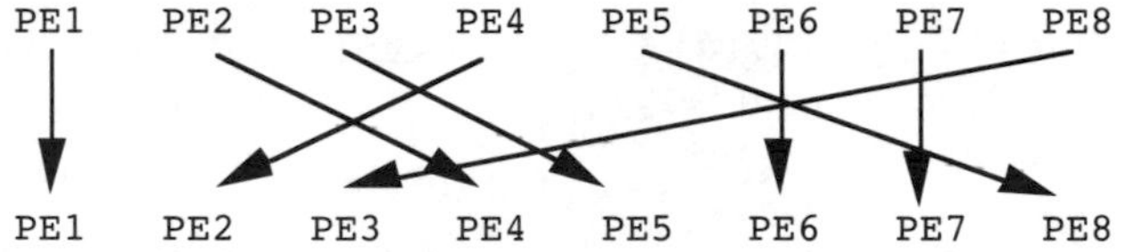

Figure 12.4 Data exchange as a vector permutation

The application of a global connection structure is much easier to program and can be automated without any trouble. The global connection structure is, however, considerably slower than the local (grid) connection structure. The correct use of the local or global connection structure is an important problem in SIMD programming.

The communication problem is rendered even more difficult by the use of virtual PEs (see Sections 11.3 and 13.2). A complex and unstructured connection topology can easily emerge from a very simple one through the segmented distribution of virtual PEs among the physical PEs. The extra buffer areas required for all of the virtual PEs also complicate the automatic mapping of virtual connection structures onto physical connections to perform efficient data exchanges.

12.2 Connection Structures of SIMD Systems

The connection structures of the Connection Machine CM-2 and the MasPar MP-2 are presented in detail in this section. As already mentioned, both systems have a global connection structure, allowing connections between any selected pairs of processors, in addition to a local (nearest neighbor) grid structure. The local grid structure is the significantly faster structure on both systems (e.g. suited for problems in image processing), while the slower global network allows dynamic selection of any possible connection topology.

Connection Machine CM-2 with 65,536 Processors

a) The local grid structure on the CM-2 is a dynamic grid with 4-way nearest neighbor connections (known as 'NEWS', after the compass points north, east, west and south) that can be configured within certain limitations for any number of dimensions with specifiable measurements. This fast local connection structure is implemented using parts of the global hypercube structure (see below) with special hardware support. The two-dimensional connection structure (with 256 × 256 PEs) is sketched in Figure 12.5.

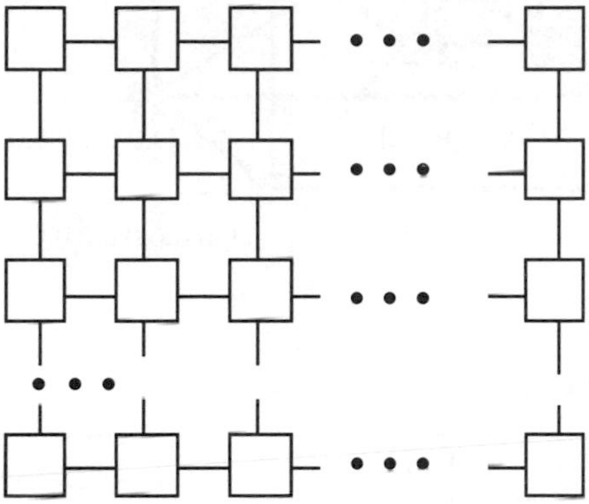

Figure 12.5 Connection Machine CM-2 grid network

b) A twelve-dimensional hypercube is used for the global connection structure in the CM-2. Accordingly this hypercube contains only 2^{12} = 4,096 elements, therefore the 65,536 PEs are divided into 4,096 clusters, each of which contains 16 PEs (see the cluster structure in Figure 12.6, with a four-dimensional hypercube only, due to space limitations). Each cluster has twelve connections into the hypercube, but the 16 PEs within the cluster are connected directly to the cluster router. If all of the PEs within the cluster need to send or receive data from outside the cluster, then the entire data exchange must be unwound into 16 steps due to this bottleneck.

The cluster solution used in the Connection Machine CM-2 restricts the global connection structure to some extent; however, it allows the construction of a parallel computer with 64K processors while holding the number of connections down to a reasonable value. The cluster solution implemented here requires altogether:

$\frac{1}{2} * 4{,}096 * 12$ =	24,576	connections for the hypercube
$65{,}536 * 1$ =	65,536	connections for the individual cluster elements
	90,112	connections

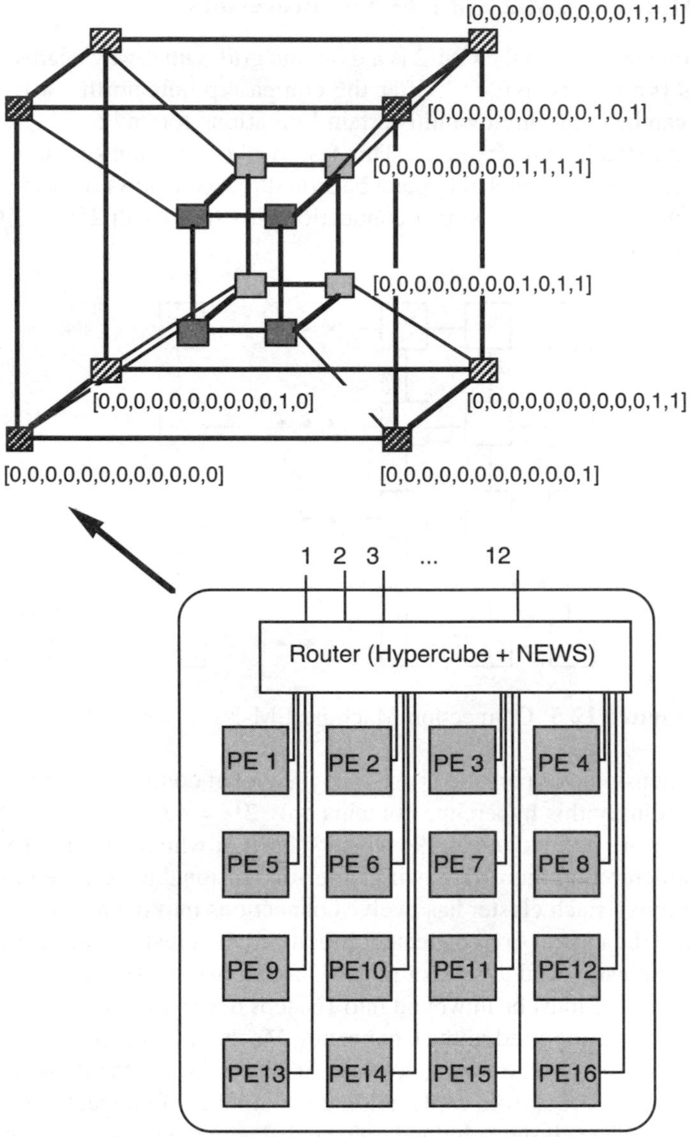

Figure 12.6 Connection Machine CM-2 hypercube network

On the other hand, considerably more connections would have been required for the implementation of a full 16-dimensional hypercube:

$\frac{1}{2} * 65{,}536 * 16 = 524{,}288$ connections

That would have required six times as many connections as the cluster solution, and would therefore have been considerably more expensive!

MasPar MP-2 Model MP-2216 with 16,384 Processors

a) The MP-2 local grid structure is a fixed, two-dimensional torus in which the PEs are arranged in a square measuring 128 × 128. Every PE is connected to its 8 neighbors (8-way nearest neighbor, known as 'x-net' after the X-shaped connections to the diagonal neighbors).

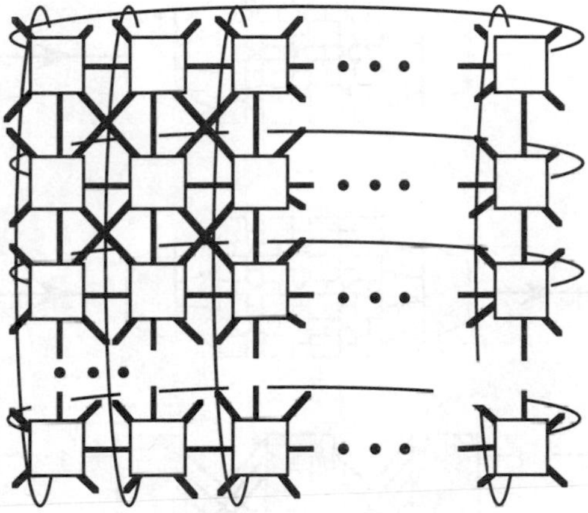

(Diagonal border connections not shown)

Figure 12.7 MasPar MP-2 grid network

b) The MP-2 global connection structure is known as the 'global router' and consists of a three-stage Clos network with 1,024 inputs and outputs. This means that 16 PEs (a 'cluster') always share a router entry and exit attachment (see Figure 12.8). Of the 16,384 PEs, only 1,024 can simultaneously set up connections. If all of the PEs need to exchange data simultaneously, the entire process requires 16 steps, assuming that no further collisions occur.

A compromise similar to that of the Connection Machine CM-2 was selected in the global connection structure. The connection costs of a three-stage Clos network are approximately $\sqrt{32} * n^{3/2}$ for n I/O connections (see Section 5.2). A full Clos network for all PEs would therefore require 16 times the size and would give rise to 64 times the costs. In comparison, a crossbar switch (costs n^2) with diameter 1,024 would cause 5.7 times the connection cost of the small Clos network, while a full crossbar switch for 16,384 PEs would require 1,448 times the cost!

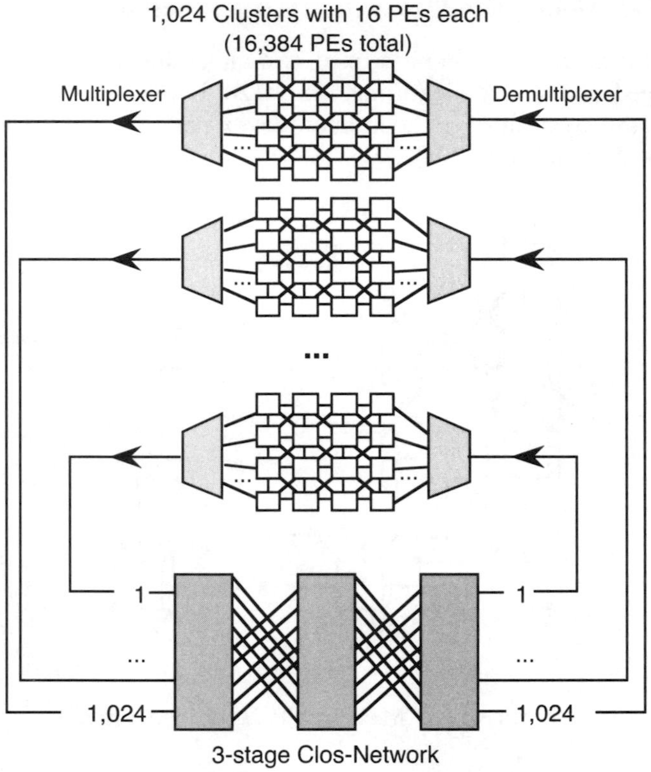

Figure 12.8 MasPar MP-2 router

12.3 Vector Reduction

A fundamental operation of vector computers and SIMD systems is vector reduction. Therefore, it is usually a primary operation or even has special hardware added for its efficient implementation. In this operation, a vector (or the individual components which are distributed among the PEs) is reduced to a scalar value (see Section 2.3). This occurs via a specific dyadic (two operand) operation such as addition, multiplication, maximum, minimum, logical AND, logical OR, etc. However, one should ensure that the reduction operation is associative and commutative (e.g. not subtraction or division), otherwise different results can be produced depending on the execution sequence.

Figure 12.9 Vector reduction via addition

The components of the vector are added up; the resulting sum is a scalar value. Any execution sequence (by using parentheses) can be used with associative operations; however, tree-shaped processing allows a much more efficient parallel execution than sequential execution (see Figure 12.10).

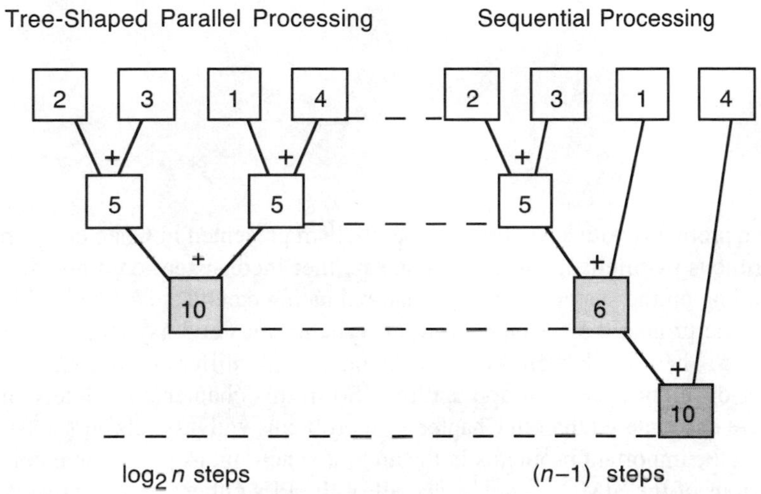

Figure 12.10 Vector reduction

In contrast to sequential execution, requiring $n-1$ steps, tree-shaped processing allows the same number of additions to be distributed among tree levels of parallel processors. Thus the result can be calculated in only $\log_2 n$ steps.

The reduction of a vector `v` into a scalar `s` using the `SUM` operation is expressed in Parallaxis notation in the following way:

```
s := REDUCE.SUM(v)
```

Vector reduction is implemented either in software through explicit data exchanges with arithmetic operations in between, or in special hardware (as with the Connection Machine CM-2) allowing execution of the reduction operation in parallel to the data transfer.

CHAPTER 13

Problems with Synchronous Parallelism

None of the problems with asynchronous parallelism presented in Chapter 8 is relevant for synchronous parallelism. Here, there are neither inconsistent data nor deadlocks, and, depending on the system, not even load balancing can be performed. This shows once again the principle difference between synchronous and asynchronous parallel programming. These models are based on fundamentally different approaches and are suitable for different classes of applications. So in this chapter completely different problems are encountered than in Chapter 8 on problems with asynchronous systems.

Many of the important problems in the area of synchronous parallelism come from the restrictions of the SIMD model. Since all of the PEs either carry out the same operation or are inactive, certain vector operations cannot be sufficiently parallelized. The introduction of a level of abstraction in order to provide virtual processors, independent of the number of physical processors available, can also lead to efficiency problems. Another problem is the attachment of peripheral devices which very often causes bottlenecks. These problems will be handled more carefully in the following chapters.

13.1 Indexed Vector Operations

The terms *gather* and *scatter* denote two fundamental vector operations (see [Quinn 87]), which create problems for the implementation of synchronous parallelism. In principle, problems arise from the vectorization of indexed data access.

Gather:

```
for i:=1 to n do
    a[i] := b[index[i]]
end;
```

Scatter:

```
for i:=1 to n do
  a[index[i]] := b[i]
end;
```

Each vector is distributed component-wise onto the PEs. The gather operation reads a vector, which is indexed by another vector, while the scatter operation writes a vector, which is indexed by another vector. This functionality is here presented in pseudocode.

In both cases the access is data-dependent upon the values contained in a third (index) vector, which means that an unstructured permutation of the vector elements is being executed. In other words, an unstructured, random access to data located on other processors occurs. Such access behaviour naturally cannot be parallelized with the typical nearest neighbor grid of a SIMD system. However, executing this important function sequentially is not desirable.

Several vector computers solve this problem with the help of special hardware; the rest require time-consuming software solutions. Indexed access such as gather and scatter can be dealt with using the slow but universal router connection structure in massively parallel systems, if such a structure is available. Otherwise, time-consuming sequential processing and routing over a local neighborhood network are the only remaining options.

Even an indirect vector access to an array on the *same* PE may cause problems for some SIMD computer systems:

Example:

```
SCALAR s   : INTEGER;
VECTOR a   : ARRAY[1..10] OF INTEGER;
       u,v: INTEGER;
...
u := a[s];  (* scalar index *)
u := a[v];  (* vector index *)
```

Both statements assign an element of vector array a to vector variable u. All SIMD systems allow access of a vector array with a scalar index (each PE using the *same* index), since otherwise vector arrays would be impossible. However, using a vector index for addressing a vector array (each PE may have a *different* index) is not possible for the Connection Machine CM-2 because of insufficient hardware, while this type of addressing causes no problems on a MasPar MP-2 system.

13.2 Mapping Virtual Processors onto Physical Processors

The importance of virtual processors for SIMD systems has already been explained in Section 11.3. The introduction of this level of abstraction provides the application programmer with an unlimited number of processors with an arbitrary connection structure. Only with this abstraction from the physical hardware can machine-independent, data parallel programs be written.

Mapping virtual processors onto physical processors with the correct connections is done either transparently through special hardware components or through an 'intelligent compiler'. During this process, a series of problems must be dealt with:

- The virtual processors must be divided equally among the available physical processors.

  This problem is resolved through iteration in special hardware, or with extra code generated by the compiler. An intelligent distribution of the virtual processors simplifies the construction of the required virtual connections for data exchanges between the processors.

- When possible, the fastest of the available network structures (usually a grid structure) should be used.

- Automatically finding the optimal mapping of the virtual topology onto an available physical structure is a very hard problem and ranges, depending on the programming language used, from difficult to impossible (due to insufficient language constructs).

  There are algorithms for certain classes of connection structures, which map one connection structure onto another (see Section 5.4 and [Siegel 79]); however, the problem of recognizing the network type in an application program from the data exchange statements or (if available) the network declarations is considerably more difficult.

- If more virtual PEs are required than there exist physical PEs, data exchange operations can only be carried out using large buffer regions and with a considerable program-dependent overhead that might considerably slow down execution.

  Data exchange between processors is the critical problem in virtualization and can be solved for complex connection structures in justifiable time only if a general global connection structure (router) exists. Since each physical PE may contain multiple virtual PEs, all of which might participate in a data exchange, each communication operation must be resolved in multiple steps.

13.3 Bottlenecks from Peripheral Attachments

The most important characteristic of data parallel SIMD systems is the avoidance of the 'von Neumann bottleneck' present in traditional single-processor computers. Through the removal of the imbalance between *one* active computing component (the CPU) and a *large number* of passive components (the memory cells), as well as the introduction of high performance communication networks for parallel connections between processors, data can flow very quickly between the PEs of SIMD computer systems. This eliminates the von Neumann bottleneck.

Unfortunately, the attachment of peripherals in order to access very large data sets can easily lead to a new bottleneck (see Figure 13.1).

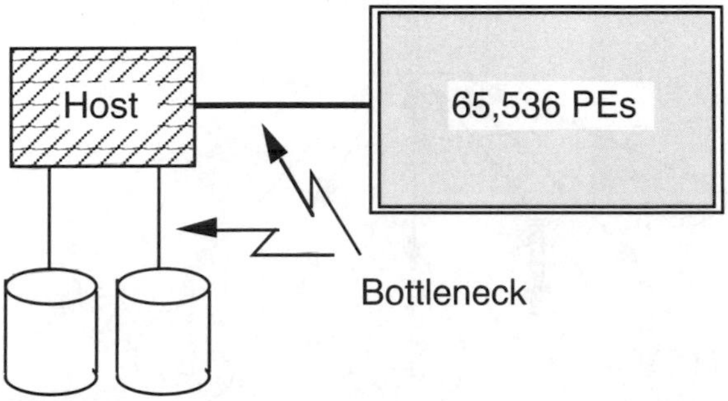

Figure 13.1 Peripheral attachment in massively parallel system

There are two problem areas here. First, the connection between the parallel PEs and the central control processor (host). The other problem area is the attachment of peripherals, such as large disk drives and high resolution graphics terminals, which may in the simplest case be connected directly to the control processor. Due to the structure of SIMD systems, the bottleneck during data exchange with the control processor cannot be resolved. Therefore data parallel application programs should always be designed to minimize both the storage of vector data onto the control processor and the reading of scalar values into the PEs during program execution. If possible, these functions should be restricted to the beginning and the ending of data parallel programs.

The bottleneck from the attachment of peripherals, as with the disk drives shown in Figure 13.1, arises from the intermediate routing through the serial control processor. Due to this connection, the data has to flow serially before reaching the PEs. This problem can be remedied by attaching the peripherals directly to the parallel PEs. This technique is known as *data vault* on the Connection Machine CM-2 and *parallel disk array* on the MasPar MP-2. The parallel connection is accomplished on the MasPar MP-2 using a high speed bus which is connected directly to the PEs through the router. This means that all of the PEs can read data from the peripherals or write data to them in parallel. Since a disk drive is principally a sequential device, parallelization is achieved through simultaneous access to many individual drives (see Figure 13.2). This technique allows fast movement of data to and from the PEs without having to move the data through the control processor.

RAID systems (redundant array of inexpensive disks) are similar disk arrays. These are also offered for sequential computer systems for increases in speed and fault tolerance.

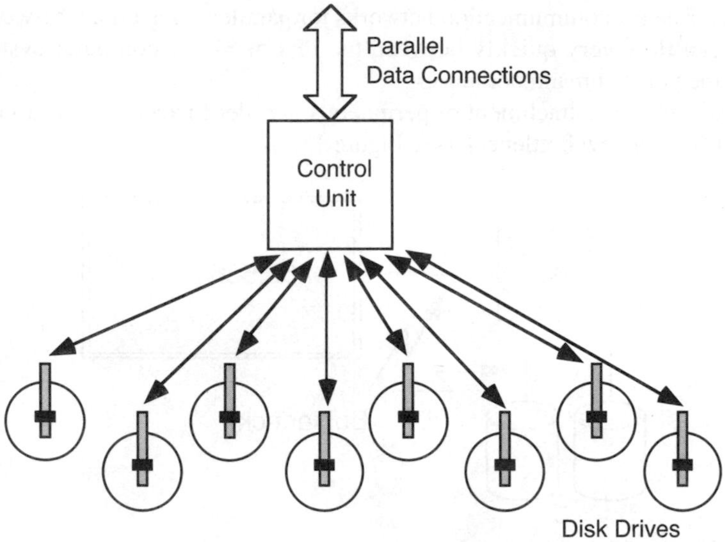

Figure 13.2 Parallel disk array

13.4 Network Bandwidth

The throughput of the connection network in a SIMD system determines to a high degree the performance of the entire system. Indeed, the time required on SIMD systems for connection set-up and execution of a communication is shorter by orders of magnitude than on MIMD systems. In addition, SIMD networks are set up to allow massively parallel data exchange. The time taken to execute a local data exchange of *all* PEs in a system with a physical neighbor PE is usually comparable to that of a parallel arithmetic operation. However, an unstructured global data exchange often requires one order of magnitude more time. SIMD computers with both a local and a global connection structure therefore have two different network bandwidths, whose weight or usage depends solely on the application program. In a program with complex network structures, the network bandwidth of the global connection structure takes on more importance and can under certain circumstances become a critical factor. Therefore, this bandwidth should be as high as possible.

Due to the restricted bandwidth of the global network, applications programs should meet certain requirements:

- Unnecessary global data exchange operations should be avoided, since they are considerably more expensive than arithmetic instructions.
- The use of structured topologies minimizes communication costs in cases where the faster local connections can be used (maybe even after a translation into a sequence of several *local* data exchange operations).

For most application programs, the PEs' ALUs are fast enough in relation to the performance of their global network. Therefore in most cases, significantly higher performance of the entire parallel computing system can only be achieved by increasing the bandwidth of the global network.

13.5 Multi-User Operation and Fault Tolerance

SIMD computers are not exactly well suited for multi-user operation. Since just one control processor is normally available, only one program can be executed at a time. The parallel execution of independent programs is not possible. The only remaining possibility is the quasi-parallel execution of a program on the control processor through time multiplexing. However, a very large problem arises due to the immense parallel memory, which is distributed across all of the PEs (for example, a total of 1 GB for the MasPar MP-2, model 2216). These huge sets of data can no longer be swapped out to (or read in from) disk in a fraction of a second during a context switch. Due to the earlier mentioned problem of the connection of peripheral devices, even when a parallel disk array is present, every read or write operation of the entire parallel memory requires time of the order of 10 s ! The concept of virtual memory is therefore currently not applicable for the parallel memory of a SIMD computer system.

Even with large time-slices, swapping data in and out of the parallel memory is not possible. The solution consists of partitioning the available memory of each PE among the currently active users. For reasons of throughput, the number of simultaneously active programs is restricted. Every program requests the amount of parallel memory required at start-up (for example 4 KB for each PE on the MasPar MP-2). If this memory space is available, it is assigned to the program and the program can be carried out in a time-multiplexed fashion. If less memory is available than was requested, the program has to wait for the termination of other currently active programs.

Another problem is fault tolerance of SIMD systems. Usually, the failure of even a single PE leaves the system inoperable, such that the problem cannot be fixed in software only! In this case, either the defective processor board (with 1,024 PEs on the MasPar MP-2) must be replaced or the processor configuration must be reduced by half. For example, the MasPar MP-2 with 16,384 PEs, *one* of which is defective, can only be configured as a system with 8,192 PEs. However, the corresponding router boards must be manually installed in the computer cabinet, to close the communication grid to a (now smaller) torus.

CHAPTER 14

SIMD Programming Languages

As with asynchronous programming discussed earlier, only procedural programming languages for synchronous parallel programming are presented here. Non-procedural languages follow in Chapter 17. At the procedural level of abstraction it is quite useful to differentiate between programming languages for MIMD systems and programming languages for SIMD systems. Since MIMD and SIMD programs are *algorithmically* different, the development of a 'universal' parallel procedural programming language might cause problems. A program in such a language could be executed efficiently only on one of the two classes of parallel systems (or possibly on neither if concepts from both classes were mixed). A differentiation between SIMD and MIMD might not be required at a level of abstraction higher than that of procedural programming. For example, with non-procedural languages, the handling of parallelism can be completely transparent to the user.

For each of the following languages the most important parallel concepts will be presented and exemplified with sample program fragments.

14.1 Fortran 90

Developed by: ANSI Committee X3J3, 1978-1991

Even the still young synchronous parallelism, it appears, cannot do without the traditional Fortran. Every company manufacturing a massively parallel computer system provides, among other languages, a parallel Fortran dialect. Unfortunately, they are all still incompatible with each other. Among others are CMFortran for the Connection Machine, MPFortran for the MasPar, and Fortran-Plus for the DAP. All of the early parallel Fortran dialects were based on drafts of Fortran 90, the new Fortran standard of the 1990s [Metcalf, Reid 90]. So these Fortran dialects are expected to adopt the new standard.

Fortran 90 is the successor of Fortran 77. Among others, data parallel extensions have been integrated as extensions to the array concept. Nevertheless, one should not assume from this continuity that old Fortran programs (*'dusty decks'*) can be executed **in parallel** on a SIMD system by simply recompiling them! This can only be done up to a certain degree (see automatic vectorization in Chapter 16). Usually, all of the algorithms have to be redesigned according to the data parallel perspective and reimplemented.

Parallel processing in Fortran 90 occurs through vector instructions, known as 'array expressions'. Since Fortran 90 has been designed to be suitable for parallel computer architectures as well as for sequential ones, no differentiation exists in the language between whether an array should be processed as a scalar on the central control processor or as a distributed vector on parallel PEs. For this reason, the syntax of the currently available parallel Fortran dialects differs from the Fortran 90 standard. In Fortran-Plus, declaration of parallel vectors is indicated by an asterisk '*'. This differs from MPFortran, where only the usage of an array determines whether it is placed in the scalar area or distributed among the PEs; the array declaration itself has no influence. However, appropriate compiler directives may be specified.

Parallel Language Constructs

The following declaration creates a parallel vector with 50 components of type integer. The vector may be distributed component-wise among the PEs on a parallel computer system.

```
INTEGER, DIMENSION(50) :: V
```

Optionally, a lower bound may be specified, which will be set to 1 when omitted:

```
INTEGER, DIMENSION(41:90) :: W
```

The following declaration creates three two-dimensional parallel vectors with 100 × 50 elements.

```
INTEGER, DIMENSION(100,50) :: A, B, C
```

Now, a matrix addition can be described as a simple addition instruction, which would be carried out component-wise on the PEs.

```
A = B + C
```

Not all of the vector components have to be included in an instruction. Ranges or even individual components can be selected through various options, in which case the non-selected PEs remain inactive. The following instruction selects the range of vector components from 2 to 10 and assigns the value 1 to all of them (scalar data values are assignment compatible to all vectors).

```
V(2:10) = 1
```

The specification of an index increment is also optional as a third parameter to the array bounds. Here, only every second element starting with `V(1)` is assigned a value:

```
V(1:21:2) = 1
```

A selection can also be accomplished by leaving out the index. In the following case, vector `V` is assigned the value from line 77 of matrix `A`.

```
V = A(77,:)
```

By using the `WHERE` statement with a boolean expression, the programmer can easily indicate the vector elements which should participate in a statement (selection of vector elements). The following instruction assigns the new value only to those vector elements whose previous value was less than zero.

```
WHERE (V .LT. 0) V = 7
```

A range of standard functions are available for reducing a vector to a scalar, such as summing all of its components. User defined reduction functions are not possible. The following reduction instruction sums all of the components of vector `V` and assigns the value to the scalar variable `S`.

```
S = SUM(V)
```

The following reduction operators are available:

```
ALL, ANY, COUNT, MAXVAL, MINVAL, PRODUCT, SUM
```

The operators `ALL` and `ANY` are the boolean 'and' and 'or' operations, respectively. Reduction operator `COUNT` counts in parallel the number of all array elements with value `TRUE`.

There are two further standard functions for dot product and matrix multiplication (not to be confused with the element-wise multiplication of two matrices, which is specified with a simple multiplication operator):

```
DOTPRODUCT (vector_a, vector_b)
MATMUL (matrix_a, matrix_b)
```

Programming with arrays in Fortran 90 (and the dialects) allows only a very restricted use of parallelism. Mathematical formulas are relatively easy to convert, but complex algorithms may create problems due to the insufficient flexibility of the language constructs.

Two example programs written in Fortran 90 conclude this section. The first one shows the calculation of a dot product and the second one the Laplace operator for edge detection in image processing. These examples will also be used for the other SIMD programming languages presented later.

Calculation of a Dot Product in Fortran 90:

```
INTEGER D_PROD
INTEGER, DIMENSION(100) :: A, B, C
...
C = A * B
D_PROD = SUM(C)
```

Since the dot product is a standard function in Fortran 90, it may also be computed trivially using: `D_PROD = DOTPRODUCT (A,B)`
Here, first a component-wise multiplication and then a reduction by addition has been executed. No explicit data exchange is necessary between the PEs.

The Laplace operator is one possible operator for emphasizing edges in a gray-scale image (edge detection). The operator carries out a simple local difference pattern (see Figure 14.1) and is therefore well suited to parallel execution. The Laplace operator is applied in parallel to each pixel with its four neighbors.

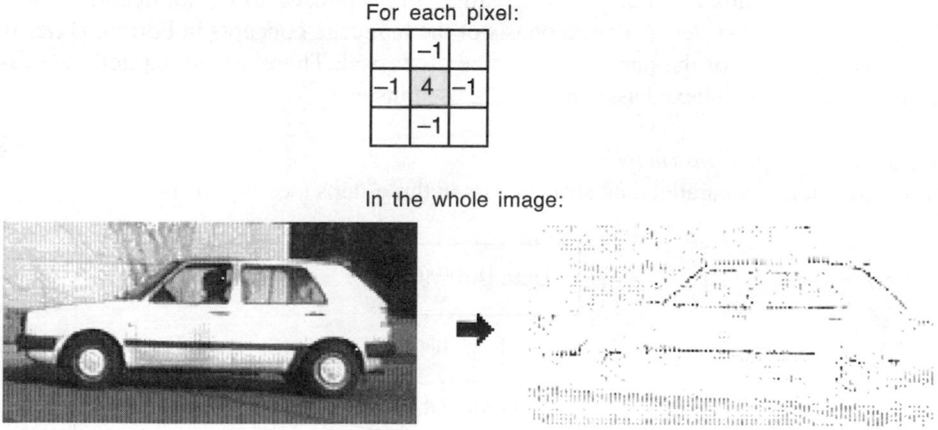

Figure 14.1 Edge detection with Laplace operator

Calculation of the Laplace Operator in Fortran 90:

```
INTEGER, DIMENSION(0:101,0:101) :: Image
...
Image(1:100,1:100) = 4*Image(1:100,1:100)
                     - Image(0: 99,1:100)  - Image(2:101,1:100)
                     - Image(1:100,0: 99)  - Image(1:100,2:101)
```

In order to facilitate the assignment via array expressions, a dummy border has been placed around the essential image of 100 × 100 elements. Here and in the following sample programs, the check of the result value against the range bounds (e.g. 0..255) has been omitted. This should be added in a complete program.

Fortran 90, with its implicit parallel constructs, is definitely a good basis as the new Fortran standard for sequential computer architectures. However, the ability of the programmer to exercise direct influence (to achieve higher efficiency) through explicit constructs in implementations on parallel architectures will be missed. For this reason, many companies producing parallel and super-computers have come together to form the 'High Performance Fortran Forum' (HPFF), which will develop a new Fortran dialect. This 'High Performance Fortran' (HPF) is supposed to use Fortran 90 as a basis and contain language concepts from Fortran D [Fox, Hiranandani, Kennedy, Koelbel, Kremer, Tseng, Wu 91].

Fortran D

Developed by: Fox, Hiranandani, Kennedy, Koelbel, Kremer, Tseng, Wu, 1991
Fortran D (*D* stands for 'data decomposition') is supposed to be applicable to both SIMD and MIMD systems. The emphasis of the language concepts in Fortran D lies in the decomposition of the parallel data to be processed. There are no explicit data exchange operations; indexed assignments are used instead.

Parallel Language Constructs
The allocation of a parallel data array occurs in three steps (see Figure 14.2):

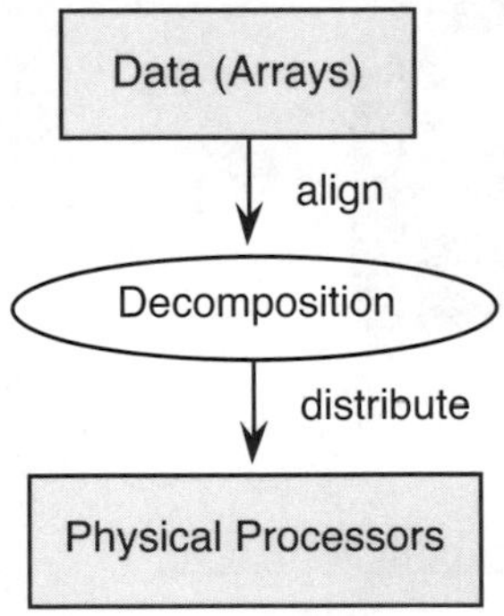

Figure 14.2 Data alignment and distribution

a) Declaration of a logic structure (`DECOMPOSITION`)
During the logic declaration of array elements, the array structure, name, number of dimensions, and size of the dimensions is specified **without** reserving memory. The following construct declares the structure `S` with two dimensions, each having 100 elements:

```
DECOMPOSITION S(100,100)
```

b) Definition of a logic mapping (ALIGN)
Arrays defined earlier can be assigned a decomposition with the ALIGN construct without a concrete association with a physical processor being involved. In the following, the array A is directly mapped onto the structure S:

```
REAL A(100,100)
DECOMPOSITION S(100,100)
ALIGN A(I,J) WITH S(I,J)
```

The mapping does not have to be exact. Using the ALIGN construct, expressions with indices are allowed on the right or an index vector can be given to specify any possible permutation:

```
ALIGN A(I,J) WITH S(I+1,2*J-1)
```

Entire columns or rows can likewise be collapsed to a single element of the structure. In the following example, each row in array A is mapped onto one element of structure T.

```
DECOMPOSITION T(100)
ALIGN A(I,J) WITH T(I)
```

When creating a mapping using ALIGN with the keyword RANGE, specified parts of an index range can be selected individually:

```
ALIGN A(I,J) WITH S(I,J) RANGE (1:100, 50:60)
```

To handle border elements of an array, that might extend beyond the border of the structure through the ALIGN mapping, one of three precautions must be taken:

ERROR (default)	Array elements outside the structure boundaries cannot be accessed, otherwise a run time error occurs.
TRUNC	All array elements outside the structure are assigned to the same border element of the structure.
WRAP	All array elements outside the structure are circularly mapped as a torus from the beginning of the column or the row.

c) Definition of a physical mapping (DISTRIBUTE)
In the third and final step, the virtual elements of a structure (with the array elements mapped to them) are distributed among the physical processors available. One of the following three distribution procedures can be selected for each of the dimensions of the structure (see Figure 14.3):

`BLOCK`	Division of the decomposition into sequential blocks of equal size for each processor.
`CYCLIC`	Every decomposition element is mapped circularly to the next processor.
`BLOCK_CYCLIC(x)`	Like `CYCLIC`, but with blocks of size `x`.
`*`	All of the decomposition elements in this dimension are mapped to the same processor.

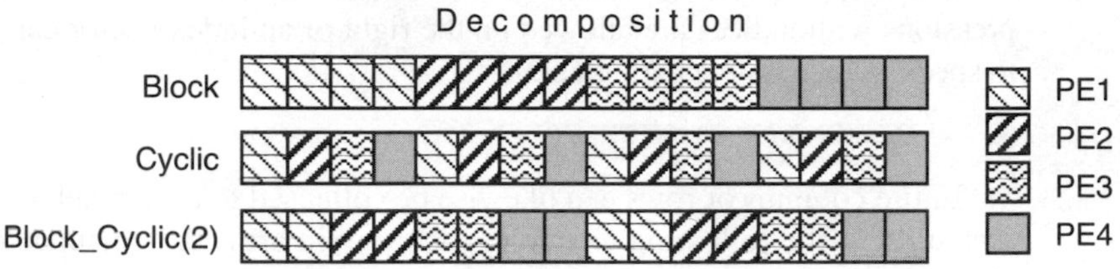

Figure 14.3 Distribution of a one-dimensional decomposition

The following example shows the mapping of the structure `S`, with 100 rows each having 100 columns, onto 50 physical processors:

`DISTRIBUTE S(BLOCK,*)`	Every processor gets two neighboring rows.
`DISTRIBUTE S(CYCLIC,*)`	Every processor gets two rows that have 50 rows in between them.
`DISTRIBUTE S(BLOCK,CYCLIC)`	The rows are mapped in block mode while the columns are mapped circularly.

In order to make the last mapping unequivocal, the keyword `BLOCK` must specify the exact number of rows of physical processors, e.g. `BLOCK(5)` for a 5×10 field of physical processors, since virtual processors are not supported in Fortran D. This makes these mapping methods somewhat difficult to understand.

The `FORALL` construct exists in Fortran D for the parallel execution of instructions. With this command, all loop iteration is executed in parallel on different processors, according to the mapping for the array specified earlier. A direct mapping of the loop passes onto physical processors can be achieved using the `ON` clause, which, however, is not used in the following example.

```
FORALL I = 1,100
  FORALL J = 1,100
    A(I,J) = 5 * A(I,J) - 3
  ENDDO
ENDDO
```

The reduction operation is also available in Fortran D as a standard operation. However – in contrast to Fortran 90 – it must be enclosed in a sequential or parallel DO loop. The following operations are predefined:

```
SUM, PROD, MIN, MAX, AND, OR
```

User defined reduction functions may also be specified here. The following example shows the reduction of a one-dimensional array Y to a scalar value X through addition. The parallel loops with reduction operators are translated into the corresponding tree structure by the Fortran D compiler.

```
REAL X, Y(N)
FORALL I = 1,N
  REDUCE(SUM, X, Y(I))
ENDDO
```

14.2 C*

Developed by: John Rose and Guy Steele, Thinking Machines, 1987–90
'C-Star' was originally developed just for the Connection Machine family [Rose, Steele 87]. However, the most recent language definition from Thinking Machines, C* Version 6 [Thinking Machines 90], is largely hardware-independent and might therefore be a promising starting point for a standard SIMD programming language.

The parallel language C* is an extension of the sequential language C with parallel constructs. Elegant programming on the level of virtual processors is possible in C*, whose translation onto physical processors occurs in hardware on the Connection Machine. C* provides the application programmer with an environment which includes a *homogeneous address space*. This means that every PE can access the local memory of every other PE through index expressions.

In the transition from C* Version 5 to C* Version 6, the language description has been changed completely. While C* Version 5 was based on C++, ANSI-C is the foundation for C* Version 6. Object oriented concepts are missing from the new language definition, the earlier parallel language constructs were replaced with others, and there is **no** upward compatibility! Programs implemented in C* Version 5 must be rewritten. Altogether one must conclude that C* Version 5 and C* Version 6 are *different parallel programming languages*.

> In ***C* Version 5***, scalar variables were declared with the keyword `mono` and vector variables with `poly`. Groups of virtual processors were defined with the `domain` construct. Data exchange between the PEs occurred through assignment operations with pointer expressions into the memory areas of the sending and receiving PEs involved.

The following text refers exclusively to **C* Version 6**.

Parallel Language Constructs

Corresponding to the SIMD architecture, a decision is made at the variable declaration whether the variable is a scalar to reside once on the host or a vector that is distributed component-wise on the virtual PEs. Scalars are declared just as in regular C. Vector variables are declared with a `shape` definition, which specifies the structure of the vector in analogy to an array. A one-dimensional vector variable `V` with 50 components is declared in the following way:

```
shape [50] one_dim;
int:one_dim V;
```

Each vector variable has to have a shape definition, but several vectors can share the same shape. The definition of three two-dimensional vectors `A`, `B` and `C` with 100 × 50 components each is as follows:

```
shape [100][50] two_dim;
int:two_dim A, B, C;
```

The vector components may be of any data type available in standard C, including structures and arrays. Each component reserves data on its appropriate virtual PE. The following declaration forms a vector with 50 components (on 50 virtual PEs), in which each component is a local array of 100 elements.

```
int:one_dim field[100];
```

In order to carry out parallel operations, the corresponding `shape` must be selected via the `with` operation. If there are more PEs in the system than the specified `shape` requires, the extra PEs will be inactive during execution of the statement block. The example starts by selecting the `two_dim` structure and then carries out a matrix addition:

```
with (two_dim)
  { A = B + C; }
```

Just as in Fortran 90, there is a `where` construct in C*, which carries out its statement block only on the virtual PEs for which the boolean condition is true. As for a sequential `if` selection, the parallel `where` selection may also contain an `else` part. This will, however, be executed only *after completion* of the `where` (‘*then*’) part. In order once again to access *all* of the vector components *within* possibly nested `where` instructions, the `everywhere` language construct is provided. In the following example, only those components of `V` that are less than zero receive a new value.

```
with (one_dim)
  where (V < 0)  { V = 7; }
```

Only vectors that belong to the same `shape` are allowed to appear together in an expression or an assignment. That is, they have to have the same structure and most importantly the same number of components. An assignment such as `A = V` is not possible (`A` belongs to shape `two_dim`, while `V` belongs to shape `one_dim`). One exception is the set of assignments and expressions with scalar values (such as `V<0` and `V=7` above). These are first transformed into a vector with identical components and then applied further. In the other direction, a vector can only be assigned to a scalar using type casting. However, which of the components of the vector will be assigned to the scalar is **implementation-dependent**! This is a superfluous and very error prone operation, so it should be avoided:

```
int S;
...                    Danger:
S = (int) V;   ➡    Assignment of an unspecified component!
```

In addition to the assignment operations, all of the other C operations can be carried out in parallel on vectors. The abbreviated assignment operators from C (and a few more) can be used as reduction operators from vectors onto scalars. The following abbreviated assignment calculates the sum of all vector components in `V` and assigns the result to `S`. Since the reduction value is added to the previous value of `S`, it must first be initialized to zero.

```
S  = 0;
S += V;
```

The following reduction operations exist in C*:

+= (Sum)	*= (Product)	&= (AND)	|= (OR)	^= (XOR)
<?= (Minimum)	>?= (Maximum)			

User defined reduction functions are not possible.

Unfortunately, in C* the reduction can become a problem. In contrast to ANSI-C where the assignments `S += V;` and `S = S + V;` are identical, this is no longer true in C* in the case where `S` is a scalar variable and `V` is a vector variable. If there are vectors on both sides of the assignment (`V += W`), then a simple vector addition is executed *instead* of a reduction.

```
int S;
int:one_dim V, W;
...
```

`s += v`	➡	$S := S + \sum_i V_i$	Vector reduction
`s = s+v`	➡	**Error**	(Attempt to assign a vector to a scalar, see 'type casting' above)
`v += s`	➡	$V := V + S$	Addition of a scalar to a vector
`v += w`	➡	$V := V + W$	Addition of a vector to a vector

It easily leads to confusion that these instructions have different meanings depending on their operand types.

The virtual connection structure among the PEs is not declared beforehand, instead routing is handled automatically for every data access to neighboring PEs. One differentiates between 'universal communication' and 'grid communication'. Universal communication is carried out over the Connection Machine's global hypercube, while grid communication can use the considerably faster local NEWS grid (see Section 11.1). The destination addresses are specified through so-called index variables, where the source and destination vectors may belong to different shapes. In the following example, vector `v` receives the components of vector `w` in an altered ordering (permutation), which is specified by vector `Index`. In this case, all of the components should be shifted two places to the right. The vector components `v[0]` and `v[1]` will receive *undefined* values and should therefore be deactivated with the `where` instruction in order to avoid programming errors.

```
shape [50] one_dim;
int:one_dim V, W, Index;
... /* Index has the values: 2, 3, 4, ..., 51 */
with (one_dim) {
  [Index]V = W;
}
```

The more complex the data exchange pattern becomes, the more difficult to understand will be the corresponding C* index expressions. So a structured specification of the connection structure would be of advantage. Indices can appear to the left and right of an assignment. If a `shape` is multi-dimensional, then an individual index must be specified for each dimension. Individual vector components can be selected and assigned to scalars with the help of indices:

```
s = [11]V;
```

The standard function `pcoord` facilitates the use of the fast grid structure. It returns the position of a vector component within its shape (the coordinates of its virtual PE) with respect to the dimension given in the parameter.

```
shape [100][50] two_dim;
int:two_dim A, B;
...
```

```
with(two_dim) {
  A = pcoord(0);
  B = pcoord(1);
}
```

Matrix A receives the position of each component with respect to the row and B receives the position with respect to the column:

$$A = \begin{pmatrix} 0 & 0 & \ldots & 0 \\ 1 & 1 & \ldots & 1 \\ \ldots & & & \\ 99 & 99 & \ldots & 99 \end{pmatrix} \qquad B = \begin{pmatrix} 0 & 1 & \ldots & 49 \\ 0 & 1 & \ldots & 49 \\ \ldots & & & \\ 0 & 1 & \ldots & 49 \end{pmatrix}$$

The use of the function `pcoord` in an additive index expression will be recognized by the compiler and leads to the generation of efficient data exchange code for the physical grid structure. The shifting by two places of a vector shown above can also be defined in the following way:

```
shape [50] one_dim;
int:one_dim V, W, Index;
...
with (one_dim) {
  [pcoord(0) + 2]V = W;
}
```

In order to simplify data parallel programming, there are a number of operations which are mentioned here. They have a large variety of options, controlled by parameters, which will not be discussed in detail.

- `scan`
  Calculation of the partial results of an operation on a vector.

  Example: Calculation of all of the partial sums of the vector `val`

  ```
  part_sum = scan(val, 0, CMC_combiner_add, CMC_upward,
                  CMC_none, CMC_no_field, CMC_inclusive);
  ```

- `spread`
  Distribution of the results of a parallel operation on the components of another vector variable with a possibly different structure (through replication of the corresponding data value).

- `enumerate`
  Calculation of the position of every *active* vector component (more general version of the `pcoord` operation), controlled by various parameters.

- `rank`
  Calculation of the position of every vector component with respect to the position of the component within the sorted list of the components.

The two data parallel sample algorithms for the dot product and the Laplace operator conclude the section.

Dot product in C*:

```
shape [max] list;
float:list x,y;
float s_prod = 0.0;
...
with (list) {
  s_prod += x*y;
}
```

The PEs are arranged as lists. After the selection, they are multiplied together component-wise and the results are reduced to a scalar through addition.

Laplace Operator in C*:

```
shape [100][100] grid;
int:grid pixel, dim1, dim2;
...
with (grid) {
  dim1 = pcoord(0);
  dim2 = pcoord(1);
  pixel= 4*pixel -[dim1-1][dim2  ]pixel -[dim1+1][dim2  ]pixel
                 -[dim1  ][dim2-1]pixel -[dim1  ][dim2+1]pixel;
}
```

There are abbreviations for the use of the `pcoord` function, which simplify the statement above to:

```
with (grid) {
  pixel = 4*pixel - [. - 1][.]pixel - [. + 1][.]pixel
                  - [.][. - 1]pixel - [.][. + 1]pixel;
}
```

14.3 MasPar Programming Language

Developed by: MasPar Computer Corporation, 1990
Like C*, MPL is an extension to the sequential programming language C with parallel concepts. It was developed by MasPar especially for the MP-1 computer system [MasPar 91], which meanwhile has been succeeded by the compatible but faster MP-2 system. Since the MasPar MP-2 has two different communications networks available, MPL also contains special machine-dependent language constructs to allow the efficient use of the fast grid network ('x-net') along with language constructs for accessing the universal communications network ('router'). Furthermore, MPL does not allow virtual

processors, that is, an MPL program cannot have more PEs declared than the associated MP-2 computer system physically provides. These language constructs restrict the portability of the language. The available parallel concepts in MPL are more primitive than those in the C* programming language.

Parallel Language Constructs

The variable declaration differentiates, as do almost all SIMD languages, between scalar data, which is declared exactly like variables in sequential C, and vector data, which is indicated with the keyword `plural`. The following declaration reserves two integer variables `i` and `j` on **all** of the physically available PEs.

```
plural int i,j;
```

Virtual processors are not supported, and different groups of PEs (structures, configurations or topologies) cannot be defined. The physical structure of the MasPar MP-2, a two-dimensional grid, is always implicitly assumed.

In order to implement the connection between the sequential control program on the workstation (front end) and the parallel program on the MasPar (back end), individual variables can be indicated with the keyword `visible`. These variables can be accessed from both sides.

Data exchanges between PEs can take place in two different ways corresponding to the two connection structures of the MasPar MP-2: fast, local data exchanges in the grid with eight-way nearest neighbor connections are carried out with the `xnet` command, while communication over an arbitrary connection structure is carried out through the slower, global router with the `router` command. Eight different commands for the x-net connections corresponding to the cardinal directions are available:

```
xnetN, xnetNE, xnetE, xnetSE, xnetS, xnetSW, xnetW, xnetNW
```

In the following communication statement over the x-net, the value of vector variable `i` is shifted two places to the left (west) and assigned to vector `j`.

```
j = xnetW[2].i;
```

The same effect can be achieved with communication over the router, assuming the vector `index` is pre-loaded with the corresponding identification numbers of the destination PEs.

```
j = router[index].i;
```

In order to use the positions of the PEs in parallel statements, the following scalar and vector constants are available in MPL:

Scalar Constants

`nproc`	Total number of PEs in a MasPar system	(= `nxproc * nyproc`)
`nxproc`	Number of columns in a MasPar system	(= row length)
`nyproc`	Number of rows in a MasPar system	(= column length)

Vector Constants

iproc	PE Identification Number	(0..nproc - 1)
ixproc	PE Position within a row	(0..nxproc - 1)
iyproc	PE Position within a column	(0..nyproc - 1)

Parallel instructions are carried out on all of the PEs by default; however, groups of PEs can be selected via a simple `if` or `while` instruction with vector conditions implicitly selected. Unlike sequential execution, the `then` and `else` branches of a vector `if` selection may both have to be carried out (subsequently, **not** in parallel). This is the case when the vector condition evaluates to `true` for (at least) one PEs and `false` for another PE. Using the `all` command, all of the PEs can be reactivated within a selection or loop. An explicit PE selection is not available.

Access to an individual PE can be accomplished using the `proc` command (for example, in order to read specific data from a PE or write to it from the control processor). Either one singular index corresponding to the `iproc` number of a PE can be specified or the two indices corresponding to the `iyproc` and `ixproc` (row, column) positions can be specified.

```
int s;
plural int v;
...
s = proc[1023].v;    Component no. 1023 of vector v
s = proc[5][7].v;    Component in the 5th row and 7th column of vector v
```

The reduction of a vector onto a scalar can be carried out with the following predefined reduction operations:

```
reduceADD, reduceMUL, reduceAND, reduceOR, reduceMax, reduceMin
```

For every operation, a suffix indicating the type of the operands must be specified. For example, `reduceADDf` indicates the reduction of a floating-point vector via addition. User defined reduction operations are not possible in MPL.

A disadvantage of MPL is the machine-dependent implementation of the data exchange operations, which was selected on the basis of higher efficiency. Higher language concepts for programming with virtual processors and connection structures would also be desirable.

<u>Dot Product in MPL:</u>

```
float d_prod (a, b)
plural float a,b;
{ plural float prod;
  prod = a*b
  return reduceAddf (prod)
}
```

The two vectors are multiplied component-wise and reduced to a scalar by addition.

Laplace Operator in MPL:

```
plural int pixel;
...
pixel = 4 * pixel - xnetN[1].pixel - xnetS[1].pixel
                  - xnetW[1].pixel - xnetE[1].pixel;
```

Data exchanges in the two-dimensional grid can be carried out with the machine-dependent 'x-net' commands, which provide altogether eight connection directions (north, south, east, west, and the four directions in between). The parameter in square brackets indicates the number of displacement steps.

14.4 Parallaxis

Developed by: Thomas Bräunl, 1989

Parallaxis [Bräunl 89], [Bräunl 90], [Bräunl 91b] is based on Modula-2 [Wirth 83], extended by data parallel concepts. The language is completely machine-independent; therefore programs written in Parallaxis can be ported between SIMD parallel computers. For a large number of (single-processor) workstations and personal computers, there is also a Parallaxis simulation system with source level debugging and tools for visualization and timing. Parallel programs with small data sets can be developed, tested and debugged with this simulation system. Then, Parallaxis compilers can be used to generate parallel code for the MasPar MP-2 or the Connection Machine CM-2. The simulation environment allows both the study of data parallel fundamentals on simple computer systems and the development of parallel programs which can later be executed on expensive parallel computer systems. The programming environment for Parallaxis is available as public domain software [Barth, Bräunl, Engelhardt, Sembach 92].

The central points of Parallaxis are programming on a level of abstraction with virtual PEs and also with virtual connections. In addition to the algorithmic description, every program includes a semi-dynamic connection declaration in functional form. This means that the desired PE network topology is specified in advance for each program (or for each procedure) and can be addressed in the algorithmic section with symbolic names (instead of complicated arithmetic index or pointer expressions).

Parallel Language Constructs

In contrast to all of the data parallel programming languages presented up to this point, a 'virtual machine' consisting of processors and a connection network is defined for every program (or separately for each procedure) in Parallaxis. This happens in two simple steps. First, the keyword `CONFIGURATION` is used to specify the number of PEs and their arrangement in analogy to an array declaration. However, no specification has been made as to the connection structure between the PEs. This follows in a functional form, which is introduced with the keyword CONNECTION. Every connection has a symbolic name and defines a mapping from a PE (*any* PE) to the corresponding neighbor PE. The specification of this *relative* neighbor is accomplished by providing an arithmetic expression for the index of the destination PE as well as a name for the entrance port. Data exchanges can now be carried out using these symbolic connection names in the parallel program.

Figure 14.4 shows as a PE arrangement as a two-dimensional grid structure in a simple Parallaxis example. The CONFIGURATION declaration provides 4 × 5 virtual processors, which are virtually connected to one another in the following CONNECTION declaration. Since symmetric connection structures or topologies are supported primarily, four connection declarations are sufficient to construct a grid of any size. One connection is defined for each cardinal direction. The connection to the north, for example, increments the first index and specifies the south port as entrance port to the neighboring PE. Some connections from the border PEs lead 'nowhere', which means that these connections do not exist, and would not participate in any data exchange operation.

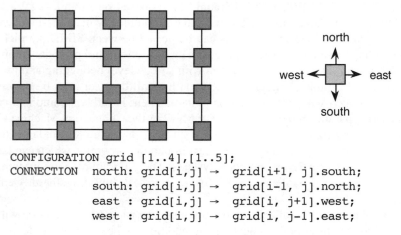

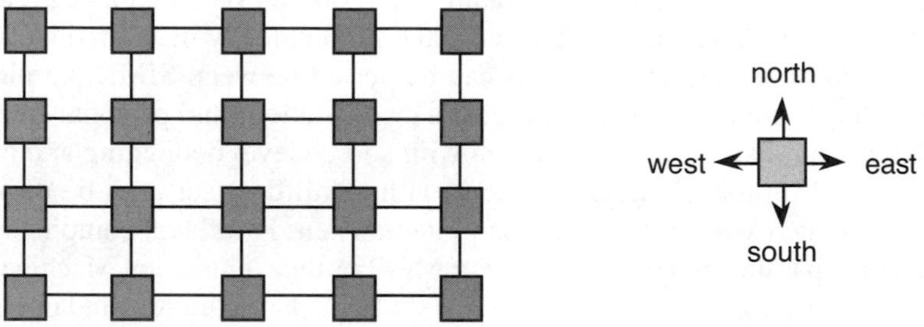


```
CONFIGURATION grid [1..4],[1..5];
CONNECTION  north: grid[i,j] →  grid[i+1, j].south;
            south: grid[i,j] →  grid[i-1, j].north;
            east : grid[i,j] →  grid[i, j+1].west;
            west : grid[i,j] →  grid[i, j-1].east;
```

Figure 14.4 Two-dimensional grid topology with representative PE

There is a list of extensions to this simple process of defining virtual computer structures: Connections may be *parameterized*, as with the hypercube in Figure 14.5. Then it is possible to perform a data exchange in a *computed* direction. For the definition of the binary tree network in Figure 14.5, *bi-directional* connections have been used.

When using uni-directional connections only, the definition of a binary tree has to make use of 'compound connections':

```
CONFIGURATION  tree [1..15];
CONNECTION  lchild: tree[i] →  tree[2*i].parent;
            rchild: tree[i] →  tree[2*i+1].parent;
            parent: tree[i] →  {even i} tree[i DIV 2].lchild,
                               {odd  i} tree[i DIV 2].rchild;
```

A case distinction is made for the `parent` connection. If the PE number is even, a connection to the left child is established, while if it is odd, a connection to the right child is established. Using compound connections, arbitrary connection structures, even with irregularities, may be defined.

In addition to the constructs shown so far, the definition of multiple topologies in a program is possible. These may be defined independently of each other on separate groups of PEs – in which case the topologies may have different vector data structures. Or the topologies can be defined as 'different views' of the same set of PEs with identical data structure. Furthermore, in non-overlapping procedures, local topologies may be defined, thus allowing semi-dynamic connection structures.

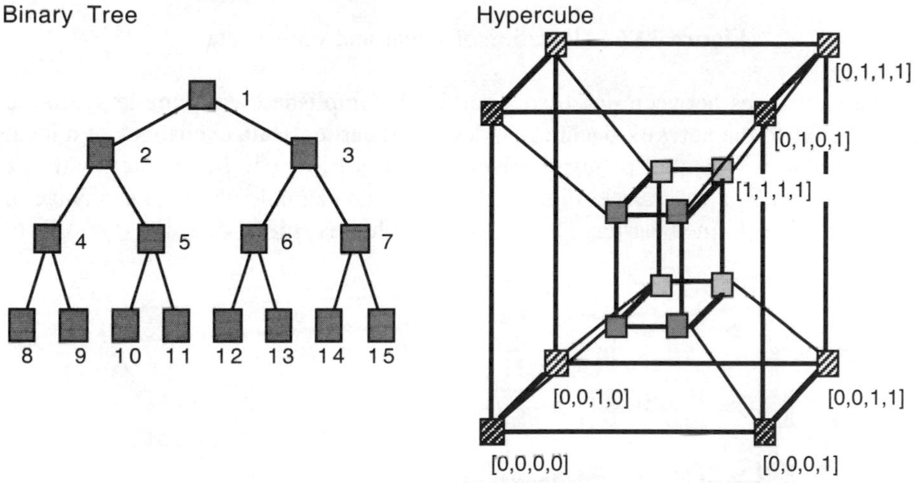


```
CONFIGURATION  tree [1..15];
CONNECTION
 lchild: tree[i] ↔ tree[2*i].parent;
 rchild: tree[i] ↔ tree[2*i+1].parent;
```

```
CONFIGURATION  hyper [2],[2],[2],[2];
CONNECTION
 go(1): hyper[i,j,k,l] →
        hyper[(i+1)mod 2, j, k, l).go(1);
 go(2): hyper[i,j,k,l] →
        hyper[i, (j+1)mod 2, k, l).go(2);
 go(3): hyper[i,j,k,l] →
        hyper[i, j, (k+1)mod 2, l).go(3);
 go(4): hyper[i,j,k,l] →
        hyper[i, j, k, (l+1)mod 2).go(4);
```

Figure 14.5 Tree and hypercube topology

Parallaxis differentiates between scalar and vector variables in data declarations as well as in procedure parameters and results. Scalar data is placed on the control processor (host), while vectors are distributed component-wise among the virtual PEs (see

Figure 14.6). In place of the `VAR` keyword from Modula-2, Parallaxis uses `SCALAR` and `VECTOR`, respectively (here, `VAR` is used only to distinguish reference parameters from value parameters).

```
SCALAR  s,t: REAL;
VECTOR  x,y: REAL;
        c,d: CHAR;
```

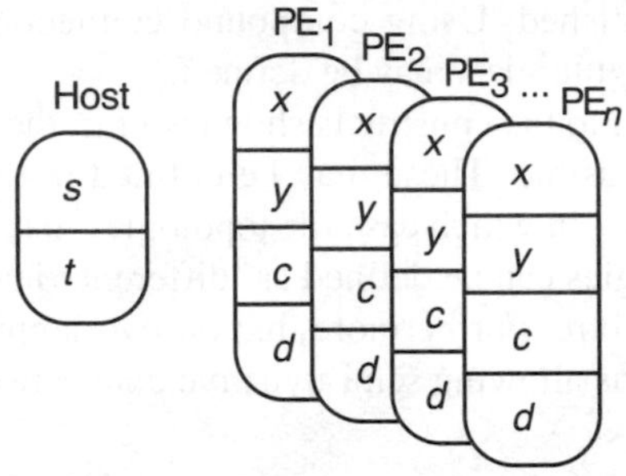

Figure 14.6 Allocation of scalar and vector data

Data exchanges between processors can be accomplished with simple symbolic names, thanks to the network declaration described earlier. Data exchanges of a local vector variable between all or just a selected group of PEs can be invoked with the standard procedure `PROPAGATE`. Figure 14.7 shows an example of a data exchange in the grid structure defined earlier. The vector variable `x` is shifted one step (one PE) to the east.

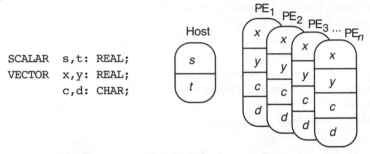

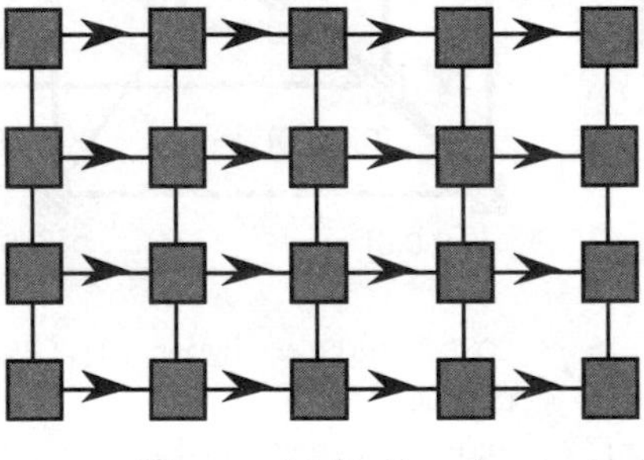

```
PROPAGATE.east(x);
```

Figure 14.7 Synchronous data exchange

The data exchange operation may also have two parameters. The first parameter contains the vector expression to be sent, while the second parameter is the receiving variable.

<u>Example:</u> `PROPAGATE.east (4*y, x);`

For the `PROPAGATE`-operation, sender *and* receiver of a data exchange have to be active. For the operations `SEND` and `RECEIVE`, it is sufficient for *only* the sender (or *only* the receiver, respectively) to be active. These operations are especially needed for the data exchange between different topologies, since due to the SIMD model only one PE structure can be active at a time.

<u>Example:</u>

```
SEND grid.east(4*y) TO grid.west(x);
RECEIVE tree.parent(t) FROM grid.east(x);
```

In contrast to other SIMD languages, in Parallaxis parallel instructions are explicitly indicated by embedding them in a '`PARALLEL`...`ENDPARALLEL`' block. There are many options for selecting PEs in such a block. They can be explicitly specified as a sub-region, subset or boolean expression for the block; or they can be implicitly selected within a parallel block by using a parallel selection or iteration instruction (`IF`, `WHILE`, `REPEAT`, `CASE`). Figure 14.8 shows the data parallel execution of a statement on an explicitly selected group of PEs.

```
VECTOR x,a,b: REAL;
...      (* only a subrange is active *)
PARALLEL grid[2..3],[1..4]
  x := a+b
ENDPARALLEL;
```

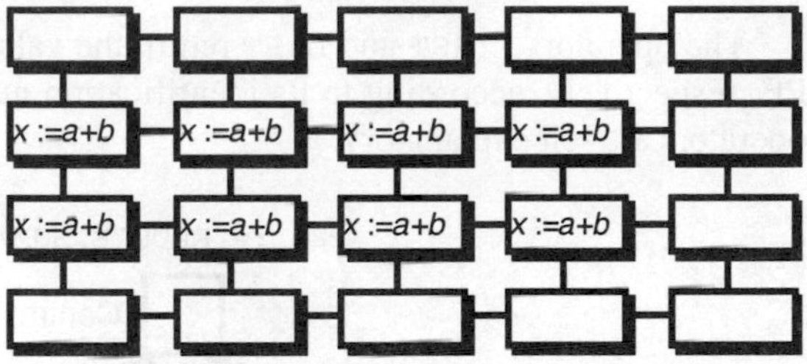

Figure 14.8 Data parallel instruction

In addition to local data, the unique PE number (`id_no`) and the position of the PE within a dimension of the predefined PE configuration (`DIM1`, `DIM2`, ...) can occur in vector expressions. These values are predefined as vector constants.

```
CONFIGURATION list[1..n];
CONNECTION ...;
SCALAR  s: ARRAY[1..n] OF INTEGER;
        t: INTEGER;
VECTOR  v: INTEGER;
```

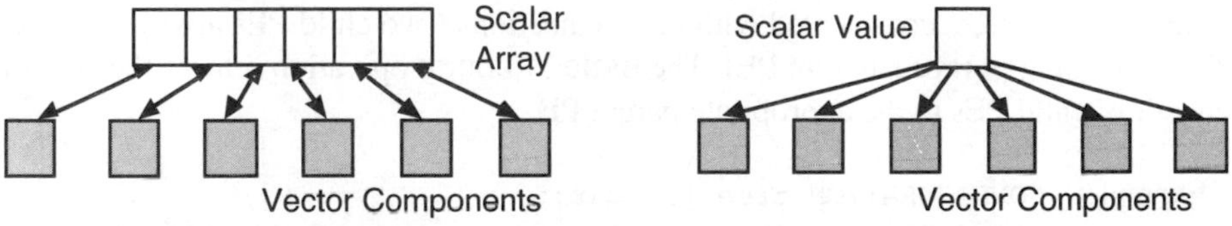


```
LOAD (v, s);                                v := t;
STORE(v, s);
```

Figure 14.9 Data exchanges between PEs and host

Communication between the control processor and the parallel PEs also requires additional language constructs or in some cases an adapted semantics. Transferring a scalar field into a parallel vector is invoked with the `LOAD` procedure, while transferring data back into a scalar field from a vector is accomplished with STORE (see Figure 14.9).

Figure 14.9 (on the right-hand side) also shows an assignment in which a (constant or variable) scalar data value is copied into all or a group of PEs. Every component of the vector contains the same value as the scalar. This operation is implemented by an implicit *broadcast*.

The reduction of a vector to a scalar is the last important operation. The REDUCE operation handles this task in conjunction with a predefined or user defined (programmable) reduction operation (see Figure 14.10). Predefined operators are:

```
SUM, PRODUCT, MAX, MIN, AND, OR, FIRST, LAST
```

The operators FIRST and LAST return the value of the first or last currently active PE, respectively, according to its identification number (id_no). All other reduction operators are self explanatory.

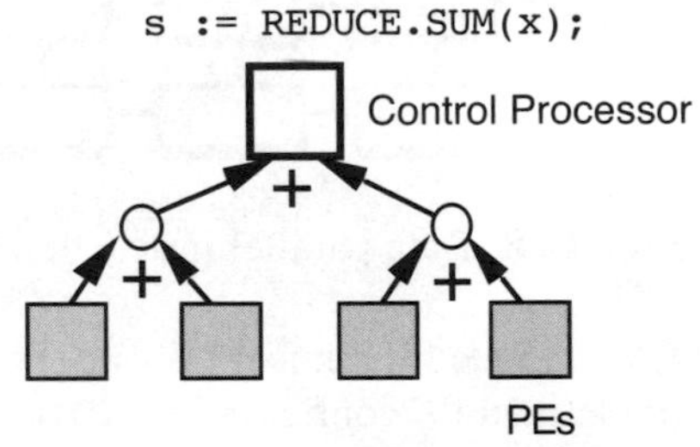

Figure 14.10 Vector reduction in Parallaxis

The connection structures as defined by the CONNECTION declaration do not have to be 1:1 connections. For 1:*n* connections, an implicit broadcast is executed. However, for *n*:1 connections (and the general *m*:*n* connections) one must ensure that only a single value arrives at any PE's entry port. Therefore, each data exchange operation (PROPAGATE, SEND or RECEIVE) may be followed by a vector reduction. The following example shows a tree, constructed with *n*:1 connections (two child PEs always connect to the same input port of a parent PE). The SEND...REDUCE operation returns the sum of each pair of child PEs to the appropriate parent PE.

Example:
```
CONFIGURATION tree [1..max];
CONNECTION parent: tree[i] <-> tree[2*i  ].children,
                   tree[i] <-> tree[2*i+1].children;
...
SEND tree.children(y) TO tree.parent(x) REDUCE.SUM;
```

The implementation of two previously shown sample algorithms in Parallaxis concludes this section.

Dot Product in Parallaxis:

```
CONFIGURATION list[max];
CONNECTION;    (* none *)
SCALAR d_prod:   REAL;
VECTOR x,y,prod: REAL;
...
PARALLEL
  prod   := x*y
  d_prod := REDUCE.SUM(prod);
ENDPARALLEL;
```

The component-wise multiplication is carried out in a parallel block. Then the partial products are summed with the reduction operation.

Laplace Operator in Parallaxis:

```
CONFIGURATION grid [1..100],[1..100];
CONNECTION  north: grid[i,j] →  grid[i+1, j].south;
            south: grid[i,j] →  grid[i-1, j].north;
            east : grid[i,j] →  grid[i, j+1].west;
            west : grid[i,j] →  grid[i, j-1].east;

VECTOR pixel,n,s,w,e: INTEGER;
...
PARALLEL
  PROPAGATE.north(pixel,s);
  PROPAGATE.south(pixel,n);
  PROPAGATE.west (pixel,e);
  PROPAGATE.east (pixel,w);
  pixel := 4*pixel - n - s - w - e;
ENDPARALLEL;
```

The data from neighbor PEs is obtained by `propagate` operations and is stored in auxiliary vector variables `n`, `s`, `e`, and `w` (according to the directions). Then they are used in an arithmetic expression to compute the new pixel value.

CHAPTER 15

Massively Parallel Algorithms

With the current state of the art in processor integration, massive parallelism refers only to data parallel SIMD systems. Totally new programming techniques are required for these fine-grained parallel systems as compared to the 'conventional' coarse-grained parallel algorithms. In addition to data exchanges, selections and program loops also have different semantics on SIMD systems, all of which influences the efficiency of a program. High processor load is no longer the main goal of program development. Because of their different system architecture, the load of SIMD systems is always lower than that of MIMD systems. However, SIMD systems usually compensate and even top this disadvantage through their much larger number of PEs.

The *natural formulation of algorithms* with inherent parallelism is the most important goal of program development. Data parallel programs are easier to design and to understand, since sequentialization, which is the restriction of the von Neumann computer model, is not present.

All of the following sample programs are implemented in the data parallel language Parallaxis (see Section 14.4). A large collection of parallel algorithms (at least for SIMD systems) can be found in [Akl 89], [JáJá 92] and [Gibbons, Rytter 88].

15.1 Numerical Integration

The following example algorithm from [Babb 89] uses the rectangle rule for approximating π. The same problem was solved with a coarse-grained parallel algorithm for MIMD systems in Section 11.3 .

The x-axis in the range [0,1] is divided into as many intervals as required for accuracy, with one virtual PE assigned to each interval. Every PE calculates the function value `f` in the middle of its interval and multiplies this value by the interval width. Summing the rectangles in $\log_2 n$ steps (as compared to n–1 steps for the MIMD algorithm in Section 10.3) provides the desired approximation of π.

$$\pi = \int_0^1 \frac{4}{1+x^2}\,dx$$

$$\approx \sum_{i=1}^{\text{interv.}} \frac{4}{1+((i-0.5)*\text{width})^2} * \text{width}$$

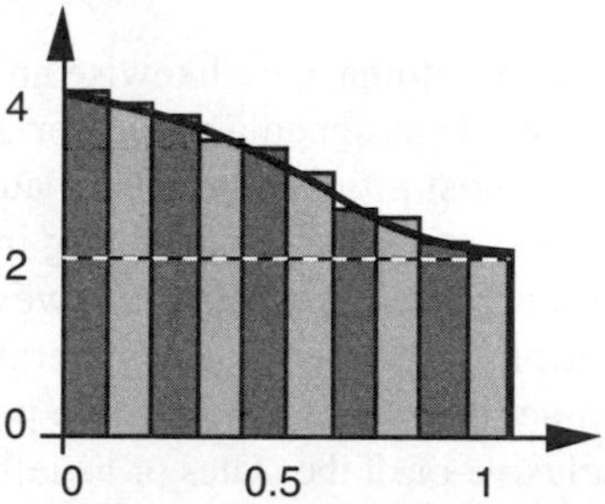

Figure 15.1 Approximation method for integral calculation

```
SYSTEM compute_pi;
(* parallel algorithm from R. Babb *)
CONST intervals = 1000;
   width        = 1.0 / float(intervals);
CONFIGURATION list [1..intervals];
CONNECTION (* none *);

VECTOR val: real;

PROCEDURE f (VECTOR x: real): VECTOR real;
(* function to be integrated *)
BEGIN
  RETURN(4.0 / (1.0 + x*x))
END f;

BEGIN
  PARALLEL (* Integral approximation with rectangle rule *)
    val := width * f( (float(id_no)-0.5) * width );
  ENDPARALLEL;
  WriteReal(REDUCE.SUM(val), 15);
END compute_pi.
```

The function to be integrated is calculated with the vector valued function `f`. The block beginning with `PARALLEL` activates all of the PEs, since there is no restricting selection present. The vector constant `id_no` returns the unique PE identification number from 1 to `intervals` for each individual PE.

15.2 Cellular Automata

Cellular automata are likewise an application area well suited to SIMD systems. Every cell can be assigned a processor and carries out the same processing instructions. One of the most prominent cellular automata is Conway's 'Game of Life', which is a two-dimensional structure changing in time. The cellular automaton shown here is simpler and only one-dimensional; however, it generates a two-dimensional image during execution (one line on every iteration). The processing instructions are conceptually simple: Every cell has only two possible states and computes its successor state from an exclusive-or of the states of its left and right neighbor. The middle cell is initialized with `TRUE` (printed as '`X`'), while all of the other cells are initialized with `FALSE` (printed as empty spaces).

```
SYSTEM cellular_automaton;
CONST n = 79;  (* number of elements *)
      m = 32;  (* number of loop passes *)
CONFIGURATION list [1..n];
CONNECTION left:  list[i] -> list[i-1] .right;
           right: list[i] -> list[i+1] .left;

SCALAR i      : integer;
VECTOR val,l,r: boolean;

PROCEDURE out;
VECTOR c: char;
BEGIN
  IF val THEN c:="X" ELSE c:=" " END;
  Write(c); WriteLn
END out;

BEGIN
  PARALLEL                          (* Initialization:        *)
    val := id_no = (n+1 DIV 2);     (* middle element = TRUE  *)
  ENDPARALLEL;                      (* all others = FALSE     *)

  FOR i:= 1 TO m DO
    PARALLEL
      out;
      PROPAGATE.left (val,l);
      PROPAGATE.right(val,r);
      val := l<>r;
    ENDPARALLEL;
  END;
END cellular_automaton.
```

The CONFIGURATION and CONNECTION declarations define a doubly linked list of PEs. The procedure out serves as screen output of the current state of the row of PEs. It converts every boolean state to a symbol of type CHAR. The complete character vector is then written to the screen sequentially by a vector valued Write operation. The initialization of the main program assigns the value TRUE only to the middle PE with number (n+1 DIV 2); all other PEs receive the value FALSE. Finally, there is a scalar loop which prints the current state and calculates the next cell state in each pass, using the data exchange (PROPAGATE) with the left and right neighbors.

Figure 15.2 shows the states of this cellular automaton, in which time progresses from top to bottom.

```
                               X
                              X X
                             X   X
                            X X X X
                           X       X
                          X X     X X
                         X   X   X   X
                        X X X X X X X X
                       X               X
                      X X             X X
                     X   X           X   X
                    X X X X         X X X X
                   X       X       X       X
                  X X     X X     X X     X X
                 X   X   X   X   X   X   X   X
                X X X X X X X X X X X X X X X X
               X                               X
              X X                             X X
             X   X                           X   X
            X X X X                         X X X X
           X       X                       X       X
          X X     X X                     X X     X X
         X   X   X   X                   X   X   X   X
        X X X X X X X X                 X X X X X X X X
       X               X               X               X
      X X             X X             X X             X X
     X   X           X   X           X   X           X   X
    X X X X         X X X X         X X X X         X X X X
   X       X       X       X       X       X       X       X
  X X     X X     X X     X X     X X     X X     X X     X X
 X   X   X   X   X   X   X   X   X   X   X   X   X   X   X   X
X X X X X X X X X X X X X X X X X X X X X X X X X X X X X X X X
```

Figure 15.2 Output of cellular automaton

Quite a number of new application areas have recently been opened up for cellular automata. One such area is 'lattice gas automata', a model used for simulation of fluid or gas dynamics (see [Doolen 90] and [Chen, Doolen, Matthaeus 91]). The solution of differential equations, as done conventionally, is not required here, for the fluid or gas is modelled by a grid of discrete cells (e.g. a hexagonal grid for two-dimensional currents). Each cell determines its time-discrete successor state from a set of rules, which are usually coded in a table. The current state of a cell and the data from local neighbors in the grid are used as indices for table look-up. Figure 15.3 (from Pätzold and Brenner, Univ. Stuttgart) shows airflow on a wing profile, simulated with lattice gas automata.

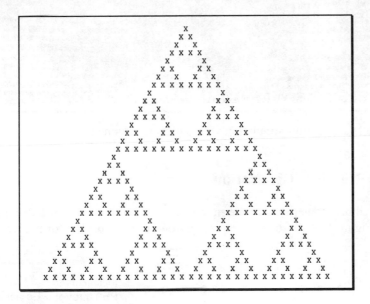

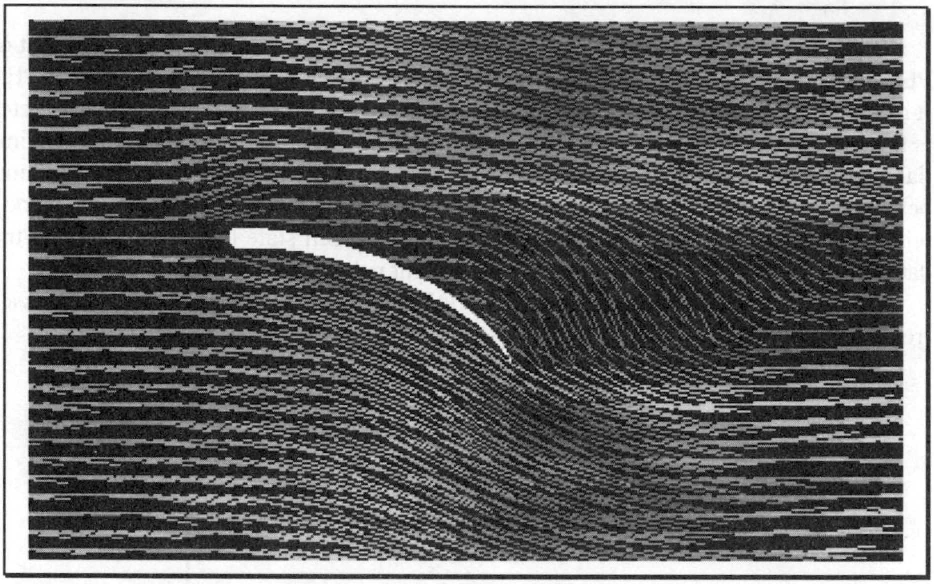

Figure 15.3 Air flow simulation with lattice gas automata

15.3 Prime Number Generation

The process used here to generate prime numbers is a parallel version of the sieve of Eratosthenes. Figure 15.4 illustrates the progression of the algorithm for twelve elements.

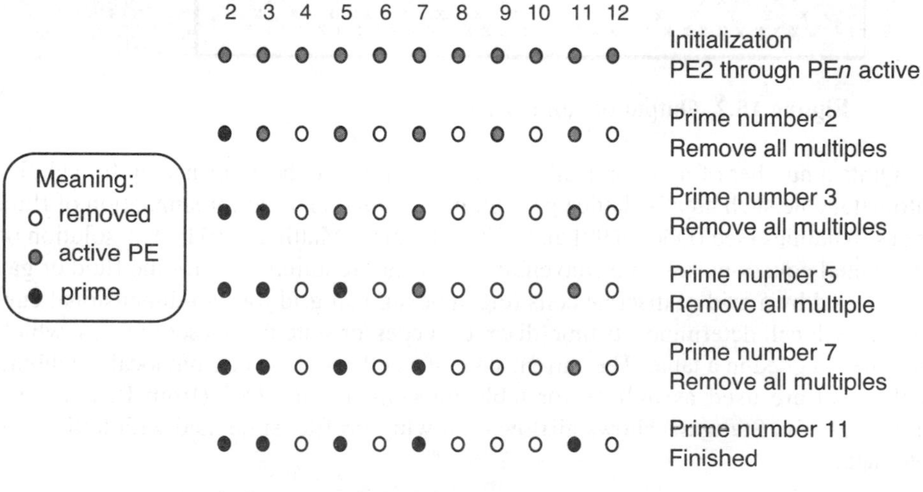

Figure 15.4 Parallel prime number generation

Using $n-1$ processors, all of the prime number between 2 and n are determined. Every PE represents an integer between 2 and n, corresponding to its position `DIM1`. Each PE remains active as long as its number is still a potential prime. In each step the smallest still active number is printed as a prime number, and all of the remaining PEs test whether their number is a multiple of this value. If so, they become inactive for all following rounds. So in each step, all of the remaining multiples of a prime are eliminated in parallel.

```
SYSTEM sieve;
CONFIGURATION list [2..200];
CONNECTION   (* none *);

SCALAR  prime   : INTEGER;
VECTOR  removed: BOOLEAN;

BEGIN
  PARALLEL
    REPEAT
      prime:= REDUCE.FIRST(DIM1);
      WriteInt(prime,10); WriteLn;   (* print prime       *)
      removed := DIM1 MOD prime = 0 (* remove multiples *)
    UNTIL removed
  ENDPARALLEL
END sieve.
```

15.4 Sorting

A number of different SIMD algorithms exist for the problem of sorting. The 'odd-even transposition sort' (OETS) is presented here as a representative, which can be understood as a parallel version of bubble-sort. OETS sorts n data elements with n PEs in n steps. Figure 15.5 shows the progression of the parallel algorithm. Every PE holds one of the numbers to be sorted. During processing, the algorithm differentiates between odd and even steps. In odd steps, all of the PEs with uneven identification numbers compare their element values with that of their right neighbor (PEs: 1–2, 3–4, 5–6, etc.) and carry out a data exchange if the value of their own element is larger than that the one of their neighbor. In the even steps, all of the PEs with even identification numbers carry out an analogous comparison and, if necessary, a data exchange with their right neighbor (PEs: 2–3, 4–5, 6–7, etc.). After n iterations, the list is sorted.

In the Parallaxis program, first the variable `lhs` determines whether a PE is in the role of the left or the right partner of a comparison. This role changes for each loop iteration. During each pass, the PEs get the data values of their left and right neighbor in `l` and `r`, respectively. The partner on the left-hand side uses the right neighbor's value for comparison, while the partner on the right-hand side uses the value of its left neighbor. The complicated comparison '`lhs = (comp<val)`' is true for the left PE partner when the right comparison value is greater than its own value; it is **also** true for the right PE partner, if the left comparison value is smaller than its own value. So a single key comparison is sufficient for all PEs to find out where swapping of data values are required. By applying a more complex compound topology, the program could be optimized further, such that only a single data exchange operation would be required for each pass through the loop.

```
SYSTEM sort;
(* Odd-Even Transposition Sorting (parallel bubble-sort) *)
CONST n = 10;
CONFIGURATION list [1..n];
CONNECTION left : list[i] -> list [i-1].right;
           right: list[i] -> list [i+1].left;

SCALAR step: INTEGER;
       a:    ARRAY[1..n] OF INTEGER;

VECTOR val,r,l,comp: INTEGER;
       lhs:          BOOLEAN;

BEGIN
  WriteString('Please enter values: ');
  FOR step:=1 TO n DO ReadInt(a[step]) END;
  LOAD(val,a);

  PARALLEL
   lhs := ODD(id_no); (* PE is left-hand side of a comparison *)
   FOR step:=1 TO n DO
    PROPAGATE.right(val,l);
    PROPAGATE.left(val,r);
    IF lhs THEN comp:=r ELSE comp:=l END;
    IF lhs = (comp<val) THEN val:=comp END; (* lhs&(comp<val) *)
    lhs := NOT lhs;                         (* or rhs&(comp≥val) *)
   END;
  ENDPARALLEL;

  STORE(val,a);
  FOR step:=1 TO n DO WriteInt(a[step],10); WriteLn END;
END sort.
```

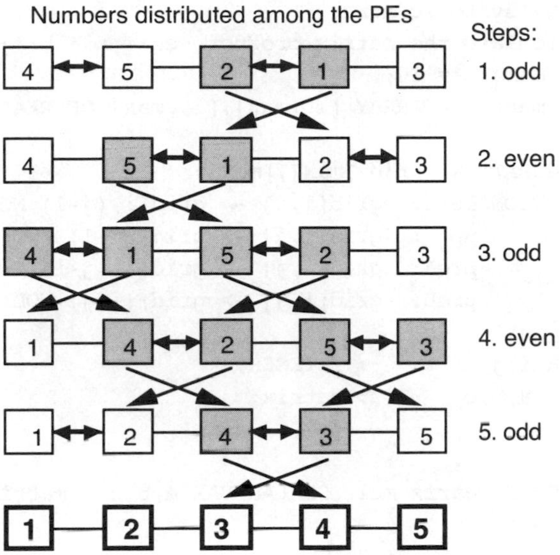

Figure 15.5 Example of odd-even transposition sorting

15.5 Systolic Matrix Multiplication

The multiplication of two matrices is one of the most important and most frequently used parallel operations. It is one of the fundamental operations in computer graphics and robotics. The so-called 'systolic multiplication' of two matrices is an efficient version of the multiplication algorithm for SIMD systems. Figure 15.6 illustrates the process. The input matrices are shifted diagonally and then brought into the solution matrix one step at a time. In each step, all PEs of the solution matrix multiply an element from input matrix **A** with an element from input matrix **B** and add the result to an accumulating value for the solution of this matrix element. In this way, $(3*n - 2)$ steps are required on n^2 PEs to multiply two $n \times n$ matrices.

This parallel algorithm is somewhat optimized in the Parallaxis program, so that only n steps are necessary. In the procedure `matrix_mult` the two input matrices are first completely loaded into the PEs, and as a preparatory step they are diagonally rotated to the left or upward, respectively. In the following iterations, matrix **A** is shifted left, and matrix **B** upward. The final result is stored in a scalar array.

```
SYSTEM  systolic_array;
(* Calculate the matrix product  c := a * b *)
CONST max    = 10;
TYPE  matrix = ARRAY [1..max],[1..max] OF REAL;

CONFIGURATION  grid [max],[max];
CONNECTION left:  grid[i,j] -> grid[i,(j-1) MOD max].left;
           up  :  grid[i,j] -> grid[(i-1) MOD max,j].up;
           preA:  grid[i,j] -> grid[i,(j-i) MOD max].preA;
           preB:  grid[i,j] -> grid[(i-j) MOD max,j].preB;

SCALAR i,j           : INTEGER;
       a,b,c         : matrix;


PROCEDURE matrix_mult(SCALAR VAR a,b,c : matrix);
(* c := a * b *)
SCALAR k: INTEGER;
VECTOR ra,rb,rc : REAL;
BEGIN
  LOAD (ra,a);
  LOAD (rb,b);
  PARALLEL
    PROPAGATE.preA(ra);
    PROPAGATE.preB(rb);
    rc := ra * rb;
    FOR k := 2 TO max DO
      PROPAGATE.left(ra);
      PROPAGATE.up(rb);
      rc := rc + ra * rb;
    END;
  ENDPARALLEL;
  STORE(rc,c);
END matrix_mult;

BEGIN
... (* read matrices a and b *)
  matrix_mult(a,b,c);
... (* write matrix c *)
END systolic_array.
```

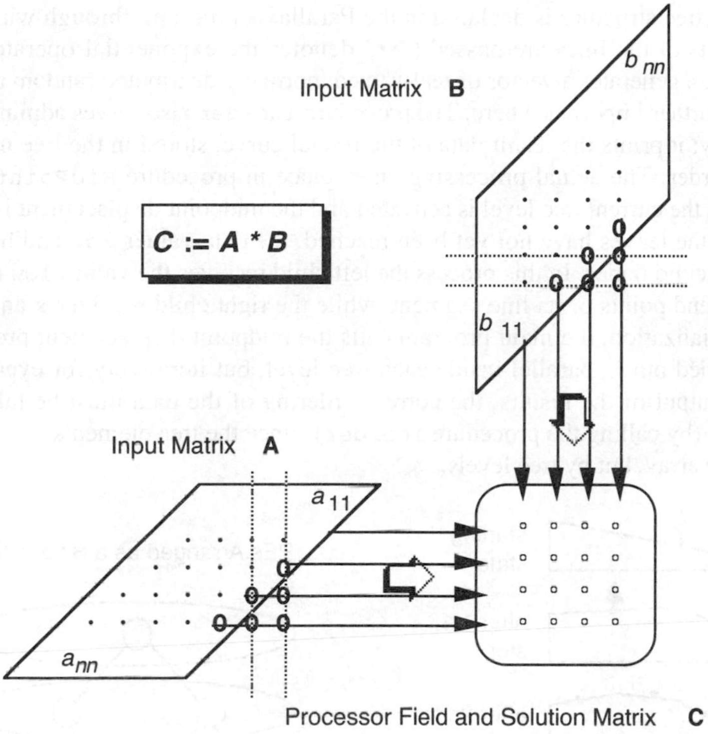

Figure 15.6 Systolic matrix multiplication

15.6 Generation of Fractals

The algorithm presented here is a problem that can be solved by a data parallel program with the 'divide-and-conquer' method. This is, however, not possible with all divide-and-conquer algorithms since the different branches usually have to carry out different program segments. The algorithm presented here generates a one-dimensional fractal curve using midpoint displacement (see [Peitgen, Saupe 88]). It starts with a straight line, which has its midpoint displaced up or down according to a weighted random value. Two line segments with different slopes arise from this process, and these are handled recursively in parallel in exactly the same way during the following steps (see Figure 15.7). The number of line segments to be processed doubles at every step, until the required resolution is reached. The processor structure used here is a binary tree structure. Beginning with the root, in each step the following tree level is activated until the leaves are reached. Since with the exception of the communication there is *only* one tree level active at a time, only half as many PEs would be sufficient with a more complicated connection structure.

A simple tree structure is declared in the Parallaxis program, through which start and end points of the lines are passed ('**' denotes the exponential operator). The function `Gauss` generates a vector of real-valued, normally distributed random numbers and is of no further importance here. The procedure `inorder` also serves administrative purposes only: it prints the result data of the fractal curve, stored in the tree nodes, in the correct order. The actual processing takes place in procedure `MidPoint`. In the parallel block the current tree level is activated and the midpoint displacement is carried out. Then, if the leaves have not yet been reached, the data values `low` and `high` are passed to the child nodes. In this process the left child receives the values `low` and `x` as the start and end points of its line segment, while the right child receives `x` and `high`. After the initialization, the main program calls the midpoint displacement procedure, which is carried out in parallel inside each tree level, but iteratively for every level. During the output of the results, the correct ordering of the data must be taken into consideration (by calling the procedure `inorder`), since the tree elements are not store linearly in the array, but by tree levels.

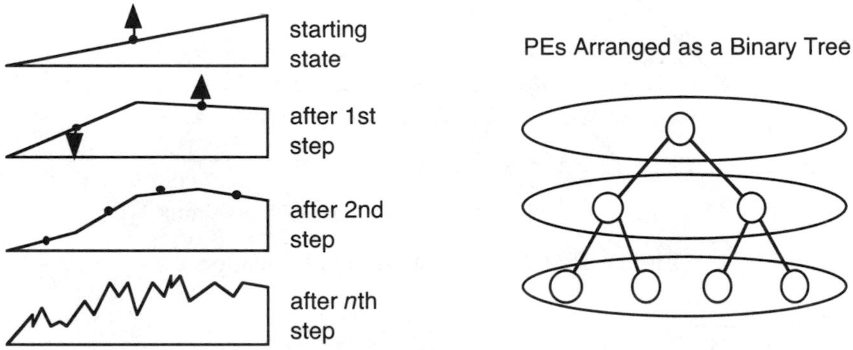

Figure 15.7 Divide-and-conquer implemented with tree topology

The computation time required for this program is relatively small: for n leaf nodes it only requires $\log_2 n$ steps (equal to the tree's height). Figure 15.8 shows a fractal curve generated by this program with 127 PEs.

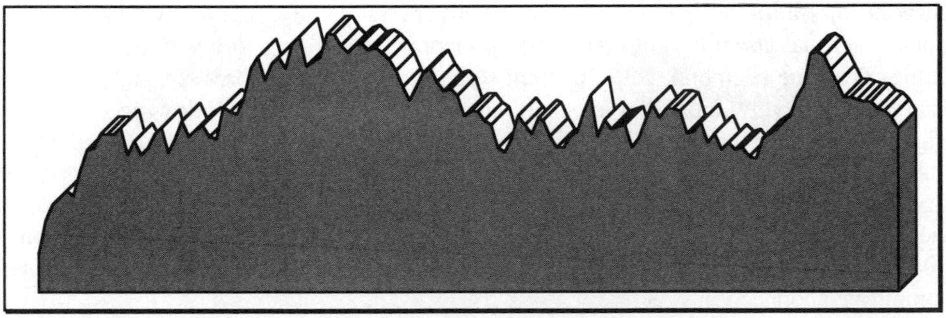

Figure 15.8 Fractal curve generated by program

```
SYSTEM fractal;
CONST  maxlevel = 7;
       low_val  = 0.0;
       high_val = 1.0;
       maxnode  = 2**maxlevel - 1;
(* declaration of the tree structure *)
CONFIGURATION tree [1..maxnode];
CONNECTION    child_l: tree[i] <-> tree[2*i].parent;
              child_r: tree[i] <-> tree[2*i+1].parent;
SCALAR  i              : INTEGER;
        delta          : REAL;
        field          : ARRAY [1..maxnode] OF REAL;
VECTOR  x, low, high   : REAL;

PROCEDURE Gauss(): VECTOR REAL;
(* generation of a random value vector with Gauss dist. *)
...
END Gauss;

PROCEDURE inorder(SCALAR node: INTEGER);
(* output of the tree elements in linear sequence *)
...
END inorder;

PROCEDURE MidPoint(SCALAR delta:REAL;SCALAR level:INTEGER);
BEGIN       (* select current tree level *)
  PARALLEL [2**(level-1) .. 2**level - 1]
    x := 0.5 * (low + high) + delta*Gauss();
    IF level < maxlevel THEN   (* values for children *)
      SEND tree.child_l (low)  TO tree.parent(low);
      SEND tree.child_l (x)    TO tree.parent(high);
      SEND tree.child_r (x)    TO tree.parent(low);
      SEND tree.child_r (high) TO tree.parent(high);
    END;
  ENDPARALLEL;
END MidPoint;

BEGIN (* main program *)
  PARALLEL  (* starting values *)
    low  := low_val;
    high := high_val;
    x    := 0.0;
  ENDPARALLEL;
  FOR i:=1 TO maxlevel DO
```

```
      delta := 0.5 ** (FLOAT(i)/2.0);
      MidPoint(delta,i);
    END;
    STORE(x,field);
    WriteFixPt(low_val,  10,3); WriteLn;
    inorder(1);  (* print values in correct sequence *)
    WriteFixPt(high_val, 10,3); WriteLn;
  END fractal.
```

15.7 Stereo Image Analysis

Spatial vision is a fascinating phenomenon, especially considering that this activity which people take for granted can only be implemented on computer systems with huge computational costs. However, the fundamental stereo image analysis algorithms can be easily translated into synchronous parallel programs. The three-dimensional impression in human vision comes from the fact that the left and right eyes see images that have slight differences due to the slightly different viewing angle of each eye (see Figure 15.9: Line *A'B'* appears longer to the left eye than line *A"B"* appears to the right eye.). The displacement of points in the left and right image is known as 'disparity' and can be used to determine the difference in distance from the observer of the corresponding points in the physical world. Unfortunately, it is not very easy to match points in the image of the left eye with points in the image of the right eye.

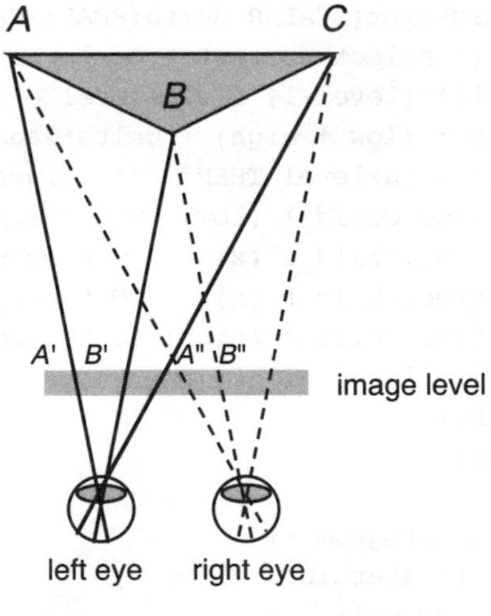

Figure 15.9 Stereo vision

Quite a while ago, Julesz used 'random dot stereograms', to show that the brain is able to interpret stereograms, with each monocular image by itself lacking any image contents (see [Julesz 60] and [Julesz 78]). Each of the left and right images considered alone appears to be completely randomly generated and contains no information. The 3D effect emerges from the interaction of the two images inside the brain, where the stereo disparity in the random patterns are analyzed and converted into spatial sensations. Random dot stereograms are very easy to generate on a computer and do not have the disadvantage of photographs, such as imprecision and alignment problems. Neither do they require any edge detection, since random dot stereograms consist of edges only.

Generation of random dot stereograms

1. *Fill the left and right images with the* same *random values*

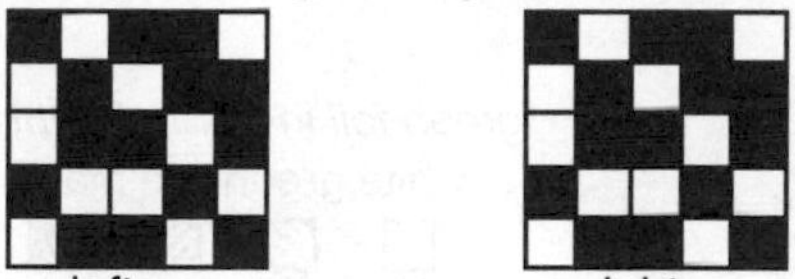

left right

2. *Raising or sinking areas*

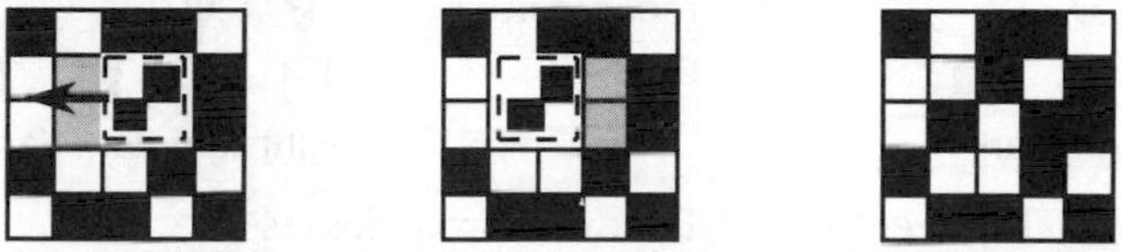

right image before rlght image after right image filled

An object can be raised to a certain altitude by shifting it only in the **right** image a corresponding number of pixels to the **left** (or lowered to some depth level by shifting to the right). The gap created in this process is then filled with a random dot pattern. *The left image remains unchanged.* This step is repeated for every area that will be elevated or lowered from the original image plane.

Display of Stereograms

There are a quite a number of possible techniques for viewing stereograms, all of which ensure that only the left picture is seen by the left eye and only the right picture by the right eye. Examples are prisms, LCD shutter displays, polarization filters, red/green filters, head mounted displays (two screens) or simply by concentrated viewing of each image with one eye. Red/green glasses (*anaglyph method*) represent the easiest option to implement. First the left image is colored green/white and the right image is colored red/white. Then the images are printed on top of each other, but slightly out of alignment so that the displacement cannot be recognized without the glasses. If two colored pixels are to be printed on top of each other, they should appear on paper or on the screen as a black pixel.

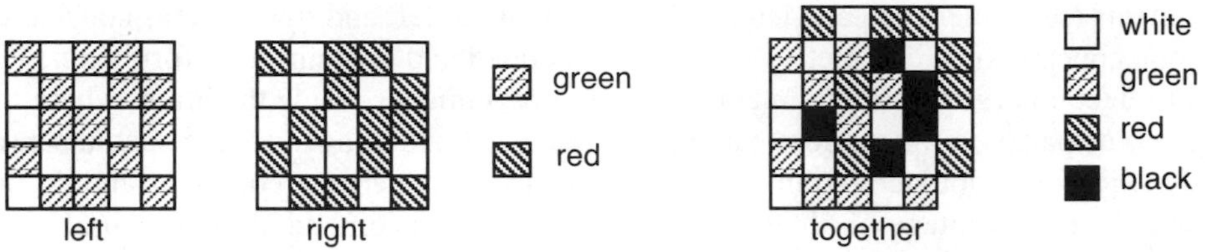

The red filter in front of the left eye only allows the red light to pass through and therefore makes the green and black points appear dark and the white and red points light. This corresponds exactly to the original left image. The green filter in front of the right eye only allows the green light to pass through, therefore the red and black pixels appear dark. The green image is thereby filtered out of the mixed image stereogram (see Figure 15.10).

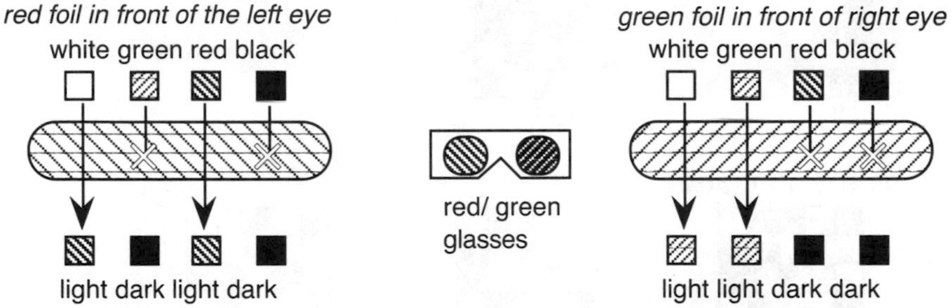

Figure 15.10 Effect of stereo glasses

The ensuing reverse calculation from the stereograms (e.g. regenerating the depth information from the left and right images) is much more difficult and computationally expensive than the generation of the stereograms. In addition, the reverse calculation can never be 100% correct. Usually, there are individual points which are assigned false depth values.

Analysis of random dot stereograms
(Reverse calculation of depth information from stereograms)

1. *Comparison of the right image to the left image and search for matching pixels*

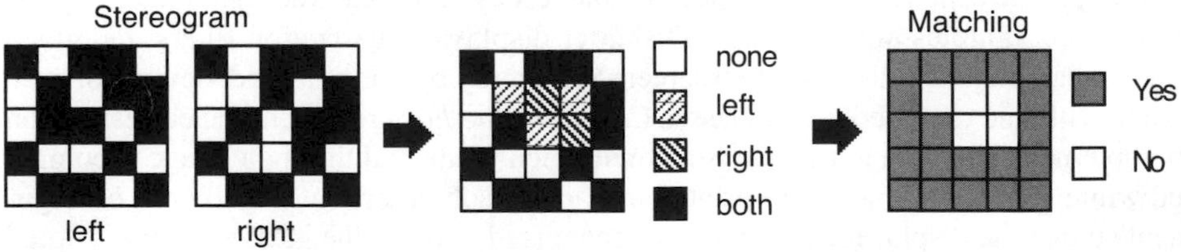

A pair of corresponding pixels (one pixel from left and right image each, at the same position) match if both pixels are black or both are white. This operation can be performed in parallel on all pixels.

2. *Shifting of the left image one pixel to the left and comparison with the right image*

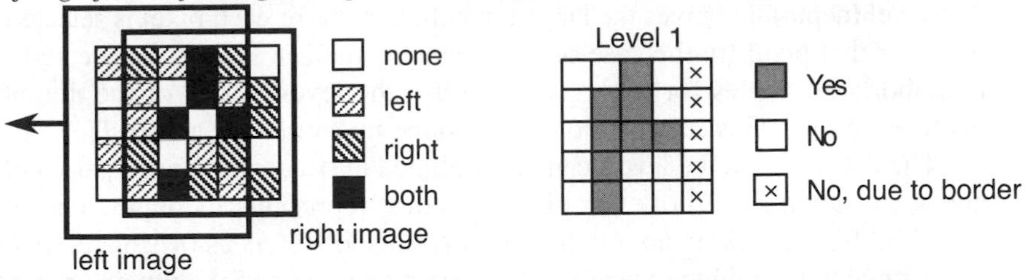

This shift step with subsequent comparison of left and right image (see step 1) is carried out iteratively for each depth level. This gives the matching pixels for all height levels.

3. *Determining the depth of each Pixel*

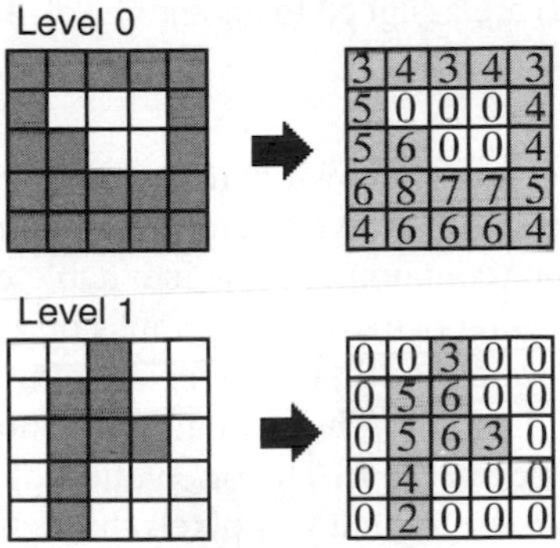

This step is also carried out iteratively for each depth level, but in parallel for all pixels. Data from a 5 × 5 local neighbor field (only a 3 × 3 field is shown in the figure) with eight-way grid connections is used to determine the matching neighborhood for all pixels. Pixels not matching receive the value zero, while pixels matching receive the sum of all neighbor pixels that also match, plus one for themselves.

4. *Selection of the best fitting level (depth) for each pixel*

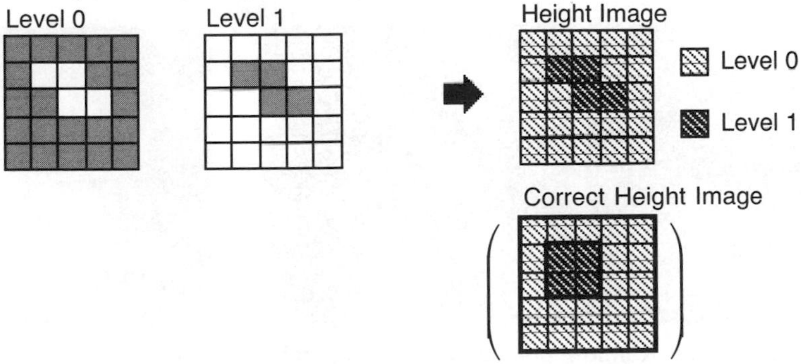

The level (depth) that gives the largest matching sum for each pixel is selected as the level for that pixel (in the case of equal values, the lower level is selected). If the neighborhood values for all levels are zero, the level of one of the neighboring pixels is chosen. This computation can be done in parallel for all pixels.

The data from all the levels can be combined into a depth image ('false color image'), as shown here. For each pixel, its color represents its depth. The solution found in the example is not totally correct, since differences of isolated pixels are not avoidable with this procedure. The correct depth image is shown in parentheses below it.

5. *Filter (optional)*
   In order to eliminate single pixel errors, a local 3 × 3 matrix can be used in each level, to sum the number of pixels already in that level. Pixels having too few neighbors in this level (number < threshold) are assigned to another level. The filter operation can be performed in parallel for all pixels.

The algorithm for analyzing random dot stereograms shown here can very easily be translated into a data parallel program. Figure 15.11 shows a sample stereogram and the corresponding calculated depth information (containing a few inevitable defects), each having a size of 128 × 128 pixels. When using pairs of photographs or video images that have been loaded into a computer system with a scanner or frame buffer, stereo image analysis becomes much more difficult. These images are no longer monochrome, instead they have gray levels or even color. The orientation of the two pictures to each other cannot be accomplished to the accuracy of pixels through camera adjustment alone. Many other distortions and inaccuracies show up as well, which do not occur with computer generated random dot stereograms. Therefore, two preparation steps are required for photographic images. First, the calculation of the 'relative orientation' of the two images to each other and the corresponding adjustment of one of the images has to be computed. Second, the edges in both images have to be detected, because these are much more expressive than the raw image data. The stereo matching algorithm can then be applied to these edge stereograms.

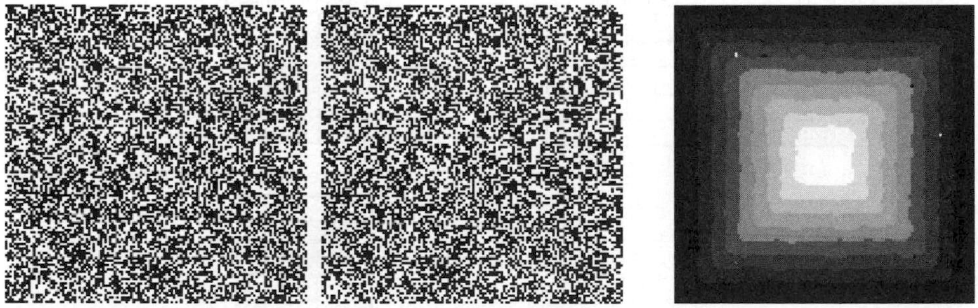

Figure 15.11 Random dot stereogram with calculated depth information

Exercises III

1. A connection structure is defined in the following way in Parallaxis:

```
CONFIGURATION strange [0..n-1];
CONNECTION     a: strange[i] <-> strange[3*i+1].d;
               b: strange[i] <-> strange[3*i+2].d;
               c: strange[i] <-> strange[3*i+3].d,
```

a) Sketch the network `strange` for n = 10 .

b) What is the number of connections per PE for `strange` ?

c) What is the maximum distance between two PEs for `strange` ?
(depending on n, the number of PEs)

2. With respect to the Parallaxis program fragment below:

a) What is the result, when variable `v` is pre-loaded with the following matrix:

$$v = \begin{pmatrix} 3 & 2 & 5 \\ 4 & 7 & 8 \\ 9 & 1 & 6 \end{pmatrix}$$

b) Which operation does this program carry out on a general matrix?

```
CONFIGURATION field [1..max],[1..max];
CONNECTION right: field[i,j] <-> field[i,j+1].left;

SCALAR i, result: integer;
VECTOR buffer, v: integer;
```

```
BEGIN
  PARALLEL
    ... (* load data in vector v *)
    FOR i:= 1 TO max-1 DO
      buffer:=v;
      PROPAGATE.left(v);
      IF buffer > v THEN v:= buffer END;
    END;
  result := REDUCE.MIN [*],[1] (v);
  ENDPARALLEL
END
```

3. Translate the following FORTRAN 90 program into a Parallaxis program. ('.LT.' stands for 'less than' or '<')

Fortran 90:

```
INTEGER, DIMENSION(100,500) :: matrix
...
matrix(1:50,1:500) = matrix(2:51,1:500);
WHERE (matrix .LT. 7) matrix = 10;
```

Parallaxis:

```
SYSTEM FtoP;
CONFIGURATION field [1..100],[1..500];
CONNECTION right: field[i,j] <-> field[i,j+1].left;
           up   : field[i,j] <-> field[i+1,j].down;

VECTOR matrix: INTEGER;

BEGIN
  .............
END FtoP.
```

4. With respect to the Parallaxis program fragment below:

a) What is the result from the following program input:
3 2 5 3 9 9 1 2 3 7 2 4 8 5 6 2
Write down the contents of the vector `f` at the beginning and end of each pass through the loop.

b) What operation does this program carry out on its input ?

c) How many data exchange operations (PROPAGATE) are carried out for one execution of the program ?

```
SYSTEM what_am_i;
CONST levels = 5;
      size = (2**levels)-1;
      start = 2**(levels-1);
      finish  = size;
CONFIGURATION tree [1..size];
CONNECTION child_l: tree[i] <-> tree[2*i  ].parent_l;
           child_r: tree[i] <-> tree[2*i+1].parent_r;
VECTOR f,left,right: integer;
SCALAR field: ARRAY [1..size] OF integer;
       z,x,result: integer;

BEGIN
  (* load data in vector f *)
  FOR z:=1 TO start-1  DO field[z]:=0 END;
  FOR z:=start TO finish DO ReadInt(field[z]) END;
  LOAD(f, field);
  FOR x:= 1 TO levels-1 DO
    PARALLEL
      PROPAGATE.parent_l(f,left);
      PROPAGATE.parent_r(f,right);
      IF left < right THEN f:=left ELSE f:=right END;
    ENDPARALLEL;
  END;
  STORE[1](f,result);
  WriteInt(result, 4);
END what_am_i.
```

5. Write a program in Fortran 90 for systolic matrix multiplication.

6. Write a program in C* to generate prime numbers with the sieve of Eratosthenes.

7. Write a program in C*, MPL, or Parallaxis to solve a system of linear equations in parallel.

8. Write a program in Parallaxis, which reads data for rectangles out of a description file and creates a parallel field of image data (see figure below). Files can be opened and closed with the following standard operations for reading and writing, respectively:

```
OpenInput("filename")   CloseInput
OpenOutput("filename")  CloseOutput
```

Every line of the file contains an entry of the following form:

<starting position *x*> <starting position *y*> <width> <height>

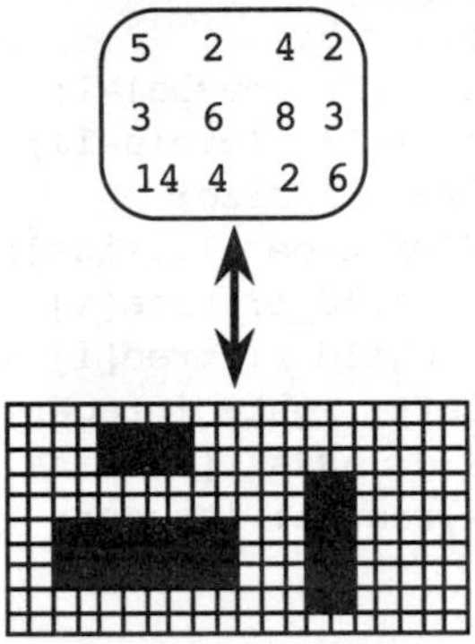

9. Write a program in Parallaxis, which uses the image data in problem 8. The rectangles in the parallel field should be recognized and once again written into a description file.

10. Write a program in Fortran 90, C*, or Parallaxis to perform a data parallel calculation of the Mandelbrot set. Use a virtual PE for each pixel.

11. Implement a cellular automaton for Conway's 'Game of Life' in Fortran 90, C*, or Parallaxis. Use a virtual PE for each cell.

12. In the odd-even transposition sort (OETS) in Section 15.4, two data exchange operations were carried out for every step, even though each PE only required a value from one neighbor. Rewrite the program using compound (conditional) connection structures so that only one data exchange operation is needed.

13. Write a program in Parallaxis to generate random dot stereograms. The parameterless standard function VBRandom() can be used to generate a random boolean vector.

14. Write a program in Parallaxis to analyze random dot stereograms (determination of depth information).

15. The following local image operator is to be applied in parallel to an image with 500×500 pixels:

–1		–1
	4	
–1		–1

a) Outline a synchronous parallel implementation of this problem in Parallaxis with 250,000 PEs.

b) Outline an asynchronous parallel implementation of this problem in Modula-P with 50 processors. Use the following monitor entries (of monitor `mon`) as given:

```
ENTRY get(i,j: INTEGER): INTEGER;
```
returns pixel value of input image in position (i,j)
```
ENTRY put(i,j, pvalue: INTEGER);
```
writes computed pixel value in position (i,j) to a different monitor variable

16. The synchronously parallel program shown below requires 1 million PEs. However, the SIMD computer system available has only 12,345 PEs.

a) Outline the mapping of virtual PEs to physical PEs for the Parallaxis program below in pseudo program notation. (Vector constant `id_no` returns the unambiguous identification number of each PE.)

b) Each of the two parallel assignment operations and the evaluation of the parallel selection condition shall require the same execution time. With these prerequisites, what is the average number and percentage of active virtual PEs for the program fragment below ?

c) What is the average number and percentage of active physical PEs for the program fragment below *(after mapping of the virtual PEs)* ?

```
CONFIGURATION abc [1..1000000];
CONNECTION (* none *);
VECTOR x,y: INTEGER;
...
PARALLEL
  x := y;
  IF ODD(id_no) THEN x := x-1 END;
ENDPARALLEL;
```

17. Implement a program to simulate voting behaviour in Fortran 90, C*, or Parallaxis. Use a two-dimensional configuration with 100 × 100 voters; each voter is to be simulated by a virtual processor.

Each voter is initially assigned a random boolean value. This represents his preference for party *T* or party *F*; other parties or undecided voters are not permitted here. In each step each voter consults *one* of his eight neighbors in the grid and takes over his neighbor's preference. A random number generator is to be used for each voter in each step to determine which neighbor to select.

PART IV

Other Models of Parallelism

In all of the procedural parallel programming languages introduced so far, direct control of parallelism is provided through special language structures for this purpose. However, ideally the programmer would not have to worry about the details of parallel execution. Instead, a compiler or the operating system should handle these problems in a way transparent to the programmer. The automatic parallelization or vectorization of sequential procedural programs is only a stopgap measure on the way to this goal, since often sufficient performance improvement is not achieved. For non-procedural languages, there exist both an implicit handling of parallelism, and also explicit parallel concepts, similar to those for procedural languages. Performance evaluation of parallel systems is of paramount importance for all parallel models and for the usage of parallel computer systems in general.

CHAPTER 16

Automatic Parallelization and Vectorization

As has been shown at least for MIMD systems, the creation of parallel programs is much more expensive, complicated, and therefore error prone than the creation of sequential programs. Moreover, the huge number of already existing libraries of sequential programs, owned by many users, should be further used in parallel systems. However, due to their enormous size (and maybe also due to a lack of reasonable documentation), they cannot be converted to a parallel programming language easily. The immense cost of creating new software packages seriously restricts the potential users (and customers) of parallel computer systems, since in comparison to mainframes, special purpose computer systems for computationally intensive problems have a very small market share. One of the biggest hopes for the success of parallel computers on the market is therefore the automatic parallelization or vectorization of sequential programs. Then, all existing sequential programs could be used *unchanged* after re-compilation, without the need to write new parallel programs. However, automatic parallelization and vectorization do not presently deliver results of satisfactory quality. It remains doubtful whether they ever will.

It would not make sense to write new programs for a parallel computer system in a sequential programming language and then rely on the automatic parallelization or vectorization. For example, a dot product is lengthy when programmed sequentially with a loop (and will look different for each application programmer!). The parallelizer/vectorizer now has to recognize this pattern and translate it into the appropriate parallel or vector operation. The same algorithm may be much easier to implement using a parallel programming language. An easy to implement 'automatic sequentializer' would complement such a system by translating parallel programs into their sequential equivalents, in the case where a parallel program is also to be executed on a sequential computer system.

A commercially available vectorizer for translating Fortran 77 programs to MPFortran (a Fortran 90 dialect) is 'VAST-2' from MasPar Computer Co. [MasPar92]. VAST-2 translates sequential Fortran `do` loops and `if` selections into the appropriate array constructs; nested loops will be translated into operations on multidimensional arrays. Data dependences (see below) between statements are analyzed and an attempt is made to minimize the number and length of dependent regions through statement reordering. The performance of this vectorizer depends to a high degree on interaction with the programmer. For the vectorization process, the tool expects compilation directives from the programmer and its diagnostics recommend rewriting certain code sections. So the generation of a parallel program is an iterative process. Generating efficient parallel programs with the VAST-2 vectorization tool might therefore be too complex a demand for a programmer inexperienced in parallel programming.

This chapter covers both the **parallelization** of sequential programs for **MIMD** computer systems (*asynchronous parallelism*) and the **vectorization** of sequential programs for **SIMD** computer systems (*synchronous parallelism*).

In addition to a pseudo-notation, Fortran 90 notation will be used in the following [Metcalf, Reid 90], which is well suited for vector programming on SIMD or MIMD systems. Fortran 90 is described in Section 14.1 .

The following example shows the vectorization of a `for` loop:

```
for i:= 1 to n do                          A(1:n) = B(1:n) + C(1:n)
  A[i]:= B[i] + C[i];  } in Fortran 90 :   D(1:n) = A(1:n) * 5
  D[i]:= A[i] * 5;
end;
```

Since the same operations are applied to the array elements for each loop pass and these operations are independent of one another, each statement inside the `for` loop can be translated into a vector statement in Fortran 90. The notation `A(1:n)` represents a vector with n components.

However

```
for i:= 1 to n do
  A[i]:= B[i] + C[i];        ⇏     A(1:n) = B(1:n) + C(1:n)
  D[i]:= A[i+1] * 5;               D(1:n) = A(2:n+1) * 5
end;
          ↑                                  ↑
  uses the old value of A          uses the new value of A

                  The correct solution has a different execution order:
                                   D(1:n) = A(2:n+1) * 5
                                   A(1:n) = B(1:n) + C(1:n)
```

Just changing a single index (`A[i+1]` instead of `A[i]`) makes the vectorization considerably more difficult in this example. In each pass through the loop, the second statement accesses the old, not yet changed value of the array `A`. Therefore there exists a data dependence that must be taken into account when vectorizing this loop. Through 'close inspection' one realizes that by reversing the order of the two vector statements the desired result can be achieved. These data dependences and rules will be placed on a firmer basis and treated more deeply in the following sections.

16.1 Data Dependence

Before the parallelization or vectorization of a sequential program can be performed, the data dependence between the individual statements must be determined. The following definitions and procedures are based on the work of Kuck and Wolfe, and are contained in [Kuck, Kuhn, Leasure, Wolfe 80] and [Hwang, DeGroot 89].

Auxiliary Definitions

Input set of a statement S:
IN(S) = 'Set of all data elements, whose value is read by S'

Output set of a statement S:
OUT(S) = 'Set of all data elements, whose value is altered by S'

The two auxiliary definitions are further explained through an example of a simple `for` loop:

```
    for i:=1 to 5 do
S:    X[i]:=A[i+1]*B
    end;
```

The IN set contains all the input data elements from the entire loop area for statement S, and the OUT set contains the corresponding output data elements:

IN(S) = {A[2], A[3], A[4], A[5], A[6], B}
OUT(S) = {X[1], X[2], X[3], X[4], X[5]}

Definition of Execution Sequence

When a statement S is in a loop with index i, then $S^{i'}$ indicates the **instance** (operation) of S during the $i{=}i'$ pass through the loop.

$S_1 \ \Theta \ S_2$:⇔ An instance of S_1 can be carried out before an instance of S_2.

$S_1^{i'} \ \Theta \ S_2^{i''}$:⇔ S_1 and S_2 are both inside a loop and $S_1^{i'}$ will be carried out before $S_2^{i''}$.

Ascertaining the ordering of two statements is highly important to the determination of the data dependences. The following simplifying assumptions apply here and in the following sections:

a) The loop increment is always equal to one.

b) Only assignment statements will be considered.

Definition of Data Dependence Relations

Data dependence is first defined for *instances of statements* (operations within a specific loop execution: the loop indices are omitted for clarity) and for statements that are not enclosed within a loop.

1) $\exists x\colon\ x \in \mathrm{OUT}(S_1)\ \wedge\ x \in \mathrm{IN}\ S_2)\ \wedge$ $S_1 \ominus S_2\ \wedge\ \nexists k\colon\ (S_1 \ominus S_k \ominus S_2 \wedge x \in \mathrm{OUT}(S_k))$ $\Leftrightarrow$: S_2 is **flow-dependent** on S_1: $\mathbf{S_1\ \delta\ S_2}$	*S_2 uses the value x, which was calculated in S_1*
(2) $\exists x\colon\ x \in \mathrm{IN}(S_1)\ \wedge\ x \in \mathrm{OUT}\ S_2)\ \wedge$ $S_1 \ominus S_2\ \wedge\ \nexists k\colon\ (S_1 \ominus S_k \ominus S_2 \wedge x \in \mathrm{OUT}(S_k))$ $\Leftrightarrow$: S_2 is **anti-dependent** on S_1: $\mathbf{S_1\ \bar{\delta}\ S_2}$	*S_1 uses the value x, before it is altered by S_2*
(3) $\exists x\colon\ x \in \mathrm{OUT}(S_1)\ \wedge\ x \in \mathrm{OUT}\ S_2)\ \wedge$ $S_1 \ominus S_2\ \wedge\ \nexists k\colon\ (S_1 \ominus S_k \ominus S_2 \wedge x \in \mathrm{OUT}(S_k))$ $\Leftrightarrow$: S_2 is **output-dependent** on S_1: $\mathbf{S_1\ \delta^\circ\ S_2}$	*S_2 overwrites the value x, which was calculated earlier in S_1*
If neither (1) nor (2) nor (3) holds, then S_1 and S_2 are **data-independent**.	

Two statements that are enclosed in a loop with index `i` are data-dependent, if there exist two instances of these statements, which are data-dependent. Data dependence is defined for nested loops in an analogous way.

$$S_1\ \delta\ S_2 \quad :\Leftrightarrow \quad \exists\ i', i'':\ S_1^{i'}\ \delta\ S_2^{i''}$$

$$S_1\ \bar{\delta}\ S_2 \quad :\Leftrightarrow \quad \exists\ i', i'':\ S_1^{i'}\ \bar{\delta}\ S_2^{i''}$$

$$S_1\ \delta^\circ\ S_2 \quad :\Leftrightarrow \quad \exists\ i', i'':\ S_1^{i'}\ \delta^\circ\ S_2^{i''}$$

So data dependence between two statements in a program can take on three different forms: flow dependence, anti-dependence and output dependence.

Flow Dependence
Statement S_2 reads a data value, which was earlier written by S_1. Due to this dependence, the ordering S_1 before S_2 must be maintained in the parallelized (or vectorized) code as well. Otherwise, S_2 might read a false data value.

Anti-Dependence
Statement S_2 overwrites a data value, which was earlier read by S_1. The ordering S_1 before S_2 must be maintained in this case as well by automatic parallelization/vectorization. Otherwise, S_1 might read a false data value.

Output Dependence
First statement S_1 writes a data value, then S_2 later overwrites it. Once again, the ordering S_1 before S_2 must be maintained by the automatic parallelization/vectorization. Otherwise, the data element would have the wrong value after execution of the assignments (the data value from S_1 instead the one of from S_2).

Simplified Rules

These definitions of the dependence relations are quite complex and, furthermore, costly to implement, due to the negative existence rules ('there exists no k with...'). In contrast to these necessary and sufficient rules ('if and only if'), weaker rules for the data dependence may sometimes suffice, as in the following rules, which are necessary but not sufficient. The check for statements occurring between S_1 and S_2 can then be omitted in a simplified data dependence test. The conditions on the new left-hand side (see below) follow from the data dependence on the right side. However, the reverse is not necessarily true.

In a restricted implementation one could use these simplified rules; however, in this case 'too many' dependences would be found (e.g. statement pairs that are not actually data-dependent). Consequently, under these circumstances the optimal parallelization may not be found. On the other hand, these simplified rules will not overlook any actual data dependences. So the parallel programs automatically generated from these rules would be correct, but probably not as efficient as they could be.

1')	$\exists x\colon x \in \mathrm{OUT}(S_1) \;\wedge\; x \in \mathrm{IN}\; S_2)$	$\wedge\; S_1 \Theta S_2$	$\Leftarrow$	$S_1 \,\delta\, S_2$
(2')	$\exists x\colon x \in \mathrm{IN}(S_1) \;\wedge\; x \in \mathrm{OUT}\; S_2)$	$\wedge\; S_1 \Theta S_2$	$\Leftarrow$	$S_1 \,\bar{\delta}\, S_2$
(3')	$\exists x\colon x \in \mathrm{OUT}(S_1) \;\wedge\; x \in \mathrm{OUT}\; S_2)$	$\wedge\; S_1 \Theta S_2$	$\Leftarrow$	$S_1 \,\delta^{\circ}\, S_2$

The difference between the two sets of rules can be clarified in the following example:

S_1: `A := B + D;`
S_2: `C := A * 3;`
S_3: `A := A + C;`
S_4: `E := A / 2;`

As one can easily derive, this sequence of statements has the following dependences:

$S_1 \,\delta\, S_2$ (due to `A`)
$S_1 \,\delta\, S_3$ (due to `A`)
$S_2 \,\delta\, S_3$ (due to `C`)
$S_3 \,\delta\, S_4$ (due to `A`)

$S_2 \,\bar{\delta}\, S_3$ (due to `A`)
$S_1 \,\delta^{\circ}\, S_3$ (due to `A`)

However,
it does *not* hold that: $S_1 \,\delta\, S_4$
although: $S_1 \Theta S_4$ and $\mathrm{OUT}(S_1) \cap \mathrm{IN}(S_4) = \{$`A`$\}$

In this case the 'simplified rule' (1') would detect a dependence, even though according to the definition of the original rule (1) no dependence exists. Although the value of the variable `A` is read by S_4 and written by S_1, it is overwritten by S_3 in between.

Definition of Indirect Data Dependence

This definition combines the three types of data dependence and expands them to chains of dependences (transitive closure).

S_2 is **data-dependent** on S_1:

$$S_1\ \delta^*\ S_2 \quad :\Leftrightarrow \quad S_1\,\delta\,S_2 \ \vee\ S_1\bar{\delta}\,S_2 \ \vee\ S_1\,\delta^\circ\,S_2$$

S_2 is **indirectly data-dependent** on S_1:

$$S_1\ \Delta\ S_2 \quad :\Leftrightarrow \quad \exists\, S_{k1}, S_{k2}, ..., S_{kn} \quad n \geq 0):$$
$$S_1\,\delta^*\,S_{k1}\,\delta^*\,S_{k2}\,\delta^*\ ...\ \delta^*\,S_{kn}\,\delta^*\,S_2$$

Definition of Directed Data Dependence

The direction of a data dependence specifies whether the two instances of statements involved are located in the same pass through the loop or one of them was carried out in an earlier pass through the loop (with a corresponding different index value). Since the statements can be contained in several nested loops, a direction must be given for each containing (surrounding) loop.

Assume S_1 and S_2 are embedded in loops with indices $i_1, ..., i_d$

If there exist two specific loop instances $I' = (i_1', ..., i_d')$ and $I'' = (i_1'', ..., i_d'')$ for the loop indices $i_1, ..., i_d$ such that the following holds for the appropriate instances of S_1 and S_2 :

$$S_1{}^{i_1' ... i_d'}\ \delta^*\ S_2{}^{i_1'' ... i_d''}$$

and if further the following relation is valid for the index vectors (loop instances):

$$I'\ \Psi\ I''$$

(that is: $\Psi = \psi_1, ..., \psi_d)$ where $\psi_i \in \{<, =, \leq, >, \geq, \neq, ?\}$,
['?' represents an unknown relation]

with $i_1'\ \psi_1\ i_1''$
$i_2'\ \psi_2\ i_2''$
...
$i_d'\ \psi_d\ i_d''$)

then the following definition holds:

$\Leftrightarrow$: S_2 is **data-dependent with direction** ψ on S_1: $S_1\ \delta^*_\psi\ S_2$

The directed data dependences δ_ψ , $\bar{\delta}_\psi$ and $\overset{\circ}{\delta}_\psi$ are defined analogously.

<u>Example of Data Dependence Direction:</u>

```
      for i:=2 to n do
        for j:=2 to m do
S1:       A[i,j]:= B[i,j];
S2:       C[i,j]:= A[i,j-1];
        end;
      end;
```

Here the data dependence $S_1\ \delta_{\Psi}\ S_2$ exists, since an instance of S_1 writes the value of `A[i,j]` which is read by an instance of S_2. The data dependence direction can be determined by comparing the indices of the two instances involved. For example, data element `A[2,2]` is *written* in the loop pass with `i=2` and `j=2`, whereas in the loop pass with `i=2` and `j=3` the same element `A[2,2]` is *read*. Comparing the indices results in:

for the surrounding loop with index `i`: $2 = 2$
for the inner loop with index `j`: $2 < 3$

This indicates that the following directed data dependence exists between S_1 and S_2:

$S_1\ \delta_{(=,<)}\ S_2$

A coarse simplification is the following:

Note to Remember

> When for a data dependence the index of a variable for the write access is `i` and for the read access is:
>
> (`i+1`) then the **old value** of a variable is being read,
>
> (`i–1`) then the **new value** of a variable is being read.

The following sections show the vectorization (synchronous parallelism, SIMD system) and the parallelization (asynchronous parallelism, MIMD system) of a sequential loop. For nested loops, the outer loop is normally chosen for parallelization due to efficiency considerations (such as the fact that start and termination of MIMD processes are expensive operations), while only the innermost loops (or all loops completely) may be vectorized.

16.2 Vectorization of a Loop

In the following the actual methods for automatically translating sequential programs into parallel programs are presented:

Vectorization Rules

a) If a data dependence relation $S_x\ \delta^*\ S_y$ exists inside the loop to be vectorized, then in the vectorized code, statement S_x has to *precede* statement S_y (by changing the statement execution order, if necessary).

b) Data dependences with direction '<' or '>' in *surrounding* loops (if any) do not have to be taken into consideration.

c) If data dependence relations do not permit a consistent statement execution order, the loop cannot be vectorized directly.

Vectorization Example:
(adapted from Wolfe in [Hwang, DeGroot 89])

```
    for i:=2 to n do
S1:   A[i]:= B[i]+C[i];
S2:   D[i]:= A[i+1]+1;
S3:   C[i]:= D[i];
    end;
```

To start with, the data dependences between all three of the statements in the loop must be determined. Then a restriction on the parallel execution sequence can be derived from each of the dependences.

The following must hold in the vectorized code:

$S_1\ \bar{\delta}_{(=)}\ S_3$ (due to C) $\Rightarrow$ S_1 before S_3

$S_2\ \bar{\delta}_{(<)}\ S_1$ (due to A) $\Rightarrow$ S_2 before S_1

$S_2\ \delta_{(=)}\ S_3$ (due to D) $\Rightarrow$ S_2 before S_3

There are three data dependences that must be taken into account during the vectorization of the loop in this example. The two anti-dependences $S_1\ \bar{\delta}_{(=)}\ S_3$ and $S_2\ \bar{\delta}_{(<)}\ S_1$ as well as the flow-dependence $S_2\ \delta_{(=)}\ S_3$ each force a specific ordering of two dependent statements in the vectorized code. The following must hold in the vectorized code:

S_1 before S_3, S_2 before S_1, and S_2 before S_3

These can only be resolved through the sequence:

S_2, S_1, S_3

The vectorized version of the original example in Fortran 90 notation results from the statement reordering according to the data dependences. Each sequential statement was converted into a vector statement based on the loop parameters:

```
S2:  D(2:N) = A(3:N+1) + 1
S1:  A(2:N) = B(2:N) + C(2:N)
S3:  C(2:N) = D(2:N)
```

16.3 Parallelization of a Loop

Parallelization of a program fragment deals with converting it for execution on an asynchronous MIMD computer system. The principle method here is the assignment of individual loop passes to different processors, which is known as 'doacross'. Often there are fewer processors available than there are passes through the loop to carry out. Therefore, another level of abstraction is required, which deals with processes instead of processors.

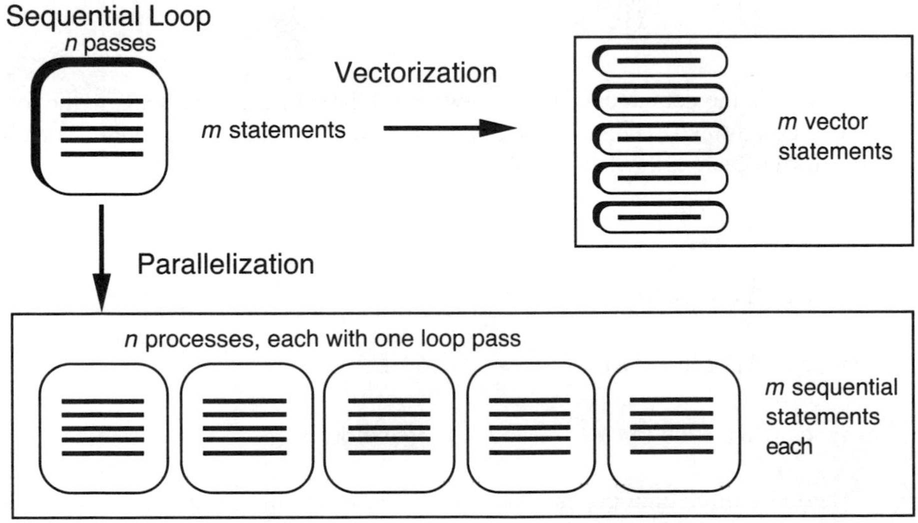

Figure 16.1 Parallelization and vectorization

In contrast to vectorizing a loop, in which an attempt is made to combine all of the occurrences of a statement in multiple passes through a loop into one vector statement, parallelizing a loop attempts to have each process (processor) execute the entire statement sequence of one pass through the loop. One can also interpret vectorization and parallelization as 'horizontal and vertical procedures' for work partitioning (see Figure 16.1).

Synchronization operations between processes may be required by the parallelization, depending on the data dependences. If, for example, a flow dependence exists between two loop passes (so this dependence now exists between two processes), then each process has to wait for the process executing the previous loop pass to generate the required data value. Such synchronization operations cause waiting time for the processes and reduce the performance of a parallel program.

However, only some of the data dependences have to be synchronized when parallelizing a loop. Since, in contrast to vectorizing a loop, the sequence of the statements inside a loop is maintained, the data dependences *within* one loop pass do *not* have to be considered. The following rules hold:

Parallelization Rules

a) Data dependences with direction '=' for the loop to be parallelized do not have to be synchronized.

b) Data dependences with direction '<' or '>' in *surrounding* loops (if any) do not have to be considered.

c) *Inner* loops (if any) do not have to be considered; they will be copied completely into the parallelized program code.

d) All other data dependences have to be synchronized between processes, each with its own array of semaphores.

e) For increasing efficiency, statement execution order inside the loop may be changed, but is restricted by existing data dependences:

If there exists a data dependence $S_x\ \delta^*_{(=)}\ S_y$ inside the loop, statement S_x has to *precede* statement S_y in the parallelized code.

Example of a):

```
  for i:=1 to n do
S1: A[i]:= C[i];
S2: B[i]:= A[i];
  end;
```

There is only one data dependence: $S_1\ \delta_{(=)}\ S_2$ (due to `A[i]`).

It occurs in the *same* loop iteration, so it will be executed by the *same* process after parallelization. Therefore, no synchronization is necessary. The parallel construct `doacross` assigns each loop iteration to a different process (ideally on a processor of its own). The parallelized loop is as follows:

```
    doacross i:=1 to n do
S1:   A[i]:= C[i];
S2:   B[i]:= A[i];
    enddoacross;
```

Example of b):

```
    for i:=1 to n do
      for j:=1 to m do
S1:     A[i,j]:= C[i,j];
S2:     B[i,j]:= A[i-1,j-1];
      end;
    end;
```

There is one data dependence: $S_1\ \delta_{(<,<)}\ S_2$ (due to `A[i,j]`).

It occurs between two iterations of the outer loop (dependence direction '<'). No synchronization is necessary, if *only the inner loop* is to be parallelized.

Parallelized loop:

```
    for i:=1 to n do
      doacross j:=1 to m do
S1:     A[i,j]:= C[i,j];
S2:     B[i,j]:= A[i-1,j-1];
      enddoacross;
    end;
```

Example of c):

The outer loop is to be parallelized:

```
    for i:=1 to n do
      for j:=1 to n do
S1:     A[i,j]:= B[i,j];
S2:     B[i,j]:= A[i,j-1];
      end;
    end;
```

Determination of all Data Dependences:

$S_1\ \delta_{(=,<)}\ S_2$ (due to A)

$S_1\ \bar{\delta}_{(=,=)}\ S_2$ (due to B)

$\Rightarrow$ no synchronization requirements

If the *outer* loop is to be parallelized, the two data dependences do not have to be synchronized according to the above rule, part a), since the direction is '=', or in the same loop pass. This means that a direct parallelization using a **doacross** can take place. In this case, the outer loop will be distributed to individual processes, while the inner loop will be performed sequentially by each individual process. A parallelization of the inner loop is not possible without more work, because of the data dependence direction '<' (second index of data dependence due to A). The parallelization of the outer loop in pseudo-notation is:

```
doacross i:=1 to n do
    for j:=1 to n do
S1:     A[i,j]:= B[i,j];
S2:     B[i,j]:= A[i,j-1];
    end;
enddoacross;
```

<u>Example of d) and e):</u>
(based on Wolfe in [Hwang, DeGroot 89])

```
for i:= 1 to n do
 S1: A[i] := B[i] + C[i];
 S2: D[i] := A[i] + E[i-1];
 S3: E[i] := E[i] + 2 * B[i];
 S4: F[i] := E[i] + 1;
end;
```

Determination of all data dependences provides the following result:

$S_1\ \delta_{=)}\ S_2$ (due to A[i])

$S_3\ \delta_{=)}\ S_4$ (due to E[i])

$S_3\ \delta_{<)}\ S_2$ (due to E[i])

The first two dependences have the '=' direction and therefore need not be synchronized. However, they specify that statement S_1 has to be executed before S_2 and S_3 has to be executed before S_4. For now, this is not relevant, since the original statement ordering of the sequential program will be retained.

Since the last data dependence exists between two loop passes, that is, between two processes, it has to be synchronized. This is shown by the data dependence direction '<'. For example, for two statement instances the following data dependence holds:

$S_3{}^4 \ \delta \ S_2{}^5$ (due to `E[4]`, and for the loop indices 4 < 5)

In pass (`i=4`), S_3 writes a value to `E[4]` and in pass (`i=5`), S_2 reads the value of `E[4]`. For this reason, statement S_2 in each loop pass (process) can only be executed after statement S_3 of the preceding loop pass (process) is finished. This leads to the following parallel program:

Parallelization of a Loop with Synchronization

```
var sync: array [1..n] of semaphore[0];

doacross i := 1 to n do
 S1: a[i] := b[i] + c[i];
     if i>1 then P(sync[i-1]) end;
 S2: d[i] := a[i] + e[i-1];

 S3: e[i] := e[i] + 2 * b[i];
     V(sync[i]);
 S4: f[i] := e[i] + 1;
enddoacross;
```

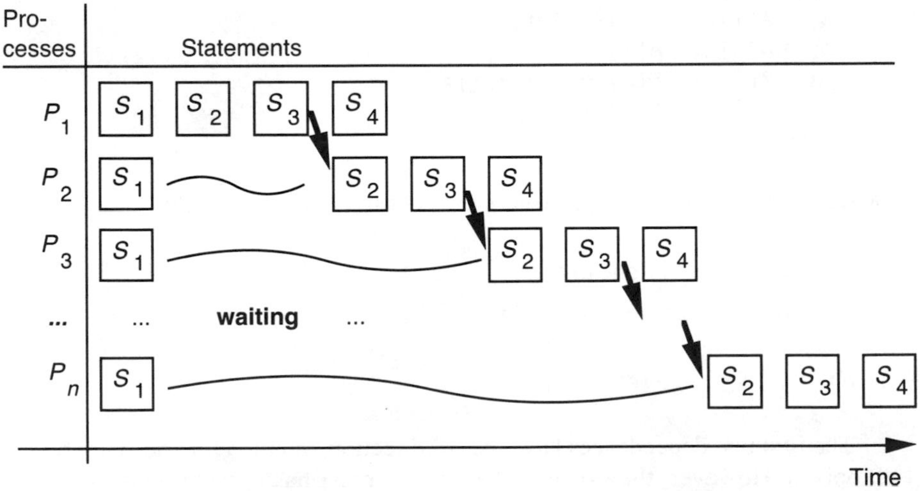

Figure 16.2 Parallelization without optimization

The processes (or possibly processors, when enough of them are available) are synchronized pair-wise, each pair with one semaphore. This is initialized to zero and must first be released by the preceding process with a V operation, before the process with the next loop pass can carry out its P operation (except for the first process). For example, process number 2 can execute its statement S_1 in parallel to all the other processes. After this, however, it has to wait in its P operation for the corresponding V operation of another process on the semaphore `sync[1]`. This V operation on `sync[1]` is carried out by process number 1 only after it has executed statements S_1, S_2 and S_3. A large time delay develops in that this waiting is chained through all of the processes. As shown in Figure 16.2, this causes a large loss of efficiency in the parallelization.

More Efficient Parallelization of a Loop
(according to rule e))

```
var sync: array [1..n] of semaphore[0];

doacross i:=1 to n do
 S3:  e[i] := e[i] + 2 * b[i];
      V(sync[i]);
 S1:  a[i] := b[i] + c[i];
 S4:  f[i] := e[i] + 1;
      if i>1 then P(sync[i-1]) end;
 S2:  d[i] := a[i] + e[i-1]
enddoacross;
```

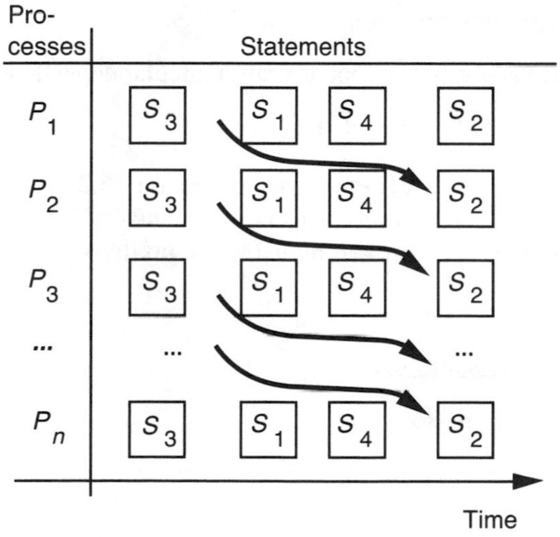

Figure 16.3 Optimized parallelization

A substantially more efficient parallelization can be achieved by reordering the statements within a loop pass while maintaining the requirements of the data dependences within the loop pass (direction '='). In this process, one always tries to place the V operation *before* the P operation in the loop pass, and in addition, one should attempt to achieve the *maximum distance* between the V and P operations (the V operation should occur as early as possible and the P operation as late as possible). The following solution achieves the maximum distance that meets the data dependence boundary conditions on the statement sequence: S_1 before S_2 and S_3 before S_4.

In this solution, the V operation is carried out after the first statement. Then every process can execute two more statements independent of the other processes, before it has to wait on its preceding process in the P operation. Since the V operation occurs before the P operation in each loop pass, the preceding process has normally already executed the required V operation before the following process (with the next loop pass) gets to its P operation. In this way, the synchronization delays (except for the cost of executing the P and V operations themselves) can be eliminated completely. Figure 16.3 shows the considerably improved run-time behaviour of the optimized parallel solution.

16.4 Solving Complex Data Dependences

The methods for vectorization and parallelization shown so far may fail because of complex data dependences. Three simple methods will be shown here to help in vectorization or parallelization of loops.

Circular Data Dependences

If the data dependence analysis of a loop reveals a circular dependence, for example:

$$S_1 \text{ before } S_2,\ S_2 \text{ before } S_3,\ S_3 \text{ before } S_1$$

then the procedure for **vectorization** shown in Section 16.2 cannot be applied, since the statements may not be reordered properly. For anti- or output dependences, this data dependence chain may be broken by using an auxiliary variable. This method is known as 'node splitting'.

Example with Circular Dependence:

```
     for i:=1 to n do
S1:   A[i]:= B[i];
S2:   B[i]:= A[i+1];
     end;
```

The data dependences are:

$S_2 \, \bar{\delta}_{(<)} \, S_1$ (due to `A`) $\Rightarrow$ S_2 before S_1

$S_1 \, \bar{\delta}_{(=)} \, S_2$ (due to `B`) $\Rightarrow$ S_1 before S_2

Thus a circular dependence exists. In this case, the dependence can be broken by using an auxiliary variable. The contents of one of the vector variables (in this case `B`) are first saved in the auxiliary variable, and then this variable can be overwritten, eliminating the previous data dependence.

```
     for i:=1 to n do
SA:   Aux[i]:= B[i];
S1:   A[i]  := Aux[i];
S2:   B[i]  := A[i+1];
     end;
```

The *new* data dependences are:

$S_A \, \delta_{(=)} \, S_1$ (due to `Aux`) $\Rightarrow$ S_A before S_1

$S_A \, \bar{\delta}_{(=)} \, S_2$ (due to `B`) $\Rightarrow$ S_A before S_2

$S_2 \, \bar{\delta}_{(<)} \, S_1$ (due to `A`) $\Rightarrow$ S_2 before S_1

Vectorization is now possible:

```
SA:   Aux(1:N)  = B(1:N);
S2:   B(1:N)    = A(2:N+1);
S1:   A(1:N)    = Aux(1:N);
```

Loop Interchanging

For vectorizing a nested loop, the *inner* loop (or several inner loops, up to *all* loops) has to be chosen, while for parallelization normally the *outer* loop is selected. The vectorized program (SIMD) then contains inside the original outer loop a number of vector statements. The parallelized program (MIMD), however, has a `doacross` statement instead of the outer loop, while the inner loop is identically contained in each process as a sequential loop.

If solvable data dependences exist for the outer loop, but unsolvable dependences exist for the inner loop, then a vectorization cannot be performed (or vice versa for parallelization). This problem may be solved by interchanging the loops, that is, exchanging the inner and outer loops. This method is applicable if no data dependence of direction (<,>) exists, which is a dependence of direction '<' in the outer and of direction '>' in the inner loop.

Loop interchanging should also be applied if it helps to generate more efficient parallel code. For two nested loops, imagine the outer loop having 1000 iterations but the inner loop having only 10. When generating vectorized code for a SIMD computer with 1000 PEs, it is much more efficient to vectorize the outer loop with 1000 operations (full PE load) than the inner loop with 10 operations (in this case 990 PEs, or 99% of the computation performance, would be inactive).

<u>Example of Loop Interchanging:</u>

(adapted from Wolfe in [Hwang, DeGroot 89])

```
     for i:=1 to n do
      for j:=1 to n do
S1:    A[i,j]:= A[i,j-1] + A[i,j+1];
      end; (* j *)
     end; (* i *)
```

The data dependences are:

$S_1 \; \delta_{=,<)} \; S_1$ (due to `A[i,j-1]`) $\Rightarrow$ S_1 before S_1

$S_1 \; \bar{\delta}_{=,<)} \; S_1$ (due to `A[i,j+1]`) $\Rightarrow$ S_1 before S_1

Due to this data dependence, the inner loop may not be vectorized. However, since no dependence of direction (<,>) exists, the loops may be interchanged.

```
     for j:=1 to n do
      for i:=1 to n do
S1:    A[i,j]:= A[i,j-1] + A[i,j+1];
      end; (* i *)
     end; (* j *)
```

The changed program has the following data dependences:

$S_1 \; \delta_{<,=)} \; S_1$ (due to `A[i,j-1]`)
$S_1 \; \bar{\delta}_{<,=)} \; S_1$ (due to `A[i,j+1]`)
$\Rightarrow$ no restriction, since surrounding loop has direction '<'

The inner loop may now be vectorized without synchronization, since the dependence extends only over the index of the outer loop, which will not be altered. The vectorized program in Fortran 90 looks as follows:

```
do j=1,n
  A(1:n,j) = A(1:n,j-1) + A(1:n,j+1)
end do
```

If the loop bounds of the inner loop use the index variable of the outer loop, then these bounds have to be adjusted for loop interchanging. In cases where the inner loop index has a non-linear dependence on the outer loop index, loop interchanging may be impossible (see [Wolfe 86]).

Example of Loop Interchanging with Interdependent Bounds:

```
     for i:=1 to n do
      for j:=1 to i do
S1:    A[i,j]:= A[j,i];
      end; (* j *)
     end; (* i *)
```

The index range of the inner loop `j` depends on the value of the outer index `i`. All loop bounds have to be adjusted properly for loop interchanging.

```
     for j:=1 to n do
      for i:=j to n do
S1:    A[i,j]:= A[j,i];
      end; (* j *)
     end; (* i *)
```

The new outer loop (index `j`) now extends over the full range from `1` to `n`, while the new inner loop (index `i`) ranges only from `j` to `n`. Figure 16.4 illustrates the changes. The vectorized program is as follows:

```
do j=1,n
  A(j:n,j) = A(j,j:n);
end do
```

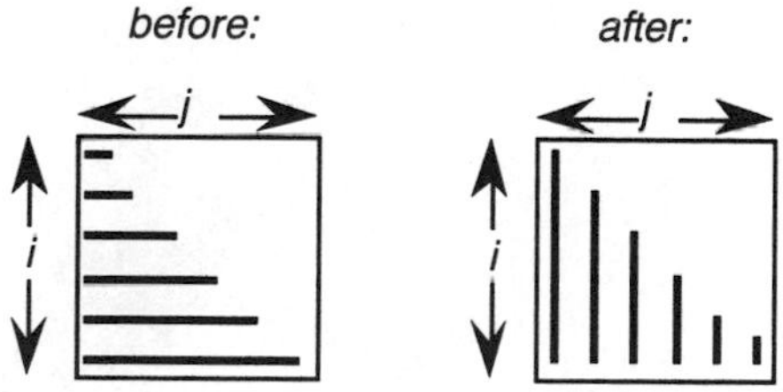

Figure 16.4 Adjusting loop indices

Complex Data Dependences

There are a number of cases where these simple methods for vectorization and parallelization are not applicable. The following vectorization example shows a loop with double indexed access:

```
    for i:= 1 to n do
S1: A[C[i]] := B[i]
    end;
```

Here, the data dependence $S_1\ \delta^{\circ}{}_{(<)}\ S_1$ (due to `A[C[i]]`) occurs.

This is due to the fact that without knowledge of the contents of `C[i]`, one has to take the possibility into account that the same array element `A[x]` will be assigned data more than once. A solution of this conflict is therefore not possible.

Another problem, easier to solve, is data dependence within the same statement:

```
    for i:= 1 to n do
S1: A[i] := A[i+1]
    end;
```

Here, the data dependence $S_1\bar{\delta}\ _{<)}\ S_1$ (due to `A`) occurs.

For parallelization, a synchronization with semaphores between processes is required. However, for vectorization this is no dependence at all, because the code generated for evaluating the right-hand side is executed before the assignment operation:

```
S1: A(1:n) = A(2:n+1)
```

One should not overlook, however, that this Fortran 90 expression contains an implicit data exchange operation (which might be expensive). Since for SIMD systems, vector data is stored component-wise on the PEs, a vector assignment with different index ranges corresponds to a data exchange between PEs (in this case from PE `i+1` to PE `i`). All PEs propagate the value of their local variable `A` to their left neighbors.

CHAPTER 17

Non-Procedural Parallel Programming Languages

Beside the procedural, *imperative* programming languages, the non-procedural, *declarative* programming languages have recently gained importance. Some parallel functional and parallel logic programming languages are presented in this chapter. The functional language Lisp was introduced in 1962 by McCarthy and is one of the oldest programming languages. So non-procedural programming languages are nothing really new.

Non-procedural programming languages exhibit a higher level of abstraction than procedural languages. So here, a distinction between sequential and parallel languages is often inappropriate. Languages like FP or APL do not need explicit parallel language constructs to describe parallel problems or to be efficiently parallelized. The parallelism is entirely hidden from the user in these languages. Due to the languages' declarative character, the management of the parallelism can be resolved transparently by the system. The database query language SQL can also be regarded as such an implicitly parallel non-procedural programming language.

Automatic parallelization/vectorization is much easier for *functional* programs with implicit parallelism than for sequential *procedural* programs (see Chapter 16). Nevertheless, there are a number of *parallel* functional languages with explicit parallel constructs. For example, imperative constructs for data parallelism from C* have been embedded in *Lisp. Other methods have been chosen for some modern parallel functional programming languages. For example, in the 'para-functional' language Haskell ([Hudak, Wadler 90] and [Szymanski 91]), code annotations are introduced for scheduling program parts to be executed in parallel.

Concurrent Prolog is presented as a representative of parallel logic programming. There are only minor differences between it and the languages Parlog, Strand, and GHC. Other prominent non-procedural approaches include the data flow language ID ([Nikhil 88] and [Szymanski 91]) and the logic (or *specification*) language Unity ([Chandy, Misra 88] and [Kurfess 91]), which is not based on Prolog. However, these languages will not be discussed further.

17.1 *Lisp

Developed by: Thinking Machines Corporation, 1986
'Star-Lisp' was developed by Thinking Machines Co. as the second parallel dialect of Lisp for the Connection Machine CM-2 SIMD computer system [Thinking Machines 86]. *Lisp has only a few similarities with CMLisp (Connection Machine Lisp), which is the original language for this computer family and was developed by Hillis [Hillis 85], [Steele, Hillis 86]. CMLisp uses many additional constructs, types and abstract mappings, which are similar to APL and are often difficult to understand. Another dialect is Paralation Lisp, developed by Sabot [Sabot 88]. Groups of virtual PEs may be declared ('paralations') and executed element-wise in parallel; data exchange is handled via different mappings. CMLisp and Paralation Lisp will not be discussed further here. *Lisp, contrary to the other parallel Lisp dialects, has the same simple parallel constructs found in C*, but embedded in the Lisp environment. The base language of *Lisp is Common Lisp.

Parallel Language Constructs

- Parallel system functions have the prefix '`*`'.
  A number of system functions exist in both a scalar and a vector version.

  Example:

`(*defvar a)`	declaration of a parallel vector

- Parallel operations have the suffix '`!!`'.
  A number of operators exist in both a scalar and a vector version.

  Example:

`(+!! a b)`	addition of two vectors
`(*!! a b)`	multiplication of two vectors
`(!! 2)`	vector constant (with identical components)
`(+!! a (!! 2))`	addition of a vector variable and a vector constant

  A comprehensible and elegant parallel programming is made possible by simply extending the well-known system functions and operators vector arguments.

- The definition of groups and the selection of general processor structures are possible using the `def-vp-set` ('define virtual processor set') and `create-geometry` functions, respectively. *Virtual processors* are supported in this manner. *N*-dimensional blocks of PEs can be defined with these functions, which correspond to the local grid ('NEWS') on the Connection Machine CM-2. The following declaration creates a three-dimensional grid called `cube` with 50 × 50 × 50 PEs:

  ```
  (def-vp-set cube '(50 50 50))
  ```

- The individual PEs can obtain their own identification numbers with each of the following functions:

`self!!`	returns an address object comprising all grid dimensions declared.
`(self-address-grid!! (!! p))`	returns an address object that comprises only the pth grid dimension.
`self-address!!`	returns the 'send address' of each PE. This in general differs from the grid address, even for one-dimensional grids.

- Corresponding to the hardware structure of the CM-2, there are two constructs for exchanging data between the PEs:

a) For local data transfer via the fast grid structure:

`*news`	performs a local data exchange along the grid structure between the source expression and destination variable.
`news!!`	returns the 'locally shifted' (or rotated) data of the source expression.
`news-border!!`	data exchange like `news!!`, in addition data references off the grid may be satisfied by using a vector parameter with 'border data'.
`*news-direction`	like `*news`, but only along a *single* grid direction (dimension).
`news-direction!!`	like `news!!`, but only along a *single* grid direction (dimension).

Example: `(news!! source 1 2)`
returns the data of vector `source` shifted by one position to the left and two positions up.

b) For global (universal) data transfer via the slower hypercube:

`*pset`	performs a global data exchange between the source expression and destination variable.
`pref!!`	returns 'globally exchanged' data of the source expression.

Example: `(pref!! source address)`
performs a data exchange (permutation) of vector `source` according to address vector `address`.

- Reduction of vectors to scalars is accomplished with standard functions:

  ```
  *and     *or      *xor     *logand  *logior  *logxor
  *sum     *min     *max     *integer-length
  ```

  These cover a number of arithmetic and boolean operations (the `log` operators carry out logic operations on integer data). However, multiplication is not supported, due to a limitation of the Connection Machine CM-2 system structure. The operation `*integer-length` determines the minimum bit-length required to represent every value of the given vector. A reduction with user defined reduction operations is possible as well in *Lisp.

- A boolean value from each of the physical PEs can be displayed on the LEDs (light emitting diodes) on the front panel of the Connection Machine CM-2 using the `*light` function.

The parallel language constructs from *Lisp are to a high degree equivalent to those in C*. One specific advantage of *Lisp is the availability of a simulator based on Common-Lisp, which allows the execution of parallel programs on sequential computers. A problem with *Lisp is the tremendous number of parallel operations, with their additional parameters. Only the most important features are presented in this section.

<u>Dot product in *Lisp:</u>

a) Using the general reduction function

```
(*defun d_prod (a b)
     (reduce!! #'+!! (*!! a b )))
```

b) Abbreviated with the standard function for summation

```
(*defun d_prod (a b)
     (*sum (*!! a b )))
```

<u>Laplace Operator in *Lisp:</u>

```
(def-vp-set grid '(100 100))
(*defvar pixel)
...
(*with-vp-set grid
  (*set pixel (-!! (*!! pixel (!! 4))
                   (news!! pixel  0  1)
                   (news!! pixel  0 -1)
                   (news!! pixel  1  0)
                   (news!! pixel -1  0) )
))
```

The communication is carried out here with the fast but machine-dependent grid communication routines. The `news!!` commands read data from a vector using a *relative* index (here –1, 0 or +1), so absolute address calculations are not required.

17.2 FP

Developed by: John Backus, 1978
FP is a purely functional programming language developed by Backus [Backus 78] and has many similarities with the language APL [Iverson 62]. The fundamental components of a universal 'FP system' are defined as follows:

1. An object domain
   (e.g. integers, reals, character, strings)
   Every object is either an atom (elementary object) or a list of objects (enclosed in angle brackets, separated by commas).

2. A set of primitive functions
   (e.g. arithmetic operations +, –, *, /)
   A call to a function is made by placing a colon between the function name and the argument (which may be an atom or a list of objects).

3. A set of program construction operations
   'program forming operations' (PFOs)
   (e.g. element-by-element application of a function to a list, sequential execution, reduction)

An FP language arises from filling-in concrete values for these three fundamental components, as in the following (based on [Eisenbach 87]):

Object domain comprises

Integer numbers, rational numbers (real), characters and strings, as well as the symbol ⊥ for 'undefined' (e.g. for incorrect application of a function, such as division by zero). The atoms `T` and `F` are interpreted as the boolean values 'true' and 'false'.

<u>Examples of atoms:</u> `10, -5.25, c, T, hello, ⊥`

<u>Examples of lists:</u> `<1, 2, 3>, <<1,2>, <a,b>, <c,1>>, <>`
(simple list, nested list, and empty list)

Primitive functions available

i) Arithmetic operations: +, -, *, / (only defined on numbers)

Examples: +:<1,2> = 3
*:<2,hello> = ⊥

ii) Comparison operations:
eq, ne, gt, ge, lt, le (only defined on numbers)
(equal, not equal, greater than, greater or equal, less than, less or equal)

Examples: eq:<1,1> = T
gt:<1,2> = F

iii) Boolean operations: and, or, not

Examples: and:<T,F> = F
not:F = T

iv) Check whether a list is empty: null

Definition: $$\texttt{null:x} = \begin{cases} \texttt{T} & \text{if } \texttt{x} = \langle\rangle \\ \texttt{F} & \text{if } \texttt{x} = \langle x_1, \ldots, x_n \rangle \text{ with } n \geq 1 \\ \bot & \text{otherwise} \end{cases}$$

Example: null:<2,3> = F

v) Determining the length of a list: len

Definition: $$\texttt{len:x} = \begin{cases} 0 & \text{if } \texttt{x} = \langle\rangle \\ n & \text{if } \texttt{x} = \langle x_1, \ldots, x_n \rangle \text{ with } n \geq 1 \\ \bot & \text{otherwise} \end{cases}$$

Example: len:<2,3> = 2

vi) Appending to a list: al, ar (append left, append right)

Definition: al:<y,<>> = <y>
al:<y, <z_1,...,z_m>> = <y,z_1,...,z_m>

ar:<<>,y> = <y>
ar:<<z_1,...,z_m>, y> = <z_1,...,z_m,y>

Example: al:<5,<7,4,7>> = <5,7,4,7>

vii) Selecting an element of a list: 1l,2l,3l,..., 1r,2r,3r,...
(Selecting the *i*-th element from left or right, respectively)

Examples: 1l:<10,11,12> = 10
1r:<10,11,12> = 12
4l:<10,11,12> = ⊥

viii) Cutting a list: `1f,2f,3f,...,` `1b,2b,3b,...` (front, back)
(Eliminating the leading or trailing *i* elements of a list)

Examples:
```
1f:<10,11,12> = <11,12>
2b:<10,11,12> = <10>
4f:<10,11,12> = ⊥
```

ix) Identity: `id`

Definition: `id:x = x`

Example:
```
id:<2,3> = <2,3>
```

x) Transposition of a matrix: `trans`

Definition:

```
trans:<<>,...,<>> = <>
```

$$\texttt{trans:}\langle\langle x_{11},\ldots,x_{1n}\rangle,\ \langle x_{21},\ldots,x_{2n}\rangle,\ \ldots,\ \langle x_{m1},\ldots,x_{mn}\rangle\rangle\ =$$
$$\langle\langle x_{11},\ldots,x_{m1}\rangle,\ \langle x_{12},\ldots,x_{m2}\rangle,\ \ldots,\ \langle x_{1n},\ldots,x_{mn}\rangle\rangle$$

Example:
```
trans:<<a,b>,<c,d>,<e,f>> = <<a,c,e>,<b,d,f>>
```

xi) Distribution of an object over a vector: `distl, distr`
(distribute left, distribute right)

Definition:

```
distl:<x,<>> = <>
```

$$\texttt{distl:}\langle x,\ \langle z_1,\ldots,z_m\rangle\rangle = \langle\langle x,z_1\rangle,\ldots,\langle x,z_m\rangle\rangle$$

```
distr:<<>,x> = <>
```

$$\texttt{distr:}\langle\langle z_1,\ldots,z_m\rangle,x\rangle = \langle\langle z_1,x\rangle,\ldots,\langle z_m,x\rangle\rangle$$

Example:
```
distl:<1,<1,2,3>> = <<1,1>,<1,2>,<1,3>>
```

xii) Generation of a list of consecutive integers (starting with one): `iota`

Examples:
```
iota:0 = <>
iota:5 = <1,2,3,4,5>
```

Program formation operations available

i) Composition (sequential execution):
```
(f ° g):x  =  f:(g:x)
```

Example:
```
(not ° and):<F,T>
        = not:(and:<F,T>)
        = not:F = T
```

ii) Condition:

$$(p \rightarrow f;\ g):x = \begin{cases} f:x & \text{if } p:x = T \\ g:x & \text{if } p:x = F \\ \bot & \text{otherwise} \end{cases}$$

Example: `(eq → +; -):<5,3>  =  -:<5,3> = 2`

iii) Construction (synchronous parallel execution):
$[f_1,\ f_2,\dots,\ f_m]:x \;=\; \langle f_1:x,\ f_2:x,\dots,\ f_m:x\rangle$

Example: `[+,*]:<1,2>  =  <+:<1,2>, *:<1,2>> = <3,2>`

iv) Apply to all (synchronous parallel execution):
$\alpha f:\langle x_1,\dots,x_m\rangle \;=\; \langle f:x_1,\dots,f:x_m\rangle$

Example: `α+:<<1,2>,<3,4>,<5,6>>`
`= <+:<1,2>, +:<3,4>, +:<5,6>> = <3,7,11>`

v) Reduction (insert left and insert right):

$$/f:x = \begin{cases} z & \text{if } x = \langle z\rangle \\ f:\langle z_1, /f:\langle z_2,\dots,z_m\rangle\rangle & \text{if } x = \langle z_1,\dots,z_m\rangle\ m\geq 2 \\ \bot & \text{otherwise} \end{cases}$$

$$\backslash f:x = \begin{cases} z & \text{if } x = \langle z\rangle \\ f:\langle \backslash f:\langle z_1,\dots,z_{m-1}\rangle, z_m\rangle & \text{if } x = \langle z_1,\dots,z_m\rangle\ m\geq 2 \\ \bot & \text{otherwise} \end{cases}$$

Example: `/or:<F,T,F> = or:<F,/or:<T,F>>`
`= or:<F,or:<T,/or:<F>>> = or:<F,or:<T,F>>`
`= or:<F,T> = T`

vi) Constant operator (e.g. 𝟙, 𝟚, 𝟛, ...):

$$\mathbb{k}:x = \begin{cases} \bot & \text{if } x=\bot \\ k & \text{otherwise} \end{cases}$$

(let k be the constant indicated by 𝕜)
(the argument x is *not* used!)

Example: `𝟝:<1,2,3> = 5`

PFOs iii) and iv) correspond to the models for asynchronous (MIMD) and synchronous (SIMD) parallelism. It is therefore possible to translate FP programs into parallel programs for the corresponding computer architecture with a compiler. In doing so, various techniques can be used such as 'eager evaluation', meaning the immediate evaluation of sub-expressions whenever possible (data driven), or 'lazy evaluation', meaning the delay of the evaluation of an expression until the result is actually required (demand driven). In place of the reduction from left or right shown here, one could also produce a synchronous parallel version, which would reduce a list object of size *n* to an atom in only $\log_2 n$ steps. Using the available operations and functions, it is possible to write application programs by defining new functions. The definition construct **def** serves this purpose. As with the languages presented earlier, the implementation of the dot product operation is shown as an example (see [Eisenbach 87]).

<u>Dot product in FP:</u>

```
def  d_prod  =  (/+∘α*∘trans)

d_prod:<<1,2,3>,<4,5,6>>
   = (/+∘α*∘trans):<<1,2,3>,<4,5,6>>      definition d_prod
   = /+:(α*:(trans:<<1,2,3>,<4,5,6>>))    sequential steps
   = /+:(α*:<<1,4>,<2,5>,<3,6>>)          transposition
   = /+:<*:<1,4>,*:<2,5>,*:<3,6>>         synchronously parallel
   = /+:<4,10,18>                         parallel execution of '*'
   =  +:<4,/+:<10,18>>                    reduction 1st step
   =  +:<4,+:<10,/+:<18>>>                reduction 2
   =  +:<4,+:<10,18>>                     reduction 3 (single elem.)
   =  +:<4,28>                            reduction 4 with '+'
   =  32                                  reduction 5 with '+'
```

The function `d_prod` is expanded step by step and applied to the argument (a list) consisting of the two vectors. So the argument is a list of lists. The following operations are carried out from right to left according to the definition:

(1) Transposition of the two vectors, which means the creation of pairs, each having one element from the first vector and one element from the second vector

(2) Synchronously parallel multiplication of all of the element pairs

(3) Summation of the results from each pair (reduction)

The set of primitive functions for FP shown here is not minimal. Function `len`, for example, may also be expressed through other functions:

```
def  new_len  =  (null → 𝟘;  (/+∘α𝟙))
```

<u>Examples:</u>

```
new_len  :  <2,4,5>
         =  (null → 𝟘;  (/+∘α𝟙))  :  <2,4,5>
         =  (/+∘α𝟙)  :  <2,4,5>
         =  /+:<1,1,1>
         =  3
```

```
new_len : <>
        = (null → ⓪; (/+°α𝟙)) : <>
        = ⓪:<>
        = 0
```

17.3 Concurrent Prolog

Developed by: Ehud Shapiro, 1983
Concurrent Prolog was developed for parallel programming as an extension to the logic programming language Prolog [Shapiro 87]. Dialects such as Parlog, Strand, GHC (Guarded Horn Clauses), Flat Concurrent Prolog and others followed (see also in [Shapiro 87]). Since these parallel extensions to Prolog do not differ much conceptually, the following presentation is restricted to Concurrent Prolog.

Since logic programming occurs on a higher, declarative level than procedural, imperative programming, it is closer to implicit, parallel execution of a logic rule base. This means that explicit parallel language constructs are not required, instead only simple (implicit) synchronization mechanisms are necessary. The possible areas for applying parallel processing can be derived from the model of sequential Prolog, shown in Figure 17.1 .

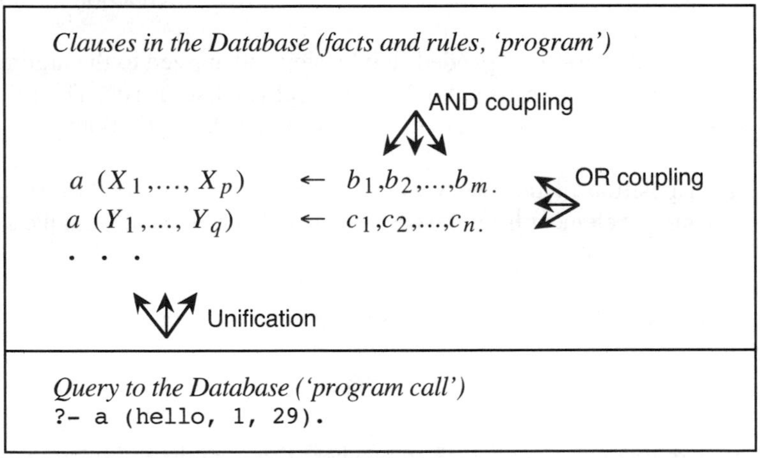

Figure 17.1 Applying parallelism in Prolog

Each of the three basic operations: AND coupling, OR coupling, and unification can be executed in parallel:

- Unification Parallelism
  Parallel matching of clause parameters can considerably reduce the time required for unification. The (top level) parameters can be processed in parallel, and

complex (structured) parameters can be processed recursively in parallel on multiple processors.

- OR Parallelism
  If multiple rules or facts are available for a clause, all alternatives can be searched in parallel. However, this is in conflict with the semantics of sequential Prolog, since the *first* matching rule is used there. The sequence of rules and facts in the database *does* carry a meaning in sequential Prolog.
  In cases where, as in sequential Prolog, only one and not all of the possible derivations (solutions) to a query to the database is needed, parallel processing of the OR variations requires in most cases an unnecessary amount of computation. This depends on the individual application program and the semantics defined for that parallel dialect of Prolog.

- AND Parallelism
  The clauses that appear in a rule (or a query) are coupled with the AND operator and can be evaluated in parallel if they are independent of each other. Independence means in this case that they contain no common, free variables. However, it is often the case that the subgoals (clauses) are dependent upon one another. In this case, the individual clauses can only be carried out partially in parallel and they have to be synchronized when free variables appear. This means that a clause may have to wait until another parallel clause places a value in this free variable.

As illustrated above, the definition of a parallel logic programming language is not without problems, as one might have assumed on this level of abstraction. The three areas of parallel logic processing discussed above rely *exclusively* on the MIMD model, because asynchronous sub-tasks with different control flows arise. The problems with parallel execution in Concurrent Prolog presented here do not allow a reliable statement on the efficiency of parallel application programs.

Parallel Language Constructs

There is a list of syntactical and semantical differences between the language definitions of Concurrent Prolog and sequential Prolog. Therefore it is not possible to execute sequential Prolog programs in Concurrent Prolog, or vice versa. Here, the clauses in a rule are divided into two groups, *guard* and *body*, which are separated by the *commit* '|' operator. Use of OR parallelism is restricted to the guards. The first successfully completed guard carries out the commit operation, and stops all of the other OR-parallel processes. The body of a rule is then processed AND-parallel to the extent allowed by the synchronization of the interdependent clauses. Explicit language constructs for unification parallelism are not provided, since they are not necessary for parallelization.

$$\underset{goal}{A} \;\leftarrow\; \underset{guards}{G_1 \ldots G_m} \;\; \underset{commit}{\mid} \;\; \underset{body}{B_1 \ldots B_n} . \qquad (m,n \geq 0)$$

- All of the OR alternatives are processed in parallel, until for one of them all of its guards are evaluated to 'true'. Only this first OR alternative is considered further ('commit'), while all others are discarded.
  → OR Parallelism,
  restricted to the guard clauses; all computation time for unused OR alternatives is wasted.

- All of the AND-coupled clauses are executed in parallel; even the interdependent clauses, which have to be synchronized (see next point).
  → AND Parallelism,
  restricted to body clauses; execution is asynchronously parallel.

- Synchronization of body clauses executed in AND-parallel mode is handled through so-called 'read-only' variables, which are indicated by a question-mark suffix, for example: `x?`
  A process which reads an uninstantiated 'read-only' variable (in Prolog: `var(X)`), is blocked until this synchronization variable is assigned a value by another clause process.

Logic programmers like to write interpreters for (parallel) Prolog extensions in sequential Prolog itself for the purposes of testing and simulation. This is shown in Shapiro's definition of the simple 'three line meta-interpreter' (see below). It is called, for example:

```
?- solve( my_task(X) ).
```

Implementation on a real parallel computer system must, however, be done on a lower level.

<u>Three Line Meta-Interpreter:</u>

```
1) solve(true)          :- !.
2) solve((Goal,Rest))   :- solve(Goal), solve(Rest).
3) solve(Head)          :- clause(Head, Body), solve(Body).
```

(1) Goal `true` is immediately fulfilled.

(2) If multiple goals are connected with AND (comma in Prolog), then these must be processed one after the other (tail recursion over variable `Rest`).

(3) In order to solve a goal, different clauses (rules or facts) that match `Head` are searched for in the database through backtracking. The meta-interpreter `solve` is recursively applied to the body of every matching rule.

This meta-interpreter can be incrementally extended and adapted to the syntax and semantics of the new Prolog dialect. The following extended unification rule with 'read-only' variables is an excerpt from [Shapiro 83].

```
1) unify (X , Y ) :- ( var(X); var(Y) ), !, X=Y.
2) unify (X?, Y ) :- !, nonvar(X), unify(X,Y).
3) unify (X , Y?) :- !, nonvar(Y), unify(X,Y).

4) unify ([X|Xs], [Y|Ys]) :- !, unify(X,Y), unify(Xs,Ys).
5) unify ([]     , []     ) :- !.

6) unify (X , Y ) :- X=..[F|Xs], Y=..[F|Ys], unify(Xs,Ys).
```

(1) checks whether one of the two variables is uninstantiated, and if so carries out a regular unification with 'X=Y' after using the 'cut' operator to stop backtracking.

(2+3) handle the 'read-only' suffix '?' symmetrically. If the variable in question already has a value (`nonvar(X)`), then the unification is recursively called without the question mark, otherwise the unification fails ('cut'-operator). This, in conjunction with the meta-predicates not shown here, leads to a temporary blocking of the caller.

(4+5) handle the unification of lists, where a unification of both heads and both tails is carried out just as in sequential Prolog.

(6) covers structured parameters, by separating functors and parameters. The functors must be identical, while a recursive call to the unification routines is executed on the parameters.

Two sample programs in Concurrent Prolog follow to end this section. The Laplace operator is not shown here, because this is a typical SIMD problem, while Concurrent Prolog is a MIMD programming language.

<u>Addition of Tree Elements in Concurrent Prolog:</u>

Definition of a tree structure: `tree`(element, subtree_left, subtree_right)
Empty sub-trees are indicated with: `empty` .

Example of a tree (see Figure 17.2):

```
tree( 7,
        tree(3, tree(5,empty,empty), tree(2,empty,empty)),
        tree(9, empty, tree(6,empty,empty)) )
```

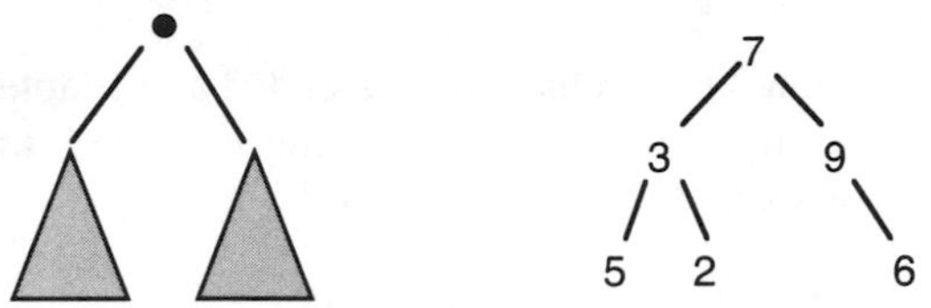

Figure 17.2 Tree representation and example in Prolog

```
add(empty,0).
add(tree(E,L,R), Sum) :-  add(L?, SL),
                          add(R?, SR),
                          Sum := E? + SL? + SR? .
```

Program Call:

```
?- add(tree(3, tree(5,empty,empty), tree(2,empty,empty)), S).
     ⇒ S = 10
```

The evaluation of the left and right sub-trees, as well as the addition of the partial results to the node element, are started as three parallel processes and are synchronized with common 'read-only' variables ('`?`'). The sub-trees `L` and `R` in the recursive call have a '`?`' in order to prevent an endless loop in the case of an uninstantiated call (`add(X,Y)`). When calculating the sum, all of the addends must already have a value, therefore the parent process must wait until the two processes summing the left and right sub-trees are done.

Dot product in Concurrent Prolog:

```
d_prod([],[],0) :- |.
d_prod([H1|T1],[H2|T2],X) :- |
       X := H1 * H2 + Rest?,
       d_prod(T1?, T2?, Rest).
```

Program Call:

```
?- d_prod([1 2 3], [4 5 6], SP).
     ⇒ SP = 32
```

The commit operator prevents the search for alternative clauses (restricting the OR parallelism), which, however, is not necessary in this case, since there are no multiple clauses with the same head. The two clauses in the rule (calculation and recursive call) are executed in parallel; however, the calculation must wait until the recursive call to the `d_prod` procedure has placed a value in the synchronization variable '`Rest?`'. Due to the recursive activation and return of results, this example program will not exhibit a large parallel speedup.

17.4 SQL

Developed by: Chamberlin and Boyce (IBM), 1974
The inclusion of the relational database language SQL ('structured query language', formerly SEQUEL [Chamberlin, Boyce 74]) among the parallel programming languages may seem somewhat unusual. However, SQL is a language with implicit parallelism, which can be exploited without requiring special language constructs, given an appropriate compiler and a distributed database system. In addition, multiple transactions from SQL programs of a large number of users are usually executed in parallel or time-sliced on one database. The compiler must therefore ensure data integrity of all transactions with appropriate locks ('semaphores'). SQL applications can either be used directly (interactively) on a database, or they can be embedded in a host programming language (e.g. Cobol or PL/I) as 'embedded SQL' (see [Date 86]).

A relational database is represented by a set of tables, in which each table contains either *entities* (objects) or *relationships* (relations between entities). Keys are defined in order to allow access to individual records of a table. One differentiates between the unique *primary key* and possibly several non-unique *secondary keys*.

Delving into all of the language constructs of SQL is not possible here. Therefore the strengths of SQL will only be briefly touched upon. In addition to the generation of tables and indices, there are four fundamental operations in SQL:

`SELECT`	Selection of a record, or a record field from a table
`UPDATE`	Alteration of a record, or a record field from a table
`DELETE`	Removal of a record from a table
`INSERT`	Addition of a record to a table

A typical SQL query in an employee database could look like the following:

```
SELECT NAME
FROM   EMPLOYEE
WHERE  SALARY > 10000
```

The search through a database can be executed implicitly in parallel. The results are the names of all entries in the employee table, whose salary field contains a number larger that 10,000. The output lists may be further arranged and sorted with the commands `GROUP` and `ORDER`, respectively.

The alteration of a table entry, for example in light of a salary increase, can be handled in the following way:

```
UPDATE EMPLOYEE
SET    SALARY = SALARY + 100
WHERE  SALARY < 2000
```

In this example, all of the 'lower income groups' (salary under 2,000) receive a raise. The update operations on possibly very many records can be executed in parallel without special language constructs (*implicit parallelism*).

The following SQL standard functions can be used in conjunction with the fundamental operations:

COUNT	Number of elements
SUM	Sum of all elements
AVG	Average of all elements
MAX	Maximum of all elements
MIN	Minimum of all elements

Probably the most powerful operations in SQL are the so-called *join queries*. These are queries in which various tables must be connected together in order to find the information requested. These queries may be computationally quite expensive, depending on the size of the tables involved, the type of access, and the presence (or lack) of indices. However, parallel processing can be used to particular advantage in this type of query. The following example shows a join over the employee table of a company and the membership table of a sports club. All persons belonging to the club and working for the company are selected (under the assumption that the name is a unique identification key, that is, the primary key):

```
SELECT EMPLOYEE.NAME
FROM   EMPLOYEE, MEMBER
WHERE  EMPLOYEE.NAME = MEMBER.NAME;
```

SQL is currently one of the most widely used database languages, while an increase in the application of parallel computer systems in the database sector is expected in the future. The use of SQL in a parallel or distributed database system means an increase in computing performance for the application programmer without having to deal with the details of the parallel implementation.

CHAPTER 18

Performance of Parallel Systems

Parallel computer systems are built for one reason in particular: high performance computation. The fact that the actual performance of a parallel system does not always agree with its theoretical performance data has been shown in the chapters on problems in parallel processing (see Chapters 8 and 13). Which class and what type of parallel computer system should be used, or whether the use of a parallel computer system makes sense at all, depends on the nature of the problem. Whether or not a reasonable speedup can be expected depends solely on the particular application.

With performance measures on a parallel computer system, one distinguishes between the speedup and the scaleup of a program (see [Reuter 92]). The *speedup* indicates how much faster the *same problem* can be computed on N processors, as compared to just a single processor. The *scaleup* indicates how much *larger problems* can be computed on N processors in the same time as the original problem on a single processor.

18.1 Speedup

As early as 1967, Amdahl employed performance considerations on parallel computer systems [Amdahl 67], which have become known as 'Amdahl's Law'. Here, the partitioning of a program into a sequential and a parallelizable part is the only parameter; the problem size always remains constant. This law is presented here in a simplified form.

Definitions for a Program of Fixed Size

P_C	Maximum Degree of Parallelization (of program A for parallel model C) Maximum number of processors, which may used in parallel at any time during the execution of program A. The model of parallelism used (e.g. synchronous or asynchronous parallelism) is also crucial.
T_k	Run time of program A with a maximum parallelization degree $P_C \geq k$ on a system with k processors.
N	Number of processors of the parallel computer system.
f	Sequential Part of the Program (of program A for parallel model C) Percentage of operations of a sequential program that **cannot** be carried out in parallel on k processors, but must instead be executed sequentially. *This simplification allows only program parts with parallelization degree 1 or N, but no intermediate values.*

Given the above definitions, the following equation holds for the run time of a parallel computer system with N processors:

$$T_N = f * T_1 + (1 - f) * \frac{T_1}{N}$$

Consequently, the speedup factor on N processors comes to:

$$S_N = \frac{T_1}{T_N} = \frac{N}{1 + f * (N-1)}$$

Since $0 \leq f \leq 1$ it follows that: $1 \leq S_N \leq N$.
So the speedup may not exceed the number of processors.

The efficiency is defined as a measure for the achieved speedup in relation to the maximum speedup N:

$$E_N = \frac{S_N}{N}$$

Consequently, the efficiency range is: $1/N \leq E_N \leq 1$. The efficiency is often given as a percentage. For example, if $E_N = 0.9$ then 90% of the maximum speedup is achieved.

Examples of the Application of Amdahl's Law:

a)
- The target computer has 1,000 processors
- The program has a maximum parallelization level of 1,000
- 0.1% of the program must be carried out sequentially (e.g. for input/output), therefore: $f = \frac{1}{1000}$

Calculating the speedup gives:

$$S_{1000} = \frac{1000}{1 + \frac{1000-1}{1000}} \approx \mathbf{500}$$

In this case, only half of the maximum possible speedup of 1,000 is achieved, in spite of a very small sequential code fraction. The efficiency comes to: $E_{1000} \approx 50\%$.

b)
- The target computer has 1,000 processors
- The program has a maximum parallelization level of 1,000
- 1% of the program must be carried out sequentially, therefore: $f = \frac{1}{100}$

Calculating the speedup gives:

$$S_{1000} = \frac{1000}{1 + \frac{1000-1}{100}} \approx \mathbf{91}$$

Only $E_{1000} \approx 9.1\%$ of the total processing capability is used here, and that with – at first glance – a still quite small sequential code fraction!

As the size of the sequential part of code in a MIMD program increases, the usage of the processors and with it the parallel speedup in comparison to a sequential system sink drastically. For a fixed sequential part of a program, the maximum possible speedup can be calculated independently of the number of processors used.

$$\lim_{N \to \infty} S_N(f) = \frac{N}{1 + f * (N-1)} = \frac{1}{f}$$

This indicates that a MIMD program with a 1% sequential part can never achieve a larger speedup than 100. This upper limit does not depend on whether 100, 1000, or 1 million processors are being used.

Figure 18.1 displays the dependence of the speedup of the number of processors N for different values of f, the sequential program part. The diagonal resembles linear speedup and may only be reached for $f = 0$. Figure 18.2 shows the dependence of the efficiency on N and f.

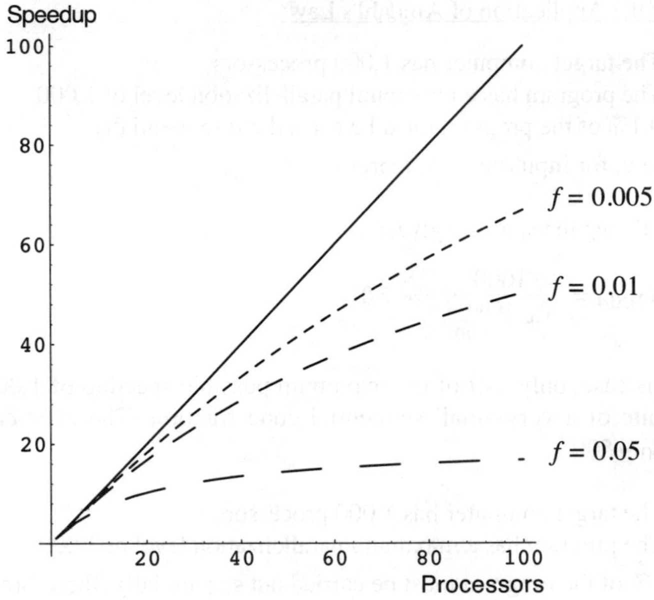

Figure 18.1 Speedup as a function of the number of processors

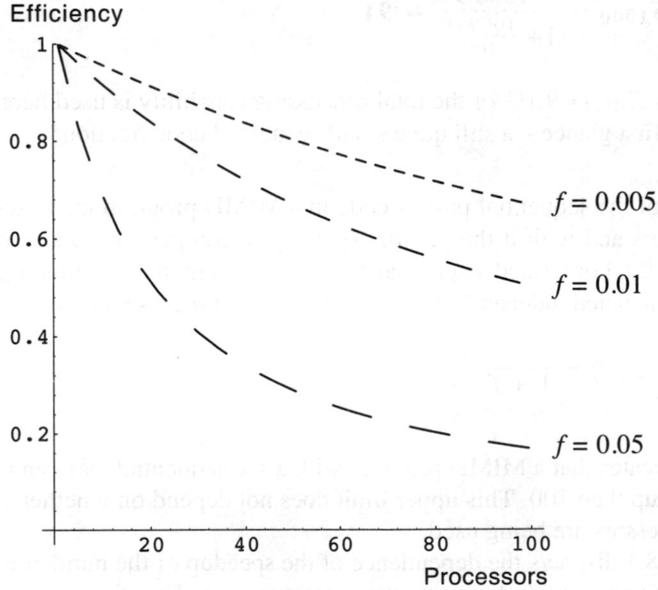

Figure 18.2 Efficiency as a function of the number of processors

18.2 Scaleup

As long as the same program is used for measurements, the factor f in Amdahl's law remains constant. However, one **cannot** assume that every parallel program, independent of its size, has to process a fixed minimum percentage of its statements sequentially. This means that the curves shown in Figures 18.1 and 18.2 no longer hold when the problem size changes! Actual measurements on a parallel computer system with a very large numbers of processors show the following [Gustafson 88]: as the problem to be solved becomes larger and thus the number of processors used increases, the relative sequential part (*not the absolute part!*) of the calculation very often becomes smaller. So high efficiency can indeed be achieved on a parallel computer with a large number of processors. So it looks promising to investigate the dependences that occur between scaled versions (versions of different 'problem size') of the same algorithm (e.g. larger data sets or higher precision calculation with more intermediate steps).

Definitions for Program Variants of Different Size

$T_k(m)$ Run time of a program with a problem size of m and a maximum parallelization degree of $P_C \geq k$ on k processors.

The scaleup of a problem of size n on k processors in comparison to a smaller problem of size m ($m<n$) on one processor is defined as follows:

If $T_1(m) = T_k(n)$ (the run time for the 'small' program on one processor is equal to the run time of the 'large' program on k processors)

then the scaleup amounts to:

$$SC_k = \frac{n}{m}$$

The scaleup curve may now be drawn in dependence of k, the number of processors. The value SC_k indicates how much larger a program may be computed on k processors in the same time as a problem of size '1' on just a single processor. The scaleup, like the speedup, always stays below the main diagonal:

$$SC_k \leq k$$

It should be noted that the run time depends on another parameter, which is not precisely defined as 'problem size'. This could, for example, be defined as the amount of data that is to be handled by the differently sized program variations of the *same* algorithm.

According to the application program, the scaleup curve may be linear or, for example, logarithmic. While local image operators have a linear scaleup (they are optimal, since they work on independent image areas), the scaleup curve for the seemingly nice summation of a vector of numbers (see reduction in Section 12.3) increases only logarithmically (see below).

<u>Example:</u> Scaling the Reduction

Assume a total of n time steps and p processors. During the initial $(n - \log_2 p)$ steps $(n+1 - \log_2 p)$ data values are added locally in each processor. The remaining $(\log_2 p)$ steps are used for adding the partial sums of all processors in a tree-like reduction.

1 PE in	5 time steps adds	6	numbers		SC_1	= 1 (by definition)
2 PEs in	5 time steps adds	10	numbers	⇒	SC_2	= 1.7
4 PEs in	5 time steps adds	16	numbers	⇒	SC_4	= 2.7
8 PEs in	5 time steps adds	24	numbers	⇒	SC_8	= 4.0
16 PEs in	5 time steps adds	32	numbers	⇒	SC_{16}	= 5.3

In general
(see curve in Figure 18.3):
1 PE in n time steps adds $n+1$ numbers
p PEs in n time steps add $(n+1 - \log_2 p) * p$ numbers, if $\log_2 p \leq n$

$$\Rightarrow SC_p = \frac{n+1 - \log_2 p}{n+1} * p$$

$$= p - \frac{p * \log_2 p}{n+1} \qquad \text{(where } n \text{ is a constant)}$$

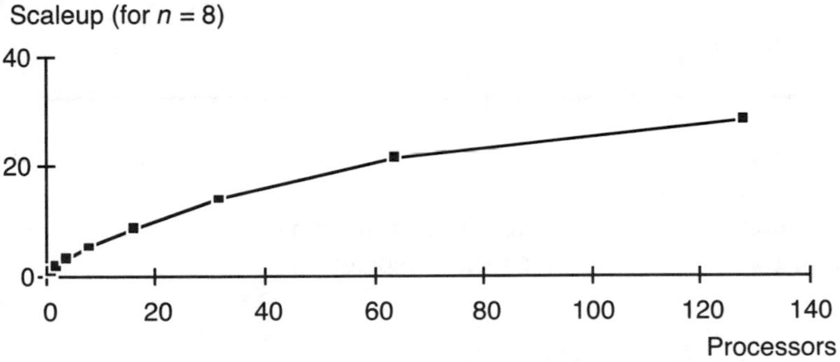

Figure 18.3 Scaleup for the reduction operation

As one can see in real-world parallel programs, larger numbers of processors are most often used to solve larger problems, instead of trying to solve the same problem faster. In this kind of situation, scaleup is more important than speedup.

18.3 MIMD versus SIMD

In the above theoretical deliberations about the performance of parallel systems there was no differentiation between MIMD and SIMD systems. Every program, however, has at least two different maximum degrees of parallelization: one for asynchronous parallel processing, P_{MIMD}, and one for synchronous parallel processing, P_{SIMD}. Due to the restrictions of synchronous parallel processing, it is always the case that $P_{\text{SIMD}} \leq P_{\text{MIMD}}$. Another point that is very important in practice is that MIMD systems can relatively easily allow the use of unused processors by other users, whereas unused processors on SIMD systems will remain idle. Therefore it is not a very good idea to use a SIMD system with, say, 16,384 processors to solve a problem that only needs 100 PEs! Due to the type of processing involved, SIMD systems usually have a considerable lower processor load than MIMD systems. Even a single `IF-THEN-ELSE` selection (with equal length branches) reduces the processor load on a SIMD system to 50%. In addition, the PEs in SIMD systems are usually much less powerful than those typically employed in MIMD systems. However, these disadvantages are usually balanced by the significantly larger number of processors employed in SIMD systems.

One quite often observes the phenomenon of MIMD systems being programmed in 'SIMD mode'. This means that the available independence of the individual processors is not needed. This occurs very often with problems that are distributed over a very large number of processors, also known as massive parallelism. Most problems that can be divided and assigned to 100, 1000 or more processors show a regular processing pattern in which a SIMD system would also suffice. This is an important argument for the SPMD model (same program, multiple data), which is a combination of SIMD and MIMD (see Section 2.1).

According to Amdahl's law, as shown earlier, efficiency sinks rapidly with the number of processors, but on the other hand a certain sequential program segment (for example, for input/output) is not avoidable. In this light, one could ask whether SIMD parallel computers with more than 65,000 processors can be fully exploited after all. As shown below, this is definitely the case. It is the *method of counting* instructions (see Figure 18.4) which can easily lead to false conclusions if Amdahl's law is improperly applied to SIMD programs.

While every elementary instruction is counted in MIMD program A in accordance with Amdahl's formula (resulting in factor f_A), both the scalar and the vector instructions in SIMD program B are treated as *a single instruction* (resulting in factor f_B). This is a natural definition, especially for SIMD systems, because every operation counted requires approximately the same amount of run time. Therefore, the following holds:

f_A indicates the sequential portion with respect to the *number of elementary operations* in a program and

f_B indicates the sequential portion with respect to the *run time of operations* of a program.

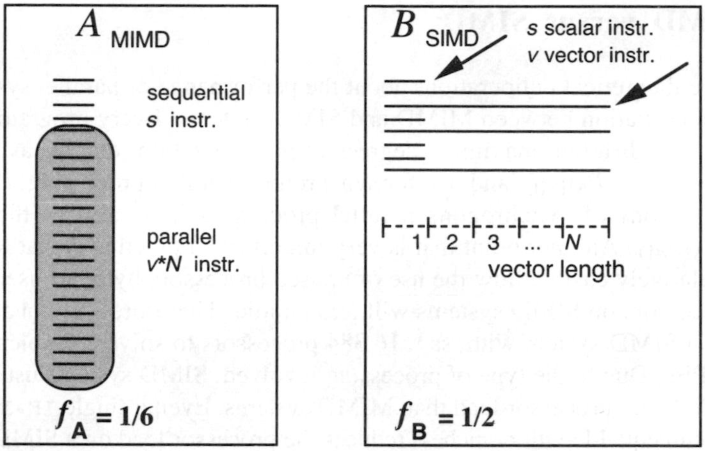

Figure 18.4 Counting methods for parallel instructions

In contrast to the fact that the SIMD example program in Figure 18.4 executes in parallel half of its run time ($f_B = 1/2$), the percentage of sequentially executed elementary instructions is considerably lower: $f_A = 1/6$. The following relationship between the two factors can be easily verified:

$$f_A = \frac{f_B}{N * (1 - f_B) + f_B}$$

In order to obtain exact values, one could use the percentage of active PEs for each *individual* SIMD instruction: this is always a value between zero (corresponding to a scalar operation on the control computer) and one (corresponding to participation of all PEs). The time-weighted sum of these percentages gives a finer measure of the usage of the parallel PEs by an application program than simply counting elementary instructions.

In order to determine the speedup of a (SIMD) parallel program, one can carry out a reverse calculation from T_N to T_1, corresponding to the question: 'How much time would a sequential computer require to process this parallel program?' (see [Bräunl 91a]).

Definition

f_B	Proportion of scalar instructions of a SIMD program with respect to the total number of instructions (scalar and vector), or identically: *proportion of run time used for sequential operations with respect to the total run time of a parallel program.*

The following reverse calculation holds for the sequential execution:

$$T_1 = f_B * T_N + (1-f_B) * N * T_N$$

Therefore the speedup factor of the parallel system with **fixed** ***N*** comes to:

$$S_N = \frac{T_1}{T_N} = f_B + (1-f_B) * N$$

Examples of the Application of the Modified Law:

a)
- The target computer has 1,000 processors
- The program has a maximum parallelization factor of 1,000
- 0.1% of the program (by the SIMD counting method) must be carried out sequentially, therefore: $f_B = \frac{1}{1000}$

Calculating the speedup gives:

$$S_{1000} = 0.1 + (1-0.001) * 1000 \approx \mathbf{1000}$$

The theoretically possible maximum speedup is almost reached ($E_{1000} \approx 100\%$). Of course, the same result would have emerged using Amdahl's formula with the appropriate f_A:

$$f_A = \frac{f_B}{N * (1-f_B) + f_B} = \frac{0.001}{1000 * (1 - 0.001) + 0.001} = \mathbf{10^{-6}}$$

Then, according to Amdahl:

$$S_{1000} = \frac{1000}{1 + 10^{-6} * (1000-1)} \approx \mathbf{999}$$

b)
- The target computer has 1,000 processors
- The program has a maximum parallelization factor of 1,000
- 10% of the program (SIMD counting method) must be carried out sequentially, therefore: $f_B = 0.1$

Calculating the speedup gives:

$$S_{1000} = 0.1 + 0.9 * 1000 \approx \mathbf{900}$$

In spite of a considerable sequential SIMD segment of code, the program execution achieves over $E_{1000} \approx 90\%$ of the maximum speedup!

The discussion here is based on a specific, *fixed* problem (with a correspondingly large maximum degree of parallelization) and a fixed, predefined number of PEs. Neither the problem size nor the number of PEs is varied, instead only a comparison against a sequential system is carried out. Considerations, such as how the speedup increases or decreases with changes in the number of PEs, are *not* possible with the above formula for S_N, because T_N was the starting point of the argument. An increase in the number of PEs would not speed up the *same* SIMD program in the range $N \geq P_{\text{SIMD}}$ (the number of PEs greater than or equal to the maximum SIMD degree of parallelization), since all of the additional PEs would be superfluous and therefore would remain inactive. By calculating all T_i, $1 < i < N$, the corresponding speedups S_i can be found:

$$T_i = f_{\text{B}} * T_N + (1 - f_{\text{B}}) * \frac{N * T_N}{i}$$

$$S_i = \frac{T_1}{T_i}$$

As expected, this results in the curve of Figure 18.1 .

The previously derived formula for S_N was used in [Gustafson 88] for the extrapolation of the time behaviour of scaled variations of a problem with linear scaleup and has been termed 'scaled speedup', which can easily be misleading. The time behaviour of **different**, *scaled variations* of a program was investigated (see scaleup in Section 18.2) and the speedup was calculated between these. However, it was assumed that the sequential portion (according to Amdahl's formula) of a 'realistic' program remains constant during scaling and only the parallel portion grows. By definition, however, this is exactly the class of programs with **linear scaleup**. For this class one can write:

$T_N(\text{A}) = T_{k*N}(k*\text{A})$ (the program variant k times as large is processed in the same time period by k times the number of processors).

In addition, the following always holds:

$T_1(k*\text{A}) = k*T_1(\text{A})$ (a program k times as large requires k times more execution time on *one* processor)

From this assumption (so for this restricted class of problems), the linear increase of the 'scaled speedup' follows of course directly:

$$\frac{S_{k*N}(k*\text{A})}{S_N(\text{A})} = \frac{\dfrac{T_1(k*\text{A})}{T_{k*N}(k*\text{A})}}{\dfrac{T_1(\text{A})}{T_N(\text{A})}} = \frac{\dfrac{k*T_1(\text{A})}{T_{k*N}(k*\text{A})}}{\dfrac{T_1(\text{A})}{T_N(\text{A})}} = \frac{k*T_N(\text{A})}{T_{k*N}(k*\text{A})} = k$$

18.4 Validity of Performance Data

As has been shown in this chapter, performance data for parallel computer systems or parallel programs should always be considered with some scepticism. There are a number of more reasons for this:

- Performance data like speedup or scaleup of a parallel computer system is always *application-dependent*. This means that it relies on a specific application, and might not be transferable to other problems (maybe not even to similar problems).

- The speedup of a program relates to a single processor of the parallel computer. On SIMD systems, the PEs are generally much weaker in terms of performance than the processors of a comparable MIMD system. This can easily amount more than an order of magnitude in speed difference.

- Processor load is one of the highest goals for MIMD systems. This is not the case for SIMD systems, since the inactive PEs cannot be used for any other purposes. However, usually the speedup is calculated based on the processor load. If a SIMD program allows the unused PEs to continue processing (sparing the unnecessary operation for turning them off explicitly), PE load and speedup values are falsified. In this case the parallel program is less efficient than the test results indicate.

- Peak performance data, for example measured in MIPS (millions of instructions per second) or MFLOPS (millions of floating point operations per second), is only of limited importance, since often only the fastest integer or floating-point operations are used for such measurements. So what kind of program would *solely* use vector addition, which is the basis for the peak performance data of some computer companies? The speed of the data exchange, for example, is not addressed in these values. Packages for comparing performance on sequential computer systems (see [Weicker 90]), like Linpack, Whetstone, Dhrystone or SPEC benchmarks, are often not applicable to parallel systems. Benchmarks for parallel computer systems are currently being developed.

- Most high level programming languages available are not able to make efficient use of all features of a particular parallel hardware. To achieve the performance data supplied by the manufacturing company, often programming at a low level (assembly language) or the use of machine-specific instructions or library routines is required.

- When comparing different types of computer system, for example a parallel system against a workstation, the compilers of the programming languages used and the I/O systems will be inadvertently included in the performance test as well. In principle, only pure execution timings may be compared in this case (*CPU time* or for single user systems also *elapsed time*).

- When comparing a parallel (or vector) computer system with a sequential (scalar) computer system, it does not really make sense to use the same algorithm on both machines (in a parallel and a sequential version). For example, OETS (see Section 15.4) is a typical SIMD sorting algorithm. However, for a sequential system, Quicksort is a much more efficient algorithm – but unfortunately it cannot be simply transformed into an efficient SIMD program. A comparison between 'parallel OETS' and 'sequential OETS' gives good results for the parallel computer system, but does not really relate to practice! On the other hand, a comparison between 'parallel OETS' and 'sequential Quicksort' (or, in general, the comparison between a parallel algorithm and the fastest ***currently known*** sequential algorithm for the same problem) also raises questions. This definition is definitely relevant in practice (e.g. for a potential customer of a parallel computer system); however, this comparison data might change over time.

Exercises IV

1. Determine all of the data dependences of the statement sequence:

```
S1:   A := B + C;
S2:   B := A + C;
S3:   D := B * C - 2;
S4:   A := B / C;
```

2. Carry out the following tasks for the program fragment below:

a) Determine all of the data dependences with directions.

b) Derive the corresponding rule from each data dependence.

c) Vectorize the loop in Fortran 90 notation for a vector computer.

```
for i := 2 to n-1 do
 S1:  A[i]     :=  B[i] + C[i];
 S2:  B[i-1]   :=  2 * D[i] + 1;
 S3:  C[i]     :=  A[i] + B[i];
 S4:  E[i]     :=  A[i+1] / 7;
end;
```

3. Carry out the following tasks for the program fragment below:

a) Determine all of the data dependences with directions.

b) Determine all of the dependences that must be synchronized.

c) Parallelize the loop (in pseudo-notation '`doacross`') for a MIMD system. Attempt to achieve maximum parallelism!

```
for i := 5 to n do
 S1:  A[i-1]    :=  2 * B[i] + 3;
 S2:  B[i]      :=  2 * D[i] + 1;
 S3:  E[i]      :=  E[i] + 5;
 S4:  C[i]      :=  A[i] + D[i];
end;
```

4. Carry out the following tasks for the program fragment below:

a) Determine all of the data dependences with directions.

b) Derive the corresponding rule from each data dependence.

c) Vectorize the loop in Fortran 90 notation (if possible).

```
for i := 1 to n do
 S1:  A[i]  :=  B[i] + D[i+1];
 S2:  B[i]  :=  D[i-1] + 1;
 S3:  C[i]  :=  A[i-1] + B[i+1];
 S4:  D[i]  :=  15;
end;
```

5. Carry out the following tasks for the program fragment below:

a) Determine all of the data dependences with directions.

b) Derive the corresponding rule from each data dependence.

c) Vectorize the loop in Fortran 90 notation (if possible).

```
for i := 1 to n do
 S1:  A[i]  :=  B[i] + D[i+1];
 S2:  B[i]  :=  D[i-1] + 1;
 S3:  C[i]  :=  A[i-1] + A[i+1];
 S4:  D[i]  :=  15;
end;
```

6. Carry out the following tasks for the program fragment below:

a) Determine all of the data dependences.

b) Parallelize the outer loop (in pseudo-notation 'doacross') for a MIMD system. Attempt to achieve maximum parallelism! (The inner loop remains the same.)

c) Vectorize the inner loop (in Fortran 90 notation) for a SIMD system. (The outer loop remains the same.)

```
for i := 1 to n do
  for j := 10 to m do
   S1: A[i,j]    :=    D[i,j] + 5;
   S2: B[i,j]    :=    2 * C[i,j] - 2 * B[i,j+1];
   S3: C[i,j]    :=    A[i+1,j] + A[i,j+2];
  end (* j *);
end (* i *);
```

7. Carry out the following tasks for the program fragment below:

a) Determine all of the data dependences with directions.

b) Parallelize the outer loop 'for i' (in pseudo-notation 'doacross') for a MIMD system. Attempt to achieve maximum parallelism!

c) Exchange the inner with the outer loop. Then determine all of the new data dependences. Vectorize the new inner loop 'for i' for a SIMD system (in Fortran 90 notation).

```
for i := 1 to 1000 do
  for j := 1 to 10 do
   S1: A[i,j]    :=    C[i,j] + j;
   S2: B[i,j]    :=    2 * C[i,j] - 2 * B[i,j+1];
   S3: A[i,j]    :=    B[i+1,j];
  end (* j *);
end (* i *);
```

8. What operation do the following program fragments apply to input vector a:

a) Modula-2

```
VAR a: ARRAY[1..max] OF INTEGER;
...
FOR i:= 2 TO max-1 DO
  a[i] := (a[i-1] + a[i+1]) DIV 2;
END;
```

b) C*

```
shape [max] one_dim;
int:one_dim a;
...
with (one_dim)
  { a = ([.-1]a + [.+1]a) / 2; }
```

c) *Lisp

```
(-!! a (/!! a (!! 2)))
```

d) FP

```
(α+ ∘ trans ∘ [id,id]) : a
```

9. Design a synchronously parallel reduction operator for the non-procedural programming language FP. For this, split the argument list into two parts, for which the reduction will be called recursively in parallel. The reduction of n elements must not require more than $\log_2 n$ steps (assuming a sufficient number of processors is available).

10. A parallel program is to be executed on a MIMD computer with 100 processors. However, 3% of all instructions during program execution must be carried out sequentially (e.g. due to synchronization, I/O, etc.), but the rest can be executed on all processors in parallel.
What is the speedup of this program for this computer system?

11. A parallel program with a sequential part of 10% is to be executed on a MIMD computer system. Is there a maximum achievable speedup, independent of the number of processors in the computer?

12. A parallel program is to be executed on an MIMD computer with 100 processors. However, the following restrictions apply:

2 % of all commands during program execution are executed sequentially,
20 % of all commands can only be executed on 50 processors,
the rest can be executed on all available processors.

What is the speedup of this program for this computer system?

13. A parallel program is to be executed on an MIMD computer with 200 processors. However, the following restrictions apply:

3 % of all commands during program execution are executed sequentially,
25 % of all commands can only be executed on 75 processors,

the rest can be executed on all available processors.
What is the speedup of this program for this computer system?

14. P is a program for computing the Laplace filter on image data in parallel. Execution of program P for an image of size 100 × 100 pixels takes 4 s on sequential computer system S. Exactly the same execution time is needed by program P for an image of size 500 × 500 pixels on parallel computer system R with 1,000 PEs.
What is the scaleup of program P at 1,000 PEs ?

15. A parallel program is to be executed on a SIMD computer with 10,000 processors. There are, however, 20% scalar commands during execution (e.g. for data transmission to the host computer). The rest are vector commands, which are executed on all PEs.
What is the speedup of this program for this computer system?

16. A parallel program is to be executed on a SIMD computer with 10,000 processors. Measurements show that on the average the PEs were active for 30% of the run time and were inactive the rest of the time (e.g. due to parallel IF–THEN–ELSE statements).
What is the speedup of this program for this computer system?

17. A parallel program is to be executed on a SIMD computer with 100,000 PEs. However:
- 20 % of all instructions executed are scalar,
- 10 % of all instructions can only be executed vectorally on 100 PEs,
- 40 % of all instructions can only be executed vectorally on 50,000 PEs,
- the rest can be executed vectorally on all PEs.

What is the speedup of this program for this computer system?

18. A parallel program is to be executed on a SIMD computer with 50,000 PEs. However:
- 10 % of all instructions executed are scalar,
- 5 % of all instructions can only be executed vectorally on 1,000 PEs,
- 35 % of all instructions can only be executed vectorally on 40,000 PEs,
- the rest can be executed vectorally on all PEs.

What is the speedup of this program for this computer system?

References

AHUJA, S., N. CARRIERO, D. GELERNTER. *Linda and friends*, IEEE Computer, vol. 19, no. 8, Aug. 1986, pp. 26–34

AKL, S. *The Design and Analysis of Parallel Algorithms*, Prentice Hall, International Editions, Englewood Cliffs NJ, 1989

AMALSI, G., A. GOTTLIEB. *Highly Parallel Computing*, Benjamin Cummings, Redwood City CA, 1989

AMDAHL, G. *Validity of the single-processor approach to achieving large scale computing capabilities*, AFIPS Conference Proceedings, vol. 30, Atlantic City NJ, Apr. 1967, pp. 483–485

BABB, R. (ed.) *Programming Parallel Processors*, Addison-Wesley, Reading MA, 1989

BACKUS, J. *Can programming be liberated from the von Neumann style? A functional style and its algebra of programs*, Communications of the ACM, vol. 21, no. 8, Aug. 1978, pp. 613–641

BARRETT, G. *occam 3 reference manual*, INMOS Limited, Bristol, 1992

BARTH, I., T. BRÄUNL, S. ENGELHARDT, F. SEMBACH. *Parallaxis Version 2 User Manual*, Second Edition, Computer Science Report, no. 2/92, Univ. Stuttgart Germany, Feb. 1992

BAUMGARTEN, B. *Petri-Netze Grundlagen und Anwendungen*, BI Wissenschaftsverlag, Mannheim Wien Zürich, 1990

BEIZER, B. *Software Testing Techniques*, Second Edition, Van Nostrand Reinhold, New York NY, 1990

BEN-ARI, M. *Principles of Concurrent Programming*, Prentice Hall International, Englewood Cliffs NJ, 1982

BLACK, U. *Data Communications and Distributed Networks*, Second Edition, Prentice Hall, Englewood Cliffs NJ, 1987

BLASGEN, M., J. GRAY, M. MITOMA, T. PRICE. *The convoy phenomenon*, ACM Operating Systems Review, vol. 13, no. 2, April 1979, pp. 20–25

BRÄUNL, T. *Structured SIMD programming in Parallaxis*, Structured Programming, vol. 10, no. 3, July 1989, pp. 121–132

BRÄUNL, T. *Massiv parallele Programmierung mit dem Parallaxis-Modell*, Springer-Verlag, Berlin Heidelberg New York, Informatik-Fachberichte Nr. 246, 1990

BRÄUNL, T. *Braunl's law*, IEEE Computer, The Open Channel, vol. 24, no. 8, Aug. 1991a, p. 120

BRÄUNL, T. *Designing massively parallel algorithms with Parallaxis*, Proceedings of the 15th Annual International Computer Software & Applications Conference, compsac91, Sep. 1991b, pp. 612–617

BRÄUNL, T., R. HINKEL, E. VON PUTTKAMER. *Konzepte der Programmiersprache Modula-P*, Internal Report No. 158/86, Univ. Kaiserslautern, Germany, 1986

BRÄUNL, T., R. NORZ. *Modula-P User Manual*, Computer Science Report, no. 5/92, Univ. Stuttgart Germany, August 1992

BRINCH HANSEN, P. *The programming language Concurrent Pascal*, IEEE Transactions on Software Engineering, vol. 1, no. 2, June 1975, pp. 199–207

BRINCH HANSEN, P. *The Architecture of Concurrent Programs*, Prentice Hall, Englewood Cliffs NJ, 1977

CARRIERO, N., D. GELERNTER. *How to write parallel programs: A guide to the perplexed*, ACM Computing Surveys, vol. 21, no. 3, Sep. 1989, pp. 323–357

CHAMBERLIN, D., R. BOYCE. *SEQUEL: A Structured English Query Language*, Proc. 1974 ACM SIGMOD Workshop on Data Description, Access and Control, May 1974

CHANDY, K. M., J. MISRA. *Parallel Program Design*, Addison-Wesley, Reading MA, 1988

CHEN, S., G. DOOLEN, W. MATTHAEUS. *Lattice gas automata for simple and complex fluids*, Journal of Statistical Physics, vol. 64, no. 5/6, 1991, pp. 1133–1162

CLOS, C. *A study of nonblocking switching networks*, Bell System Technical Journal, vol. 32, no. 2, 1953, pp. 406 – 424

COFFMAN, E., M. ELPHICK, A. SHOSHANI. *System deadlocks*, ACM Computing Surveys, vol. 3, no. 2, June 1971, pp. 67–78

CONWAY, M. *A multiprocessor system design*, Proceedings of the AFIPS Fall Joint Conference, 1963, pp. 139–146

COULOURIS, G., J. DOLLIMORE. *Distributed Systems Concepts and Design*, International Computer Science Series, Addison-Wesley, Reading MA, 1988

COURTOIS, P., F. HEYMANS, D. PARNAS. *Concurrent control with 'readers' and 'writers'*, Communications of the ACM, vol. 14, no. 10, Oct. 1971, pp. 667–668

DATE, C. *An Introduction to Database Systems* (2 vols), Addison-Wesley, Reading MA, 1986

DENNIS, J., E. VAN HORN. *Programming semantics for multiprogrammed computations*, Communications of the ACM, vol. 9, no. 3, March 1966, pp. 143–155

DIJKSTRA, E. *Cooperating Sequential Processes*, Technical Report EWD-123, Technical University Eindhoven, 1965 (also contained in [Genuys 68])

DOOLEN, G. (ed.) *Lattice Gas Methods for Partial Differential Equations*, Addison-Wesley, Reading MA, 1990

EISENBACH, S. (ed.) *Functional programming languages, tools and architectures*, Ellis Horwood, Chichester, 1987

EISENBERG, M., M. MCGUIRE. *Further comments on Dijkstra's Concurrent Programming control problem*, Communications of the ACM, vol. 15, no. 11, Nov. 1972, p. 999

FISHER, J. *The VLIW machine: A multiprocessor for compiling scientific code*, IEEE Computer, vol. 17, no. 7, July 1984, pp. 37– 47

FLYNN, M. *Very High Speed Computing Systems*, Proceedings of the IEEE, vol. 54, 1966, pp. 1901–1909

FOX, G., S. HIRANANDANI, K. KENNEDY, C. KOELBEL, U. KREMER, C. TSENG, M. WU. *Fortran D Language Specification*, Technical Report, Rice University, Houston TX, April 1991

GEHANI, N., A. MCGETTRICK (eds) *Concurrent Programming*, Addison-Wesley, International Computer Science Series, Reading MA, 1988

GENUYS, F. (ed.) *Programming Languages*, Academic Press, London, 1968

GIBBONS, A., W. RYTTER. *Efficient Parallel Algorithms*, Cambridge University Press, Cambridge, 1988

GONAUSER, M., M. MRVA (eds) *Multiprozessor-Systeme*, Springer-Verlag, Berlin Heidelberg New York, 1989

GOSCINSKI, A. *Distributed Operating Systems The Logical Design*, Addison-Wesley, Reading MA, 1991

GRAY, J., A. REUTER. *Transaction Processing: Concepts and Techniques*, Morgan Kaufmann, Los Altos CA, 1992

GUSTAFSON, J. *Reevaluating Amdahl's law*, Communications of the ACM, Technical Note, vol. 31, no. 5, May 1988, pp. 532–533

HABERMANN, A. N. *Introduction to Operating System Design*, Science Research Associates Incorporation / IBM, SRA Computer Science Series, Chicago, 1976

HILLIS, W. D. *The Connection Machine*, MIT Press, Cambridge MA, 1985

HOARE, C.A.R. *Monitors: An operating system structuring concept*, Communications of the ACM, vol. 17, no. 10, Oct. 1974, pp. 549–557

HOARE, C.A.R. *Communicating sequential processes*, Communications of the ACM, vol. 21, no. 8, Aug. 1978, pp. 666 – 677

HOARE, C.A.R. *Communicating Sequential Processes*, Prentice Hall, International Series in Computer Science, Englewood Cliffs NJ, 1985

HOCKNEY, R., C. JESSHOPE. *Parallel Computers 2*, Second Edition, Adam Hilger IOP Publishing Ltd., Bristol, 1988

HOPCROFT, J., J. ULLMAN. *Formal Languages and their Relation to Automata*, Addison-Wesley, Reading MA, 1969

HUDAK, P., P. WADLER (eds) *Report on the Programming Language Haskell, a Non-strict Purely Functional Language (Version 1.0)*, Technical Report no. YALEU/DCS/RR777, Yale University, Department of Computer Science, April 1990

HWANG, K., F. BRIGGS. *Computer Architecture and Parallel Processing*, McGraw-Hill, New York, 1984

HWANG, K., D. DEGROOT (eds) *Parallel Processing for Supercomputers & Artificial Intelligence*, McGraw-Hill, New York, 1989

INMOS LIMITED. *occam Programming Manual*, Prentice Hall International, Englewood Cliffs NJ, 1984

IVERSON, K. E. *A Programming Language*, Wiley, New York, 1962

JÁJÁ, J. *An Introduction to Parallel Algorithms*, Addison-Wesley, Reading MA, 1992

JULESZ, B. *Binocular depth perception of computer generated patterns*, Bell Systems Technical Journal, no. 38, 1960, pp. 1001–1020

JULESZ, B. *Cooperative phenomena in binocular depth perception*, Sensory Physiology, no. 8, 1978, pp. 215–252

KERNIGHAN, B., R. PIKE. *The Unix Programming Environment*, Prentice Hall, Englewood Cliffs NJ, 1984

KOBER, R. *Parallelrechner-Architekturen*, Springer-Verlag, Berlin Heidelberg New York, 1988

KRISHNAMURTHY, E. V. *Parallel Processing Principles and Practice*, Addison-Wesley, Reading MA, 1989

KUCK, D., R. KUHN, B. LEASURE, M. WOLFE. *The structure of an advanced vectorizer for pipelined processors*, Proceedings of the 4th International Computer Software and Applications Conference, compsac80, Chicago IL, Oct. 1980, pp. 709–715

KUNG, H. T., C. E. LEISERSON. *Systolic arrays (for VLSI)*, Sparse Matrix Proceedings '78, Academic Press, Orlando FL, 1979, pp. 256–282 (also contained in [Mead, Conway 80])

KUNG, S., S. LO, S. JEAN, J. HWANG. *Wavefront array processors – concept to implementation*, IEEE Computer, vol. 20, no. 7, July 1987, pp. 18–33

KURFESS, F. *Parallelism in Logic*, Vieweg Verlagsgesellschaft, Artificial Intelligence Series, Braunschweig, 1991

LEISERSON, C. *Fat-trees: Universal networks for hardware-efficient supercomputing*, IEEE Transactions on Computers, vol. C-34, no. 10, Oct. 1985, pp. 892–901

LEWIS, T. *Data parallel computing: An alternative for the 1990s*, IEEE Computer, Viewpoints, vol. 24, no. 9, Sep. 1991, pp. 110–111

LI, K., P. HUDAK. *Memory coherence in shared virtual memory systems*, ACM Transactions on Computer Systems, vol. 7, no. 4, Nov. 1989, pp. 321–359

MASPAR COMPUTER CORPORATION. *MasPar Programming Language (ANSI C compatible MPL) User Guide*, Software Version 2.2, MasPar System Documentation, DPN 9302-0101, Dec. 1991

MASPAR COMPUTER CORPORATION. *MasPar VAST-2 User's Guide*, Software Version 1.2, MasPar System Documentation, DPN 9300-9035, Feb. 1992

MEAD, C., L. CONWAY (eds) *Introduction to VLSI Systems*, Addison-Wesley, Reading MA, 1980

METCALF, M., J. REID. *Fortran 90 Explained*, Oxford University Press, Oxford, 1990

MUJTABA, S., R. GOLDMAN. *AL Users' Manual*, Third Edition, Stanford Artificial Intelligence Laboratory Report, Stanford University, Dec. 1981

MULLENDER, S. (ed.) *Distributed Systems*, ACM Press, Frontier Series, Addison-Wesley, Reading MA, 1989

NEHMER, J. *Softwaretechnik fur verteilte Systeme*, Springer-Verlag, Berlin Heidelberg New York, 1985

NIKHIL, R. *ID (Version 88.1) Reference Manual*, Compilation Structures Group Memo no. 284, MIT Laboratory for Computer Science, Cambridge MA, Aug. 1988

PARKINSON, D., J. LITT (eds) *Massively Parallel Computing with the DAP*, Pitman Publishing, London, and MIT Press, Cambridge MA, 1990

PEITGEN, H.-O., D. SAUPE (eds) *The Science of Fractal Images*, Springer-Verlag, Berlin Heidelberg New York, 1988

PERROT, R. *Parallel Programming*, Addison-Wesley, Reading MA, 1987

PETERSON, J. *Petri Net Theory and the Modeling of Systems*, Prentice Hall, Englewood Cliffs NJ, 1981

PETERSON, G. *Myths about the mutual exclusion problem*, Information Processing Letters, vol. 12, no. 3, June 1981, pp. 115–116

PETERSON, J., A. SILBERSCHATZ. *Operating System Concepts*, Second Edition, Addison-Wesley, Reading MA, 1985

PETRI, C. A. *Kommunikation mit Automaten*, Ph.D. thesis, Univ. Bonn, Germany, 1962

POUNTAIN, D., D. MAY. *A Tutorial Introduction to occam Programming*, Blackwell Scientific Publications Ltd., INMOS, 1987

QUINN, M. *Designing Efficient Algorithms for Parallel Computing*, McGraw-Hill, New York, 1987

REUTER, A. *Grenzen der Parallelität*, Informationstechnik it, vol. 34, no.1, 1992, pp. 62–74

ROSE, J., G. STEELE. *C*: An Extended C Language for Data Parallel Programming,* Thinking Machines Corporation, Technical Report, PL87-5, 1987

SABOT, G. *The Paralation Model*, MIT Press, Cambridge MA, 1988

SEQUENT COMPUTER SYSTEMS INCORPORATED. *Sequent Guide to Parallel Programming*, Sequent Computer Systems, Report no. 1003-44459, 1987

SHAPIRO, E. *A Subset of Concurrent Prolog and Its Interpreter*, Institute for New Generation Computer Technology, Tokyo, ICOT Technical Report no. TR-003, 1983, (also contained in [Shapiro 87])

SHAPIRO, E. (ed.) *Concurrent Prolog* (2 vols), MIT Press, Cambridge MA, 1987

SIEGEL, H. J. *Interconnection networks for SIMD machines*, IEEE Computer, vol. 12, no. 6, June 1979, pp. 57–65

SOMMERVILLE, I., R. MORRISON. *Software Development with Ada*, Addison-Wesley, Reading MA, 1987

STEELE, G., W. D. HILLIS. *Connection Machine Lisp: Fine Grained Parallel Symbolic Processing*, Thinking Machines Corporation, Technical Report Series PL86-2, 1986

SZYMANSKI, B. (ed.) *Parallel Functional Languages and Compilers*, ACM Press, New York NY, Addison-Wesley, Reading MA, 1991

TANENBAUM, A. *Computer Networks*, Second Edition, Prentice Hall, Englewood Cliffs NJ, 1989

TREW, A., G. WILSON (eds) *Past, Present, Parallel*, Springer-Verlag, Berlin Heidelberg New York, 1991

THINKING MACHINES CORPORATION. *Introduction to Data Level Parallelism*, Technical Report Series TR86-14, 1986

THINKING MACHINES CORPORATION. *C* Programming Guide Version 6.0*, Thinking Machines System Documentation, Nov. 1990

UNITED STATES DEPARTMENT OF DEFENSE. *The Programming Language Ada Reference Manual*, Lecture Notes in Computer Science, no. 106, Springer-Verlag, Berlin Heidelberg New York, 1981

WEICKER, R. *An Overview of Common Benchmarks*, IEEE Computer, vol. 23, no. 12, Dec. 1990, pp. 65–75

WIRTH, N. *Programming in Modula-2*, Springer-Verlag, Berlin Heidelberg New York, 1983

WOLFE, M. *Advanced Loop Interchanging*, Proceedings of the 1986 International Conference on Parallel Processing, St. Charles, IEEE CS Press, Washington D.C., Aug. 1986, pp. 536–543

Index